Environmentalism:
An Evolutionary Approach

The premise of this book is that our environmental dilemmas are products of biological and sociocultural evolution, and that through an understanding of evolution we can reframe debates of thought and action. The purpose is to explain the wide variety of environmental worldviews, their origins, commonalities, points of contention, and their implications for the modern environmental movement.

In three parts covering the origins, evolution, and future of environmentalism, it offers instructors and students a framework on which to map theory, case studies, and classical literature. It is shown that environmentalism can be described in terms of six human values—utility, stability, equity, beauty, sanctity, and morality—and that these are deeply rooted in our biological and cultural origins. In building this case the book draws upon ecology, philosophy, psychology, history, biology, economics, spirituality, and aesthetics, but rather than consider these all independently it integrates them to craft a mosaic narrative of our species and its home. From our evolutionary origins a story emerges; it is the story of humankind, how we have come to threaten our own existence, and why we seem to have such difficulty in acting together to ensure our common future. Understanding our environmental problems in evolutionary terms gives us a way forward. It suggests an environmentalism in which material views of human life include spirituality, in which our anthropocentric behaviors incorporate ecological function, and in which environmental problems are addressed by the intentional relation of humans to the nonhuman world and to one another. Aimed at students taking courses in environmental studies, the book brings clarity to a complex and, at times, confusing array of ideas and concepts of environmentalism.

Douglas Spieles is a Professor of Environmental Studies at Denison University in Granville, Ohio, USA. He teaches courses on environmental science, ecosystem management, wetland ecology, and geographic information systems. His previous works include the book *Protected Land: Disturbance, Stress and American Ecosystem Management.*

"Dr. Spieles' book is timely, ambitious, well researched, and wonderfully comprehensive. It integrates myriad perspectives on environmentalism, analyzing our current and historical relationship to the environment from biological, sociocultural, psychological, and spiritual angles. We are in an age of intense global "environmental anxiety" as we grapple with the implications of anthropogenic climate change, pollution, habitat destruction, introduction of invasive species, expansion of human populations into natural areas, and overexploitation of our natural resources. This comprehensive text helps make sense of how our relationship to the environment developed through the course of our evolution, and how current conflicts and tensions have arisen as a result of differing perspectives on environmentalism. It also provides a roadmap for how we might seek resolution to these conflicts and achieve a more unified vision of environmentalism. *Environmentalism: An Evolutionary Approach* is eloquently and concisely written and should serve as a trusted handbook for students as they navigate the complex waters of the environmental sciences."

– *Elena Berg, The American University of Paris, France*

"*Environmentalism: An Evolutionary Approach* is the first textbook to take a multidisciplinary approach to fully integrate the principles of biological and sociocultural evolution in the context of environmental issues. By exploring a diversity of worldviews and their roots in shared human values, the text seeks to understand the evolution of our place in, and dependence on, the natural world and our sometimes conflicted relationship with it. It is truly a unique and refreshing perspective, building a rich understanding of the relationship of humans and the environment, and highlights a way forward in our efforts to cope with the critical environmental issues of our time."

– *Siobhan Fennessy, Kenyon College, USA*

Environmentalism:
An Evolutionary Approach

Douglas Spieles

Routledge
Taylor & Francis Group
LONDON AND NEW YORK

earthscan
from Routledge

First published 2018
by Routledge
2 Park Square, Milton Park, Abingdon, Oxon OX14 4RN

and by Routledge
711 Third Avenue, New York, NY 10017

Routledge is an imprint of the Taylor & Francis Group, an informa business

British Library Cataloguing-in-Publication Data
A catalogue record for this book is available from the British Library

Library of Congress Cataloging-in-Publication Data
A catalog record for this book has been requested

ISBN: 978-1-138-50241-3 (hbk)
ISBN: 978-1-138-50242-0 (pbk)
ISBN: 978-1-315-14491-7 (ebk)

Typeset in Goudy
by Sunrise Setting Ltd, Brixham, UK

Contents

Boxes

Preface

Environmentalism is an ideology of concern for human behavior and advocacy for the nonhuman world. It is, however, much more than a single way of thinking. In fact, environmentalism is a diverse collection of ideas and worldviews that can appear to be contradictory and incompatible. Conceptual conflicts make it difficult to discern the fundamental principles of the movement: what sort of human behavior should be considered environmental behavior, and what exactly is it about the natural world that should be protected? In short, what does it mean to be an environmentalist?

In this book I confront the ambiguity of western environmentalism. At one level this is an exercise in deconstruction—an attempt to identify and organize the various philosophical perspectives, conceptual dimensions and ways of knowing that inform environmental thought and action. At another level it is a search for clarity. Clarity, I suggest, may be found in our evolutionary origins. The different ways in which we perceive and encounter our environment are artefacts of the processes that make us human. We are products of biological evolution and sociocultural evolution. An examination of our evolutionary legacy can tell us much about who we are and why we have such difficulty coming to consensus on solutions to global environmental problems.

Just as environmentalism is a collection of ideas, so too is it a topic of interest to many different academic disciplines. Philosophy, biology, economics, anthropology, sociology, religion, psychology, aesthetics—all bring their own frames of reference to bear on environmental questions. All of these perspectives are valid and necessary, but a disconnected multidisciplinary approach leaves environmentalism without a unifying theme. In this book I present evolution as a common foundation on which environmental arguments can be based. A firm grasp of this theoretical grounding will help us to better understand our own individual and collective behavior and to evaluate the effects of our actions on ourselves, our communities, and our planet.

Acknowledgements

This work was made possible by the collegial support of Denison University. I gratefully acknowledge the assistance, energy, and encouragement of my colleagues and students. Special thanks to colleagues who provided valuable feedback on the manuscript, including Elena Berg, Quentin Duroy, Harry Heft, Kevin Harrison, Tom Henshaw, Susan Klemetti, Justine Law, Beth Spieles, and Steve Vogel. I appreciate the contributions of students Grace Bachmann, Em Bennett, Al Dilorenzo, Craig Freeland Jr., Sophia Rodriguez, Annabel Spangler, Willie Weems, and Thomas Worm. Many thanks to the outstanding Denison librarians, who tracked down absolutely every resource I could imagine. Sincere thanks to Tim Hardwick and Amy Louise Johnston at Routledge for their assistance, advice, and vision. I also appreciate the work of several anonymous reviewers, whose comments certainly improved the final product. Finally, thanks to Beth, Jackie, and Adam for their encouragement, patience, and love.

Introduction

You're an environmentalist.

Sometimes the simplest remark can touch a nerve. This particular comment was directed at me in the summer of 1999 by a Minnesota farmer. It was not exactly hostile, but neither was it a compliment. And it was a statement, not a question. He was simply making an observation, classifying me according to his own social taxonomy just as I had probably classified him according to mine. Having categorized me, he dismissed the whole notion and moved on to the business at hand.

I had driven out his way because of a dot on a map. The map intrigued me as maps often do, especially since it depicted an area that I had not yet traveled. It held the promise of an afternoon out of the office, exploring my new home. The dot represented a special wetland called a fen—relatively rare to my previous home in Ohio but scattered all around southwest Minnesota. I'm a wetland ecologist, you see, and every now and then (especially when there is a lot of paperwork to be done) I get the urge to toss the boots in the trunk, grab the camera, and head for the lowlands. So, when I stumbled across the *Fens of Southwest Minnesota* map and saw that it was shaping up to be a pretty nice day, I was out the door.

I hopped into the car and followed the highway to a turnoff in the middle of nowhere, and several unmarked dirt roads later, there I was. He met me at the end of his driveway, which was somewhat surprising since I hadn't called ahead (I had no name or number, just a fen map). But those dirt roads kick up so much dust that he saw me coming from miles away. It is a kind of rural burglar alarm, I suppose. He didn't seem at all surprised that I was there to see the fen, so maybe he was used to a lot of fen traffic. After a brief and somewhat tense introduction during which I had to repeatedly emphasize that I was not any sort of government official, he grunted, called me an environmentalist, and agreed to walk me back to the wetland. And for the next hour or so he and I talked fen as two people enjoy a fine wine.

The wetland was excellent—certainly worthy of the dot on the map—but it is the tour guide that I'm still thinking of, all these years later. He was a farmer, complete with pickup truck and bib overalls. His plowed and planted fields surrounded us and the homestead. He was a hunter and a fisherman, and he knew his wildlife. When we got to the fen he told me all about its hydrology and how it allows for a unique community of plants. He knew that it was an old feature of the landscape, and he was immensely proud to have it on his land (though a bit annoyed that someone had published a map that would lead riffraff like me straight to his farm). This was the way the land used to be—how it should be, in his mind. He had no problem with the juxtaposition of industrial agriculture and natural area; farmland, to him, was also what this land was supposed to be. His ancestors had been on the land for a long time, and he talked with reverence about the Native American legacy of this place before his family came to own it. Now he was its steward, and he took the responsibility very seriously.

And yet he made it very clear that he wanted nothing to do with environmentalists, though he had apparently made an allowance in my case. He certainly would not consider himself to be an environmentalist. He didn't want anyone telling him what to do with his land, his time, or his money. He told me straight up not to get him started on global warming, which he then proceeded to get started on. He seemed to really resent the fact that others—politicians, foreigners, and especially environmentalists—were taking jobs from his region, affecting the market for his crops, and regulating his life. It became obvious as we talked that, while we were both wetland enthusiasts, he considered me to be one of *them*: an environmentalist.

Am I an environmentalist? At the time of my companion's characterization of me—and still today—there is abundant evidence to the affirmative. I am a student and teacher of environmental science. I support environmental causes with time, money, and expertise when I am able. While my own ecological footprint still exceeds that of the average human, I like to think that I live in an environmentally responsible manner. Still, while there are many environmental causes that I support, others give me pause. Environmentalism, it seems, does not mean the same thing to everyone, and I find myself questioning certain aspects of the movement—or, more fundamentally, wondering what exactly the basic tenets of the environmental movement are.

Don't get me wrong. I am convinced that humanity is teetering on the brink of an environmental catastrophe. The evidence is overwhelming. Biodiversity is in decline worldwide, such that many scientists consider us to be in the midst of a sixth great extinction event, this one caused not by asteroid collisions or megavolcanoes, but by human activity. Anthropogenic climate change is a reality that is altering agriculture, weather patterns, infectious disease, and coastal flooding—but it is truly playing havoc with the oceans, where acidification and increasing temperature are jeopardizing the existence of species that are the primary food source for many people. On land we have issues of freshwater quantity and quality, soil erosion and fertility, resource extraction and waste disposal. Too many people suffer from toxic chemical exposure, and too often they are poor, people of color, indigenous people, those with no voice. Too many ecosystems are degraded and disregarded, supporting far fewer organisms and far fewer functions than they once did. These are serious problems, and any human who is paying attention should be an environmentalist. And yet many are not, or at least they resist the association. Why is this? What is it about the label *environmentalism* that is so polarizing?

Actually, environmentalism itself is polarized, with wide disagreements of theory and practice. Conceptually, it runs the gamut from spiritual biocentrism to wise-use conservationism to unrestricted biological and ecological engineering. This can make concerted action difficult. Where action is attempted, it often falls short of the goal. Of course, the environmental movement has some success stories. In the last century humans have placed nearly 15% of Earth's habitable landscape under some sort of protection, along with about 12% of the territorial marine environment.[1] Many nations have regulations aimed at improving and maintaining air and water quality, food safety, and the protection of endangered species. Add to this thousands of local victories—environmental education centers, community recycling centers and gardens, dedicated parkland, and so on—and it is clear that progress is being made. Still, we humans seem to trip over ourselves. In our darker moments, we are wasteful, selfish, xenophobic over-consumers prone to the pleasures of short-term gratification with little thought to the future. Surrounding our success stories are cases of contamination, depletion, degradation, and affluence amid abject poverty. Our collective behaviors too often result in problems of human health, environmental stress, and social strife. In response, environmentalists hardly speak with one voice. Different factions are at philosophical odds with one another, and the lack of clarity hinders coordinated action. In the affluent west—arguably the demographic that most needs to reconsider its behavior—environmental concerns are too often an afterthought. Moreover, many good people, like my Minnesota farmer friend, seem to shun the movement altogether.

Here's the thing, though. I think my fellow fen-enthusiast was, and probably is still, an environmentalist—though he would be loath to admit it. He loved that farm of his more than anything. Perhaps as much as anyone I've ever met, he saw himself as being responsible for the land. He believed it to be a special place and was doing his level best to protect the unique features of his property. Despite his gruff demeanor he was pleased that I had sought him out, and he generously invited me to bring my students to see his wetland, which I did a few weeks later. Clearly, he cared for his immediate environment and was proud of it. But he was full of contradictions. Even as he expressed a real desire to protect the fen, he was growing a monoculture of corn all around it and using pesticides, fertilizers, and industrial machinery to achieve the greatest yield. Even as he understood and cherished the delicate hydrology of the fen he withdrew groundwater for his farming operation. Even as he wanted fair treatment for himself and his neighbors he did not seem to have the same concern for others around the world.

It has occurred to me that my farmer friend probably would not have balked at the term *ecologist*, for it does not seem to carry the same baggage as the term *environmentalist*. An ecologist, after all, studies living things in relation to each other and to the non-living world in which they exist. And he knew a great deal about the plants and animals with whom he shared the land. He knew when they migrate, where they nest, when they flower, and what conditions they need to thrive. In this sense my guide was an excellent ecologist. The trouble seemed to lie in the extension of ecological concepts to the human community, to the global community, to *social* relationships. Environmentalism, I suspect, is problematic for many people for this very reason: it occurs amid the conflicting priorities of the self, the nonhuman, and other people.

As I have reflected on the farmer's worldview I have pondered the uncertainties of my own. If I am an environmentalist, what am I to make of ecological habitat amid industrial agriculture? What is the proper way of caring for this delicate bit of muddy ground—should it be meticulously tended or left to its own devices? If it is managed, does it somehow become artificial? And what of the general concept of land use here? Should I favor the modern, commodity-driven lifestyle of this farm or the nature-centric indigenous culture that preceded it? What *should* our relationship with the natural world be? Further, if he and I both had a soft spot in our hearts for wetlands and wildlife, why was it so hard for us to relate to one another regarding environmental issues? What *should* be the character of our relationships with one another? It seems to me that the literature and rhetoric of the environmental movement is frustratingly ambiguous on such questions.

Now here is an interesting thought. What if, in response to "You're an environmentalist" I had responded, "No, sir, I consider myself an *evolutionist*." How might he have reacted? Since the topic didn't come up during our brief encounter, I can't be sure of his views on evolution. But considering the opinion of Americans in general and rural Americans in particular—some of whom will refuse to pick up this book because the word evolution appears on the cover—I suspect that he might have taken offense. He may have run me off his land, and I would never have gotten to see his fen. Or, perhaps he would have reacted with delight and interest; I can't be sure. Evolution is one of those things—like religion and politics—that you just aren't supposed to bring up in polite company.

For the sake of argument, let's imagine that I had self-identified as an evolutionist and that my fen contact had reacted with revulsion. There he would be, standing on his driveway, watching the cloud of dust rise from my hasty retreat up the dirt road. And there I would be, trying to keep the car out of the ditch, eyes glued to the mirror, waiting for the shotgun blast that would lead to tomorrow's headline: Young Professor and Alleged Evolutionist Slain in Fen Hunt Gone Awry.

Assuming that he and I survived to ponder the incident, we might both have been perplexed. We were both nature enthusiasts, both fascinated with ecological relationships, and—whatever misgivings we might have had about the label environmentalist—we were both in favor of protecting certain ecological systems for their beauty, unique species, and habitat quality. In these respects we were kindred spirits. And yet the concept of evolution would have driven us apart. I would be left wondering how this person could not see that evolution is entirely compatible with the ecological marvel of the fen, that it is in fact the central reason for its existence. He would be left wondering how an otherwise clean-cut, boot-toting fen lover could have gotten wrapped up in such nonsense.

Misunderstanding and mistrust of evolution are unfortunate. Considered broadly, evolution explains much about the structure, function, and interaction of living things (biological evolution) and the structure, function, and interaction of human communities (sociocultural evolution). Basic human attitudes and behaviors are thus largely attributable to our sociobiological and sociocultural heritage. Much about our mounting environmental and social problems can be understood by viewing them through the lens of evolution. As biological organisms not far removed from our humble origins, we've been thrust into a complex social and environmental context. Our confusion and conflict regarding our home and our fellow humans betray our roots. A better understanding of evolutionary processes, pressures, and outcomes could help change attitudes, guide behaviors, and potentially stimulate collective action. In short, it could help us develop a more effective environmentalism.

So it happens, all these years later, that my interactions with the farmer have led me to consider the larger issues here, issues which humans have long struggled with but not yet resolved. The first set of questions are about the world in which we live. How should people relate to the nonhuman world? Why is it so difficult to reconcile the ways in which we use the natural world with the ways in which we desire to protect it? To what extent are our relationships with the environment driven by society and culture, and how have these pressures changed over time? A related set of questions concerns our treatment of one another. How should we relate to other people, both those who are close to us and those who are not? Why do we so often fail to align our own interests with the common good? What factors influence human interaction, and how have those factors changed over time? These, I believe, are the fundamental questions of environmentalism. They are questions of resource use and social equity. They are questions of human nature amid social, cultural, and ecological change. They are evolutionary questions.

This book is an effort to link our evolutionary heritage to environmentalism and its competing modes of thought and action. I aim to make sense of the wide variety of environmental worldviews, their founding principles, commonalities, and points of contention. I explore the modern environmental dilemma—particularly in the western world—in the light of biological and sociocultural evolution. Based on these reflections, I propose a reframing of environmentalism that brings clarity to the fundamental questions posed above.

The first section of the book considers the conceptual foundations and dimensions of environmentalism. I describe some of the many perspectives that inform our understanding of the human–environment relationship. I begin with relevant philosophical perspectives of the Enlightenment, not because they mark the origin of environmentalism, but instead because they illustrate some fundamental aspects of the human condition. In the second and third chapters I apply these concepts to the diverse and conflicted state of environmentalism and ecology in the modern western world. From these various worldviews I distill a set of common—if occasionally antagonistic—environmental values that are the basis of environmentalism.

The second section of the book is devoted to the evolutionary origins of environmental worldviews. We are biological, social, and cultural organisms, and our relationships with one another and with the nonhuman world occur in biological and sociocultural context. An evolutionary framework, I propose, will help us understand the conflicting perspectives and values we hold. Chapter 4 reviews the evolutionary origins of cooperative reciprocity, mental modeling, and sociocultural norms, characteristics which give us the capacity for environmentally and socially responsible behavior. In Chapter 5 these aspects of our nature are traced through human sociocultural evolution. Economic, ecological, spiritual, and aesthetic elements of human evolution are explored in Chapters 6 through 9.

In the final section of the book I make the case that environmental problems are social problems and conceptual problems. I argue that our own sociocultural evolution has threatened ecological services and diminished equitable access to resources, even as it has separated people from natural systems and from one another. Sociocultural evolution has, in short, compromised the human traits that provide the capacity for collective action. I propose that the great task of environmentalism is to rectify conceptual misunderstandings and to build social cohesion around the ecological processes on which our species depends.

This is a multidisciplinary—and transdisciplinary—task. To comprehend some philosophical views of western environmentalism and ecology we need to consider their historical, biological, sociocultural, economic, ecological, spiritual, aesthetic, and psychological foundations. Breadth comes at the price of depth, so this book is not a treatise on any of these fields. Rather, I draw upon classical theory and current knowledge in each to craft a mosaic of our species and its home. There are outliers and exceptions, there is complexity and disagreement, but from general trends and points of consensus a story emerges. It is the story of humankind. It is the story of how we relate to one another and to our natural surroundings, how we have come to threaten our own existence, and why we seem to have such difficulty in acting together to ensure our common future.

Note

1 World Bank, World Development Indicators table 3.4. 2016, World Bank Group. http://wdi.worldbank.org/table/3.4. Accessed December, 2016.

Part 1

Foundations, dimensions, and perspectives

1 Foundations of environmentalism

Human

non-human

Key points

- Environmental thought considers our responsibilities toward other people and the nonhuman world.
- Responsibility thinking was a focal point of many scholars of the Enlightenment.
- Different perspectives on the nature of our responsibilities provide a conflicted foundation for modern environmentalism.

I sometimes pose a question to my students: what is the greatest environmental disaster ever to occur on planet Earth? The Chernobyl accident is a common response, as are major oil spills like the *Exxon Valdez* and *Deepwater Horizon*. Some suggest war-related activity, like the use of atomic weapons in Hiroshima and Nagasaki. These are all major environmental and human tragedies, to be sure. But then I ask them to consider Chicxulub—the area of the Yucatan peninsula in Mexico where an asteroid collided with Earth some 66 million years ago, effectively ending the reign of the dinosaurs. Or how about the great oxygen increase of two to three billion years ago, during which photosynthetic organisms evolved and began to oxygenate our atmosphere, killing unknowable numbers of oxygen-intolerant organisms? Shouldn't we count these among Earth's greatest environmental disasters? For the most part, my students reject these events as environmental catastrophes. Why? Because, they usually say, these were *natural* events. They were not our fault and did not harm our species. In fact, both events played a role in paving the way for human life as we know it today. An environmental disaster, my students seem to think, is something that dramatically impacts human life, and particularly something that was *caused* by humans. Whether you agree with the logic or not, the message is clear: it is difficult for some people to conceive of an environmentalism that does not prioritize our own species.

This is an example of an environmental worldview that is particularly prevalent in modern western thought. If I were to poll other people in other places or other times I may well hear an alternative perspective. In some cultures, for example,

one perspective: people cannot view environmental

elements of nature are believed to have agency. An environmental catastrophe in this context may involve the clashing forces of the universe, quite apart from human action. It's not that either perspective is wrong. They are simply different ways of conceptualizing the human place in the cosmos.

The first section of this book is a presentation and organization of many different environmental worldviews. If we are to better understand environmentalism, this is an important first step. Cultural perspectives influence the priorities and behaviors of individual people, and competing worldviews can lead to conflicted priorities and behaviors. The purpose of this chapter is to explore some of the fundamental ideas that define and confound the modern environmental movement in the western world. we have to look at Cultural factors to understand environmentalism

Responsibility thinking

If we accept—for the sake of argument—my students' notion that environmental disasters revolve around human prospects, then surely the Black Death must be counted among the greatest. The Great Mortality, as it was known at the time (it would not be called the Black Death until nearly 300 years later), killed roughly one-third of the human population of Europe, North Africa, and the Middle East from 1347–1350, and it recurred throughout the ensuing century. The causes, though still debated, are generally thought to be a combination of natural and anthropogenic factors. Major climate changes of the Little Ice Age hit Eurasia around 1300. In Europe, this took the form of torrential rains, floods, cold summers, and harsh winters. Crops failed repeatedly, resulting in malnutrition that weakened the immune systems of children born during that time. Meanwhile the steppes of Asia became drier and colder, driving rodents from their natural habitats to seek food among human travelers and settlements. Conditions were filthy everywhere, with garbage and excrement providing habitat for rats, rats providing habitat for fleas, and fleas harboring *Yersinia pestis*: the bacterium that causes the plague. The result was human suffering and death on a terrible scale (Kelly, 2005).

Our knowledge is in hindsight, of course. At the time, no one understood infectious disease, nor the human immune system, nor the life cycle of the flea, nor the relationship of climate change to agriculture. Consequently no one at the time understood this as an environmental problem. It was instead widely seen as a spiritual problem, and many innocent people were blamed and murdered for the sins that had supposedly invited God's wrath (Kelly, 2005: 12–23). Much later, after the Enlightenment and the scientific revolution, scholars would begin to understand the reasons for the plague. Rationalism and science are sometimes blamed for environmental problems, but in this case rational science, had it been known in medieval times, could have mitigated, if not prevented, the tragedy. As it happened, neither victims nor survivors of the plague had any knowledge of its source or mode of transmission. Consequently, they had no means of averting disaster.

Today, the Black Death can be considered a major environmental disaster, but as it occurred it did not give rise to *environmentalism*. Why not? The lack of a scientific understanding of the natural world is certainly part of the answer, as are the constraints of communication, the deficiencies of infrastructure, and the absence of socio-political mechanisms for change. These deficiencies began to be overcome as humanity emerged from the Middle Ages. Science and logic began to be applied to the workings of nature, and the human condition began to be scrutinized through the lens of rational philosophy. These new ways of understanding people and their environment would eventually sow the seeds for modern concerns of environmental quality and human equity.

In this chapter I trace the development of two ideas that together form the basis of modern western environmentalism in all its disparate forms. The first is the idea that humans should consider their environmental surroundings in their actions— that we have a responsibility toward the nonhuman world. This includes the contested notions that places can have spiritual value, that animals have intrinsic worth and should have rights, and that there is a proper state of nature and therefore a proper relationship between human and nonhuman. The second idea is about our responsibility toward one another: that humans have, or ought to have, certain universal rights and freedoms, that these include, or should include, fair access to ecological goods and services, and that individuals should consider the consequences of their actions for others. Together, these ideologies of responsibility have been central to the development of modern civilization. In their emergence, we can see the foundations of western environmentalism.

Where and when did such "responsibility" thinking begin? This is an unanswerable question, of course, but we may speculate that such thoughts are nearly as old as thought itself. Some of the oldest surviving written texts concern human social responsibility, often in conjunction with natural resource use. Responsibility in thought and speech, lost forever, certainly predates written record. I will make the case later in this book that such thinking is an ancient part of our evolutionary heritage. While we can never know, we have good reason to believe that some of the first human interactions revolved—and evolved—around a sense of responsibility.

Responsibility thinking provides a foundation on which the principles of environmentalism depend. I propose, then, that an effort to better understand western environmentalism should start with some philosophical ideas that have shaped the western world. For these purposes, early modern Europe is an excellent place to begin (Box 1.1). It is in this era—roughly speaking, the 17th through 19th centuries—that we see the Enlightenment, the scientific revolution, and the beginnings of industrialization, mechanization, and urbanization that would lead to some of the first expressions of environmental concern. We also see in this period a spiritual reaction to materialism and a blossoming romantic view of the natural world, even as mechanization drove invention, production, degradation, and pollution to new heights (and depths). New ideas of a mechanistic universe led some to ponder the human role on Earth and the human relationship with nature. Central to this debate were questions of rights and values: whether nonhuman life has value beyond the ways in which it serves humans, and whether ethical considerations should be extended to other species, to nonliving entities, and to

---

Box 1.1 Selected scholars of responsibility thinking, 1600–1950

	Continental European	British	American
1600		Francis Bacon, 1561–1626	
		Thomas Hobbes, 1588–1679	
	René Descartes, 1596–1650		
		Henry More, 1614–1687	
	Baruch Spinoza, 1632–1677		
		John Locke, 1632–1704	
1700			
	Carl Linnaeus, 1707–1778		
	Jean-Jacques Rousseau, 1712–1778		
	Immanuel Kant, 1724–1804		
		Jeremy Bentham, 1748–1832	
1800	Alexander von Humboldt, 1769–1859		
			Ralph Waldo Emerson, 1803–1882
		John Stuart Mill, 1806–1873	
		Charles Darwin, 1809–1882	
			Henry David Thoreau, 1817–1862
		Herbert Spencer, 1820–1903	
			John Burroughs, 1837–1921
1900			John Muir, 1838–1914
	Charles Gide, 1847–1932		
			Aldo Leopold, 1887–1948

---

natural systems. At the same time, enlightened thinkers were writing and speaking about human rights, moral obligations, and equity. These are questions of how people ought to behave toward one another. The juxtaposition of these ideas set the stage for the environmental movement of the following centuries.

What follows, then, is a brief trip through some foundational ideas of the modern western world. Beginning with mechanistic, materialistic, and utilitarian worldviews that advanced industrialization, I will then turn to spiritual and romanticized concepts of nature and the Darwinian science that simultaneously enabled and challenged them. Finally, I will consider early thoughts on property ownership, class stratification, and social responsibility.

Mechanism and materialism

A fundamental question of the human relationship with nature is whether humans are distinct from or part of the nonhuman world. This is a question of perspective, and a changing perspective was one of the many remarkable features of the Enlightenment. Perspective is informed by culture, and the dominant culture of early modern Europe was Judeo-Christian spiritualism. Christianity had by then held Europe in its unquestionable grasp for a millennium, but for much of that time it looked in many ways like the paganism it had supplanted. Slowly, Christian

Christians saw themselves above nature

churches replaced temples, Christian holy days subsumed pagan festivals, and saints replaced pagan gods (Manchester, 1992: 10–15). A thousand years of enforced doctrine has a way of shaping worldviews, and the Europe that staggered out of the dark ages was of a different mindset than the one that had entered. In contrast to earlier animistic traditions, in which spirits were thought to pervade the nonhuman world and humans alike, Christianity set humans apart from nature. Humans were the special creation of God, given power over nature to subdue it and to make it productive. Since the realm of God is not of this world, and since humans were made in God's image to seek His realm, the Christian was seen to be above nature, not of it. Human separation from nature is thus divine providence (Kaufman, 2003: 38).

Naturally, not everyone accepts this line of reasoning. Even if one accepts it, it does not necessarily follow that Christianity is therefore to blame for the environmental problems of the modern world. Nor does it mean that a pagan Europe would have been any more judicious in its use of the world's resources. What is clear is that Christianity enabled philosophical and scientific arguments for human superiority over the nonhuman world. Its domination of early modern thought is surely one of the reasons that the scientific and industrial revolutions occurred first in Europe.

Among the most important scientific worldviews of the age was the conceptualization of the universe as a machine with regular, predictable, and quantifiable properties. Mechanistic ideas were not new. In fact, they had pervaded the European world since the time of Archimedes (c.287 BCE–c.212 BCE). The universe and its components, in this view, follow fundamental principles and motions, and from these principles mechanical devices can be derived and constructed (de Solla Price, 1964: 15). In this way the world came to be seen by some as a great apparatus, created by God and operated by man. The Italian friar Thomas Aquinas (1225–1274) applied this notion to animals, stating in his *Summa theologica* (Aquinas, 1485) that the motions of animals were without soul or reason and therefore machine-like. The Aquinan conception of animals, along with the Copernican solar system, the physics of Galileo, and the physiology of William Harvey seemed to confirm what the French polymath René Descartes (1596–1650) later concluded about the natural world: that it is, in the words of a biographer, "sheer mechanism and nothing else" (Crombie, 1959: 160). Animals, in Cartesian logic, lack the ability to speak, reason, and feel pain as humans do. Therefore only humans are conscious—a quality that elevates them above nature. What this meant to Descartes is that the nonhuman world is devoid of the spiritual soul that humans possess (Harrison, 1992: 223).

In our modern world of ultra-specialization, Descartes' intellectual reach can be hard to fathom. A groundbreaking mathematician and inventor of analytical geometry, he was also a champion of rational science, an optical physicist, human physiologist, and briefly a soldier. All of this was accomplished with a penchant for spending long hours lying in bed, just thinking (a habit I intend to adopt myself). He was also known to partake in a bit of carousing and gambling, causing his father to remark at one point that he was "not good for anything but to be bound in buckskin" (Crombie, 1959: 166). Fathers can be hard to please. But it is Cartesian philosophy that is most central to this discussion. While he lived and died long before anyone spoke of an environmental ethic, Descartes is an important figure in the conceptualization of environmentalism. Driven as he was by a mechanistic view of the universe, he is credited—or cursed—with the introduction of two different philosophical dualisms into western thought. The first is that the human mind is separate from the body, and the second is that humans are separate from nature (Crombie, 1959; Nash, 1989: 18).

Descartes did not infer from the mechanistic worldview that nonhuman organisms, lacking a human soul, were therefore available for exploitation. However, many of his followers—called *mechanici* by the 18th century—took this step and reached the rational conclusion that nature was available for the taking without ethical concern (Lange, 1877: 242; Harrison, 1992: 220). The Englishman Francis Bacon (1561–1626), for example, felt that science and management would allow humans to properly exert authority over other living things, which God had created for human dominion. Cartesian and Baconian philosophy did much to advance the mechanistic worldview in their time, and the effects are still readily apparent today (Worster, 1994: 30, 106).

Even so, Descartes the mechanist was not a wholesale materialist (Worster, 1994: 40). Materialism—the philosophy that nothing exists but matter and energy—would have precluded a spiritual world, and this was a journey that few mechanists of the day were willing to take. Rather, their world was one of individual parts set in motion by a benevolent God for the benefit and industry of humans. But mechanism can lead one down a slippery path to thoughts that perhaps there is no ghost in the machine after all.[1] European materialists have explored this path for centuries, at least as far back as the atomists and Epicureans of ancient Greece. Democritus (c.460 BCE–c.370 BCE), for example, is credited with an atomic theory of the universe that bears a striking resemblance to modern Newtonian physics. It held that changes in matter are due to combination and separation of atoms, and that nothing exists but atoms and empty space. Even the soul, for Democritus, consisted only of atoms that enabled life (Lange, 1877).

Some 2,000 years later this assertion was still difficult for many to accept. But where Descartes backed away from equating consciousness with matter, others were game to venture (Lange, 1877: 246). To Bacon, for example, there was no such thing as immaterial substance. Baconian philosophy thus called the vital energy of the soul into question. The Dutch philosopher Baruch Spinoza (1632–1677) similarly diverged from Descartes on some important points. He went so far as to state that consciousness and matter are of the same substance. This was a refutation of Cartesian mind–body dualism; it was the equation of the spiritual with the material. As such it negated the need for theism and, among other of his thoughts and writings, won Spinoza the label of heretic. He was certainly dismissive of scripture. A contemporary noted of Spinoza that "the New Testament, the Koran and the fables of Aesop would have the same weight according to him" (Borch, 1996 [1661]). Spinoza was summarily excommunicated from the Church in 1656 (Klever, 1996).

Spinoza's philosophy is an interesting case, for in it we can see the beginnings of two modern contradictory viewpoints. On the one hand, we can imagine the perspective of the materialist being linked to the commodification of nature. If the vital spirit of living things is an illusion, if all living things are instead made of the same substance as nonliving things, then what makes living things worthy of protection? Why would we not proceed with harvest, extraction, even abuse of other organisms? Furthermore, Spinoza was a determinist, believing that "particular volitions cannot be called free . . . but must be as their causes have determined them to be" (Spinoza, 1996 [1661]: 2; Klever, 1996: 15). All actions, in this view, are predetermined, and all natural impulses are quite beyond our control. One could use this perspective to justify environmental exploitation. On the other hand—and probably more in line with Spinoza's actual intention—if the spiritual and the material are of the same substance, then the spirit is part of all things, and God is one with nature. In the words of his biographer, this line of thought conveys "the unity of the mind with the whole of nature" (Klever, 1996: 21). This is pantheism; it is a religion of nature (Gottlieb, 1999). In it we can see ample reason to protect the nonhuman world, for the God or gods are in it, and it is within God. We will return to these thoughts, for many still wrestle with them today.

Mechanism and materialism came of age in a continent on the brink of the industrial revolution. An emerging scientific rationalism, a political economy of production, and a spirit of imperialism arose at the same time. The historian Donald Worster (1994: 29–51) recounts the mindset of this "age of reason" from the perspective of Carl Linnaeus (1707–1778). Most well-known today for his system of species classification, Linnaeus advocated the human dominion of the Earth; he was, following the lead of Bacon, an ecological imperialist. The Linnaean worldview was of great influence on a central debate of the age: the proper relationship of humans with the natural world. Nature in this perspective was a system of "order, beauty and harmony" designed by the creator "for the sake of man" (Worster, 1994: 38). Everything in nature—every organism, species, and resource—had its use, and each was intended for the utility of God's greatest creation: the human being. It was, in Worster's words, a "triumph over the pagan view of nature, [through which] western science could proceed to study the Earth as a thoroughly profane and analyzable object" (Worster, 1994: 29). While unbridled domination of nature was tempered by others, as we shall see, the Linnaean perspective essentially won the day and set the course for much subsequent development of the western world.

Utilitarianism and Kant

Linnaeus applied mechanistic and material views of the natural world to the idea that humans can and should use nonhuman resources to advance our own individual or collective agendas. This precipitated its own line of philosophical thought. Utilitarianism, championed by Jeremy Bentham (1748–1832) and John Stuart Mill (1806–1873), holds that we should weigh the benefits of our actions against the potential harms. Thus, it is not so much the appropriation of nature as it is the consequence of appropriation that is the issue. If the action maximizes happiness, then it should be done. Whether that happiness pertains only to humans or extends to the nonhuman world is an open question. Bentham in particular drew the line at organisms that can talk, reason, and suffer; in other words, he advocated for the greatest happiness for *people*. He did allow, however, that one day humans may come to consider the rights of the nonhuman, and so we can imagine the "greatest good" being extended to animals, plants, and even abiotic entities (Kaufman, 2003: 9–12).

John Stuart Mill, protégé and godchild of Bentham, added nuance to utilitarianism. He too was the son of a hard-to-please father (one wonders if there was any other kind in early modern Europe), prompting Mill to write in his autobiography that "my father, in all his teaching, demanded of me not only the utmost that I could do, but much that I could by no possibility have done" (Mill, 1924 [1873]: 28). Following his father's philosophy and that of Bentham, Mill asserted that our actions should happen with restraint, for the "greatest good" includes things that traditional economics does not value. We might imagine this idea being applied to an issue like environmental quality, suggesting that we should limit production—and even population—to allow humans the capacity to experience the world around them. Mill did not accept that competition for the advancement of self at the expense of others was the epitome of human existence: "I am not charmed with the ideal of life held out by those who think that the normal state of human beings is that of struggling to get on; that the trampling, crushing, elbowing, and treading on each other's heels . . . are the most desirable lot of humankind" (Mill, 1848: IV6.5). Mill was optimistic that individuals have the capacity for self-restraint but realized that, to be effective, restraint must be enforced by social structure (even as he defended individual liberties over the tyranny of the state). Further, Mill argued that social action and restraint could be understood as scientific phenomena. This means that there are causal reasons for social actions, and that social change could therefore be guided. In this we can see the beginnings of social science (Mautner, 2005; Reeves, 2007).

In the logic of Immanuel Kant (1724–1804), our actions should be judged not on their consequences, but instead on motive: whether the action is being done for the right reasons according to universal standards of virtue. Thus, he held that people, being rational beings, deserve to be treated with respect on principle; we have intrinsic value because we have the capacity to act as moral agents. Nonhumans, to the contrary, have instrumental value and are not subject to the same level of respect. This does not necessarily mean that nature is therefore available for abuse, for the abuse of nature may indirectly be disrespectful of people. In Kant's vision, humans are the arbiters of the standards of virtue. People are therefore the agents of morality, and this agency means that we have moral responsibilities (Kaufman, 2003; Bustos, 2011: 295–297).

In summary, some ideas of the Enlightenment cast a shadow of uncertainty over individual responsibility toward the nonhuman world. Mechanism, materialism, and utilitarianism suggest that the world is reducible to inanimate parts of instrumental value. Persuaded by these arguments, some began to question the notion of the spiritual, considering that perhaps abiotic resources, plants, and animals did not have a spiritual component, but rather were wholly material (and that perhaps humans were not so different). Some reasoned that human appropriation of nature was right and proper, given certain conditions: that the use was done in the way ordained by God, that the outcomes of the use served the greatest good, or that the use was respectful in principle to humans. Together these philosophical perspectives—as well as their religious undercurrents—allow and even urge the human dominion over nature. It is hardly surprising that such thoughts engendered imperialism, extraction, and industrialization.

Still, there were (and are) opposing viewpoints which contend that humans should not have unlimited control over nature, that nonhuman entities do have spirits and should have rights, and that the world is not reducible to interlocking and interchangeable parts. These perspectives too have grown from early roots to influence our modern concepts of environmentalism.

Animism, romanticism, and Darwin — animals have spirits

European and Judeo-Christian material utilitarianism may have come to dominate much of the world, but it is by no means the only perspective of the human–environment relationship. Different approaches to human–nature relations have developed in other parts of the world, and these too have religious connotations. In Jainism, for example, the belief in a cyclical reincarnation of living things means that the spirit of ancestors may reside in animals. Buddhism and Hinduism similarly hold views that extend human-level respect to animals. Indeed, the fate of one's soul in the next incarnation may be determined according to how one treated other living things in the previous life. The Maori of New Zealand, like many other indigenous cultures, consider the elements of their environment to be alive, under the control of gods with whom they have an intimate relationship. These worldviews promote a spiritual kinship with nonhuman beings, resulting in a sense of equality rather than domination. The notion that the soul or vital energy of a human can inhabit the body of an animal—or vice versa—is a form of animism; it holds that all living things have a non-material essence that makes them alive. This affords intrinsic value, not just instrumental value, to all organisms. In some traditions, intrinsic value is extended even to nonliving things; thus rocks may harbor a spirit that was once—or one day may be—of human embodiment (Harvey, 2005: 50–65; Szűcs et al., 2012).

The philosopher J. Baird Callicott (1982) summarizes a similar animistic perspective held by some Native American cultures, notably the Sioux and Ojibwa. In this worldview, the abiotic and biotic aspects of nature are alive with a power, a consciousness, a vital spirit with which the attentive human might communicate. Further, this spirit is shared among beings and with the overarching Great Spirit—sometimes represented as Father Sky and Mother Earth. All things are in this way related as one spiritual family. By extension, then, good standing in the world means good relations with both human and nonhuman members of the family. It is easy to see how such a worldview results in a very different relationship with nature than the mechanistic and materialistic systems I described earlier. In the Sioux and Ojibwa traditions it is not that one is *precluded* from the use of nature, of course, but that the use is to be respectful and reciprocal, in the same way that one would approach an exchange with a relative. It is a relational concept of the natural world, one that includes the wind and the river along with animals, plants, and ancestors.

Animism was not absent from early modern Europe. In fact, there was a strong undercurrent of animism that eventually gave rise to a branch of modern environmentalism. It too grew out of Christianity—though not as an enabler for human domination over nature. Its patron is the historical and legendary St Francis of Assisi (1181–1226). Francis saw nature as God's work, but held that humans were to share peaceful fraternity with the elements of creation. Humility, respect, and care for nature in praise of God were one and the same with respect and care for one another. This idea of a harmonious relationship with nature preceded Francis—it was in fact an element of pagan literature: "a longing to reestablish an inner sense of harmony between man and nature through an outer physical reconciliation" (Worster, 1994: 10). Indeed, the "gospel of nature" was folded into the good book itself: "The wolf also shall dwell with the lamb, and the leopard shall lie down with the kid; and the calf and the young lion and the fatling together; and a little child shall lead them" (Isaiah 11:6). This is a peaceful, benevolent nature, one of pious love. In post-medieval Europe it was taken up in response to the cold, hard indifference of the new science and industry (Worster, 1994: 16).

Accordingly, animistic philosophers in both Europe and America found spirit in the animals, plants, and elements of nature. The English philosopher Henry More (1614–1687), for example, was a proponent of the organismal view of nature which, unlike the machine analogy of the mechanists, afforded nonhuman beings a soul. In fact, More considered the entire world to have a soul, and that the spirit "pervaded the whole matter of the universe" (Worster, 1994: 42). The American naturalist John Burroughs (1837–1921) similarly saw nature as a single great sentient organism. This, we can see, is not far from the animistic philosophies of major eastern and Native American religions, nor from the pantheism of Spinoza. In the Christian version, of course, the universe was created by the one God, and the spirit of that one God is alive in the works of nature. It was a nod to paganism nonetheless. As Donald Worster notes, this animism was ammunition for the romantic view of nature that sought an alternative to ecological imperialism (Worster, 1994: 17, 42).

The romantic movement has roots, oddly enough, in rational science (Thacker, 1983). Isaac Newton's astonishing work revealed to scholars of the day a universe of perfection—one that followed laws set forth by God. Wild nature had for ages been a thing to be feared and excluded; the rough, irregular shapes and dark, fearsome shadows were seen by some as signs of God's displeasure. It was instead the garden, nature tamed and walled, organized, and controlled, that was desirable. But Newton's science and the philosophy of John Locke (1632–1704) found evidence of the Deity in the perfection of nature. If God is good and God created nature, then nature must be good. The romantic mindset is one of optimism, in that nature is created for the good of mankind in praise of God. Human institutions and manipulations, to the contrary, are corruptions of nature. In the words of Jean-Jacques Rousseau (1712–1778), the inequality of society "is patently against the law of nature . . . that a handful of people should have a surfeit of luxuries, while the hungry multitude lacks the necessities of life" (Rousseau, 1992 [1755]: 891). In wild nature, to the romantic, there is equality, love, and balance. The most virtuous state of man is therefore the most primitive, as evidenced by the "noble savages" encountered by European explorers.[2]

It is not so strange that in the culture of rationalism there emerged a counter-culture of romanticism. Both were, in their own way, expressions of new freedom in thought and action. Romantics expressed feeling and emotion in response to applied science and ruthless economics. It was, in the view of historian Hoxie Fairchild, an idealistic movement, one that sought truth, beauty, and love in the world. To Fairchild (1940: 20), romanticism was born of newfound religious freedom to "sentimental deists with pantheistic hankerings." Indeed, romantic art and literature are full of animism, searching for the unifying spirit in nature, seeking to "naturalize the supernatural and supernaturalize the natural" (Fairchild, 1940: 22). Nature, seen through romantic eyes, is *sublime*—just as contemporary society is disheartening—and the romantic quest is to harmonize with, to be one with, the spirit of the natural world. In nature there is majesty, redemption, restoration, and salvation. There is a melancholy in romantic literature, but also a defiant insistence that the good and pure of the universe are immortal and eternal. To the romantic, no obstacle is too great to be overcome, and the spirit always triumphs in the end (Thacker, 1983).

The romantic notion of natural peace, harmony, and perfection was challenged in the 19th century by an Englishman who attended divinity school but ultimately spent the balance of his life as a gentleman scientist. Charles Darwin (1809–1882), somewhat adrift at the age of 22 and facing with dread a career in the clergy, hardly seemed the type to launch a revolution of thought. He was the second choice for a naturalist position on a voyage around the world, a voyage which his father forbade. Then the first choice dropped out and his father yielded. One can almost hear the paternal sigh. Having returned from the voyage with voluminous evidence for a theory of natural selection, he was reluctant to publish that which he knew would defy the religious convention of his day. But publish he did—with some reticence and much agony—and his work changed the way many people understand the world (Desmond and Moore, 1991: 101–105).

Darwin recognized that species are mutable, not fixed in form, and that their evolution is subject to environmental selection pressures. This alone does not preclude the "gospel of nature." It was the implication of Darwin's mechanism, rather, that gave his contemporaries pause and continues to do so today. Darwinian evolution, however beautiful its products, is based on population principles set forth by Thomas Malthus in 1798: it is a system of intense competition, suffering, and death. It is hard to reconcile a benevolent God and harmonious nature with Darwinian observations that many more organisms are born than can possibly survive, that chance plays a significant role in survival, and that there is no goal or direction to the process except survival and reproduction. It all seems rather violent and purposeless (Desmond and Moore, 1991).

Students of natural philosophy in Darwin's day were quick to apply this view of nature to human society. Some likened the brutality of the system to the 17th-century political philosophy of Thomas Hobbes (1588–1679), who considered the struggle for life to be a "condition called war" and had the audacity to predict that humans would be at each other's throats, "every man against every man," but for the restraints of government (Hobbes, 1994 [1651]: 62). Herbert Spencer (1820–1903), the Darwin enthusiast who first described the theory as "survival of the fittest" (Spencer, 1864: 444), incorrectly applied evolution broadly to the universe, concluding that everything develops from simple beginnings to complex maturity. In Spencer's perspective, complex entities acquire traits as they mature toward a final goal: the highest state of evolution. This, according to Spencer, applies to complex social systems just as it applies to complex biological systems. The "social organism" thus evolves toward an ideal organization—with European societies, in his estimation, advanced far beyond more primitive races (Spencer, 1864: 45, 212; Laland and Brown, 2011: 41). The idea that development of a proper social organism could be aided by selective breeding was the impetus for the horrors of social Darwinism in the late 19th and early 20th centuries.

The extension of Darwinian logic to *human* biological evolution was seen by some as blasphemy. The suggestion that humans are not of eternal form, but rather evolved from ape-like ancestors, was contrary to Genesis. How could this be true if man is created in God's image (an image that for most people is distinctly human)? It also implies that human evolution proceeds the same way that it proceeds for all other species, with a great deal of suffering and senseless death. And what of the soul, that vital spirit that some attribute only to conscious beings? If it was not bestowed upon man at the time of creation, if humans were in fact descended from the beasts, then at what point did the soul appear—or does it mean that every living creature has a soul (or that none do)? And if every creature does have a soul, why are they so brutal to one another?

Some romantics have countered this devastating Darwinian logic with more Darwinian logic. Paradoxically, evolutionary competition and the struggle for life is also a system of cooperation, mutualism, and interrelation. It makes a strong case that all species share common ancestors and that all have arisen by the same process. If this is indeed how all species have come to be, it intimates that the same vitality (to some, the same spirit of God) must be in all living things. Darwin, for his part, was not immune to romanticism. He was convinced of the kinship of living things and that morality, as it too evolves, will eventually come to embrace nonhuman nature (Worster, 1994: 182). It is true that there is cooperation in Darwinian ecology, as organisms rely on one another to survive. Even so, Darwinian evolution is seen by many as a victory for materialism, not animism. The process of natural selection is mechanistic. The chances of survival and reproduction are mundane matters of probability, and there is little room for the triumph of the spirit.

Such reasoning posed a problem for pagan animists and Christian naturalists alike. This was not the sort of fraternity with nature they had in mind. Romantics of Darwin's time (and ever since) have refused to cede the spirit to the material world, insistently finding in nature the glory of God and the source of human inspiration (sentiments, it must be noted, with which Darwin himself may have agreed, but with which many Darwinists take issue). Where science would penetrate the darkest corners of the natural world to better understand it, romantics would leave it undisturbed to fuel the human imagination.

This was the age of the great romantic naturalists. The explorer and geographer Alexander von Humboldt (1769–1859), much studied by Darwin, saw nature through romantic eyes as a holistic entity. In his travels he searched for harmony among organisms in different geographic and climatic conditions (Worster, 1994: 133–134). In the writings of Henry David Thoreau (1817–1862) and John Muir (1838–1914) there is a sensual and individual connection with nature—really with the entire cosmos—even as the science of nature is embraced. There is an appreciation for mysticism and a regard for pristine, primeval nature, unspoiled by humans. This love for wilderness was prevalent in a practical sense, manifested in efforts to secure protection for wild places, but it was also mental—a notion that humans consumed by social institutions must be re-connected with wild nature, for in such connection we find the path beyond our physical existence. There is more than a little animism here, but with some new twists. That there is a way nature is *supposed* to be; that nature can and should be protected in its pristine state; that humans can ally with nature to discover the supernatural within themselves; that nature spoiled by human encroachment loses its vitality; that humans removed from the wild and caught up in social entanglements are poorer in spirit—these are all representative of the romantic ideal in the face of Darwinian science (Nash, 1989: 39–56; Worster, 1994).

In these sentiments we can see some fundamental principles of modern environmentalism. Such ideas in various forms are what prompted the establishment of national parks, wilderness areas, and wildlife sanctuaries, first in the United States and then around the world. They are what fueled the concept of the ecological community and gave rise to efforts to control wildfires, floods, and other natural disturbances to protect ecosystems as a unit. They have driven programs to save endangered species and places, not because they have instrumental value but because they have intrinsic value. Yet Darwinian ecology has persisted alongside romantic visions of the environment like a pesky fly, asserting a host of troublesome realities: that iconic species and protected places will change despite our efforts; that ecological communities do not occur as a unit; that there is no goal of natural selection or ecological succession; that natural disturbances, however destructive to human eyes, are essential for ecological function; and that there is no such thing as intrinsic value. And looming over all of this is the mechanistic, utilitarian materialism which insists that natural products are resources for the human endeavor, that such resources can and should be used for the greatest good, and that human needs must supersede the needs of nonhuman nature.

The conflicts among these different perspectives have become amplified over time. The human population has grown. Industrialization and resource extraction have generated pollution and made scarce natural products that were once plentiful.

Places once pristine have become degraded, and the capacity for the planet to adequately support this and future generations has been strained. If we jump ahead in time to the environmental revolution of the 1960s the same themes are present, accompanied by another: environmental justice. This is the recognition that our environmental problems are not equally distributed. There is surplus amid want, cleanliness in the midst of pollution, and access alongside exclusion. There are two worlds, one of consumption and relative environmental quality, the other of exploitation and degradation. Too often these worlds are divided along lines of wealth, race, and ethnicity. Thus, the questions of material versus spiritual, appropriation versus preservation, and Cartesian dualism are not the sole foundation of the environmental movement. Environmentalism is just as much about social equity.

Rights of ownership

There is a connection between our treatment of nonhuman nature and our treatment of one another, and that connection is in the recognition of rights. To romantics and spiritual animists, as we have seen, the extension of rights to the nonhuman makes perfect sense. Not so for the material utilitarian. In a similar way, humans have long struggled with the extension of rights to other humans. Roderick Nash has noted that in recent human history the circle of ethics has widened, such that rights once extended only to white landowners, for example, have slowly become accessible to slaves, to women, and to people of color (Nash, 1989: 7). The establishment of certain protections for endangered species implies to Nash that modern affluent society may be poised to one day extend rights to all animals, plants, and nonliving nature, thus achieving what many animists have long advocated. Time will tell whether this is true or not, but the thought provides a link between the two pillars of modern environmentalism: the question of responsibility toward nonhuman nature and the question of human rights and social relations.

A peculiar aspect of many human societies is the notion of property rights, or the idea that a person can own a portion of the natural world and hold the right to use it as he or she sees fit. The concept is so ubiquitous in the modern affluent world that it is taken as a basic human right. This was not always so and is not the case in every society. Individual or collective ownership of natural resources has played a critical role in the emergence of environmentalism, for ownership and utility, however beneficial to the user, can easily lead to conflict. Such conflict can include damage of property owned by others, injury to their personal health and well-being, inequitable access to resources, or to the degradation of common resources. Environmental problems, in this sense, are at least partially problems of ownership.

The origins of private land ownership take us once again to early modern Europe. In medieval times land was owned variously by emperors and then by decentralized nobility. According to the feudal system of the age, peasants were permitted land use (and the prospect of military defense) in exchange for service or payment. Natural resources, such as arable land, forests, and streams, were inherited by those of noble birth and not available for private ownership. Therefore, private enterprise—in the manner of resource acquisition and exchange as we know it today—was inconceivable for all but the wealthiest lords. Production, in the form of crops, timber, livestock, and skilled craftsmanship, were intended for local consumption only under the auspices of the aristocracy (Mason, 2015: 234–238).

What caused this centuries-old system to break down is open to debate, but a central factor may well have been that great environmental catastrophe, the Black Death. The economist Paul Mason postulates that the climate change-driven famines of the early 1300s and the ensuing plague caused a labor shortage, resulting in higher city wages that drew workers away from feudal farms. The scale of death was so great that even this influx of laborers could not meet the demand. In the centuries following the plague, necessity stimulated invention—after a thousand years of very little technological innovation. Cranks, reels, and connecting rods were used in conjunction with water power, windmills, and flywheels to facilitate production with limited labor. So began the age of automation that, with the later invention of the spinning jenny, would usher in the mass production of the textile factory. Likewise, the invention of navigational instruments spurred exploration, and exploration facilitated imperialism. Fueled by the plundered wealth and new markets of colonial lands, and by credit from an emerging banking system, capitalism was born (O'Brien and Williams, 2013: 68; Mason, 2015: 238–242).

In this way, as Europe emerged from the plague its socioeconomic system began to change. New economic realities came in fits and starts through innovation, uprising, resistance, legislation, political pressures, or all at once. In the 18th century English agriculture (like manufacturing) shifted from production for local subsistence to production for the marketplace. Accompanying this was a change in the legal status of the land. Thousands of private enclosures were created out of land that was once common space, or land previously held by noble lords (Worster, 1994: 13). In France at the same time the system of *domaine direct*—land workers subservient to a lord—was similarly breaking down (Congost, 2003: 86). But the transition from fiefdoms to modern private ownership was not so immediate or clear; it was, in fact, part of a long period of change that continued into the 20th century. Private, heritable land rights, the right to voluntary sale of said rights, and the emergence of a class of people holding personal wealth were all part of this transition, which occurred through various stages of semi-feudalism.

A notable feature of semi-feudalistic Europe was the emphyteutic contracts issued to tenants of the land, known as copyholders in England. These contracts obligated the tenant to improve the land by construction and modification, subject to fines or loss of privileges for neglect of this duty. The term *improve* was used in the economic sense: to make the land more amenable to production. The result was widespread conversion of woodland, wetland, and wasteland into agricultural land. A similar practice was later used in the American system of homesteading. While some tenants chafed at, eluded, and eventually resisted oppressive treatment at the hands of the landlord, it was not because of any perceived degradation of the land. Rather, it was the growing sense that freedom from oppression and individual rights should be paramount. Once full owners (or freeholders in England), people were free to improve the land and enhance its production for the marketplace. This attitude, too, found its way to America and beyond (Congost, 2003: 97).

Social division and solidarity

The industrial revolution complicated social class division. Preindustrial social classes generally included the aristocracy, the clergy, artisans, and laboring peasants. With the onset of private land and private enterprise came new social structures: individual owners of natural capital, a merchant class devoted to the buying and selling of commodities, a middle class which controlled the mechanisms of production, a working class of both agrarian and industrial settings that provided (or withheld) labor, and the destitute. Urbanization and its appalling conditions for work and life, the pollution of early industrialization, and the lack of labor laws made life less than ideal for the working class. On the other hand, merchants, skilled craftsmen, and the owners of productive land or factories could do quite well in the nascent market economy. Such discrepancy increased the likelihood of class struggle, crime, and violence, and spurred Marxist visions of the future. Societies attempted to deal with class struggle in various ways, and to this end rights were slowly extended to the working class (though by no means universally). The rights of individual freedoms of speech, thought, and faith, the right to private property and justice, and the right to participate in governance all unfolded as industrial capitalism grew (Mann, 1987: 339–344; Fitzgerald, 2000: 376–381).

In further response to the casualties of social division there emerged in 19th-century Europe the concept of social citizenship, or the social economy. According to the French economist Charles Gide (1847–1932) the social economy epitomized "the natural laws that govern the spontaneous relations between people and things; it was the science of social justice" (Gide, 2005 [1912]: 10; Moulaert and Ailenei, 2005: 2040). To some the social economy was the purview of the state. It was the state's role, therefore, to protect people from the failings of the self-interest-driven market, and indeed many states have taken on this role. But the industrial revolution also spawned third-sector organizations, neither of the state nor of the market, with the sole intention of promoting social well-being. In Europe these took the form of "mutual support organizations, cooperatives and associations" that worked to protect workers against "social risks (disease, accidents, death), professional risks (unemployment, strikes), or the alienation from basic needs (shelter, food)" (Moulaert and Ailenei, 2005: 2041). Initially local and typically guild-specific, such partnerships eventually grew to regional, national, and international scale. We recognize such associations today as nonprofit organizations, non-governmental organizations, unions, and community groups. In their infancy such cooperatives primarily advocated for better wages, improved working conditions, and consumer rights. Increasingly, though, as citizens of industrialized areas faced declining personal health and degraded environmental quality, solidarity movements began to take aim at environmental concerns (Moulaert and Ailenei, 2005: 2037–2046).

The social contract

Contractual agreements for land ownership and associations for social wellness were ostensibly at odds with one another, for in the one case they promoted individual freedom, while in the other they curtailed individual freedom to promote the common good. Even so, they co-existed, and were even drawn from the same long-standing Enlightenment ideas of the social contract. Thomas Hobbes had expressed ideas on just this sort of human conflict: that as self-interested individuals we will compete, but as equals we must co-exist. Hobbes believed that humans are selfishly motivated, but also rational, and it is our rationality that allows us to follow the rules of society. These rules, both written and unwritten, are the social contract of civility. For self-interested individuals to live constructively together, the contract must be established and enforced by some authority (an absolute sovereign was Hobbes' preference). Otherwise, in Hobbes' vision, we descend into the war of nature (Hampton, 1999: 41–57).

The English philosopher John Locke had a kinder, gentler view of society. He saw the natural state of humans as a state of personal liberty, in which people were free to pursue individual desires. Of course, unlimited pursuit of our desires would quickly encroach upon the desires of others. In Locke's philosophy it is our morality—our duty to God—that curbs our behavior, and mutual recognition of moral boundaries allows us to co-exist. Locke observed that ownership of private property complicates this arrangement, for the self-interested actions of one, while they may not impact another directly, may certainly have indirect effects by encroaching on another's property. Interestingly, Locke equated property rights with utility; that is, one should have the right to procure, develop, and improve resources in the course of the human endeavor. Ultimately, obligations and responsibilities are accountable to the Creator. It is the role of government, then, to enforce rights set forth by God and to adjudicate when social contracts are breached (Simmons, 1999).

Jean-Jacques Rousseau, in his *Discourse on the origin and foundations of inequality among men* (Rousseau, 1992 [1755]), agreed with Locke that private property confounds our nature, which to the romantic Rousseau was a peaceful, harmonious existence. However, Rousseau saw what he called "naturalized" social contracts as devices that favored the wealthy and perpetuated inequality, even as they purported to promote equity. To Rousseau, the ideal social contract—what he called the "normative" contract—would require participants to sacrifice some of their self-interested desires for the collective good. By general agreement, then, greed would be held in check and equality assured, "setting the conditions of future interaction among the members of a community" (Ripstein, 1999: 224; Rousseau, 1923 [1761]). Rousseau theorized that such a system could only work in a direct democracy, in which all parties know one another and periodically confer to arrive at mutual understanding (Cohen, 1999).

Mutual understanding—easily stated but not so easily achieved—is an old idea. Spinoza argued for it in the 17th century, recognizing that one's actions or attitudes may meet with the disapproval of others, but that such differences must to some extent be borne in civil society. Spinoza appears to have anticipated Rousseau's small democratic groups, for he proposed that mutual tolerance can exist in society "only if everyone is allowed to think what he will, and say what he thinks" (Spinoza, 2007 [1670]: 32; Rosenthal, 2001: 536). Beliefs and attitudes cannot be compelled, and any attempt to do so leads to political and social instability. Spinoza saw two components to human character: the self-regarding and the other-regarding. We strive, then, simultaneously to "preserve our being" and "to aid other men and to join them to us in friendship" (Spinoza, 1950 [1677]: 59; Rosenthal, 2001: 544). Ambition, a condition of the first desire, must be held in check to achieve the second desire. When ambition can be checked, the result is social stability and mutual advantage. Ultimately, Spinoza's tolerance of others is a facet of self-preservation, for social stability is good for the individual. This is an important aspect of social contract theory in general: acting for the good of the collective is itself an act of self-interest (Rosenthal, 2001).

Private ownership of land and natural resources, social citizenship, third-sector organizations devoted to the common good, and social contracts of mutual understanding: these can all be seen in the ensuing century of developing environmentalism. The difficulties have been in the restraint of private (and state, and corporate) enterprise in the name of social responsibility, in the exploitation and degradation of common resources by those acting in their own self-interest, and in the extension (or denial) of social contracts to the marginalized poor, indigenous, people of color, and women. We see these struggles of environmentalism in John Muir's fight to keep the Hetch Hetchy valley from being dammed, in Rachel Carson's (1962) plea for regulation of synthetic pesticides, in the disastrous operation of a chemical plant in Bhopal, India, and in the contamination of Minimata Bay, Japan. Such cases and so many others, it could be argued, are breached social contracts and failures of mutual understanding.

A conflicted foundation

Here, then, is the foundation of modern western environmentalism. It is built upon two pillars. One is a question of the human–nature relationship, with particular regard to the character of the nonhuman world and the extent to which it should be granted moral consideration. The other concerns human obligations toward one another, especially considering property rights, social contracts, and civility. But these pillars are conflicted—they are the confluence of fundamentally different worldviews. Mechanism and animism, spiritualism and materialism, utilitarianism and preservationism, private ownership and the common good, self-interest and social civility—these ideas make our responsibilities ambiguous. What does such a conflicted foundation mean for modern environmentalism? In short, it means that it is multidimensional and self-contradictory.

Notes

1 The phrase "ghost in the machine" is a reference to Gilbert Ryle's assessment of Cartesian mind–body dualism.
2 The term noble savage is first attributed to the playwright John Dryden in 1672.

Bibliography

Aquinas, T. (1485). *Summa theologica*. Translation by Fathers of the English Dominican Province. Rome: Benzinger Brothers Printers to the Holy Apostolic See.

Borch, O. (1996 [1661]). Diary entry of September 1661, as per Klever, W. 1996. Spinoza's life and works. In: D. Garrett, ed., *The Cambridge companion to Spinoza*. Cambridge, UK: Cambridge University Press. pp. 13–60.

Bustos, K. (2011). Kantian philosophy and the environment. In: J. Newman, ed., *Green ethics and philosophy: an A–Z guide*. Thousand Oaks, CA: SAGE Publications. pp. 295–297.

Callicott, J.B. (1982). Traditional American Indian and Western European attitudes toward nature. *Environmental Ethics*, 4(4), pp. 293–318.

Carson, R. (1962). *Silent spring*. Boston: Houghton Mifflin.

Cohen, J. (1999). Reflections on Rousseau: autonomy and democracy. In: C. Morris, ed., *The social contract theorists: critical essays on Hobbes, Locke and Rousseau*. New York: Rowman & Littlefield. pp. 191–204.

Congost, R. (2003). Property rights and historical analysis: What rights? What history? *Past & Present*, 181, pp. 73–106.

Crombie, A.C. (1959). Descartes. *Scientific American*, October 1, 1959, pp. 160–173.

Desmond, A. and Moore, J. (1991). *Darwin: the life of a tormented evolutionist*. New York: W.W. Norton.

de Solla Price, D.J. (1964). Automata and the origins of mechanism and mechanistic philosophy. *Technology and Culture*, 5(1), pp. 9–23.

Fairchild, H.N. (1940). The romantic movement in England. *Publications of the Modern Language Association of America*, 55, pp. 20–26.

Fitzgerald, R.D. (2000). The social impact of the industrial revolution. In: J. Lauer and N. Schlager, eds., *Science and its times: understanding the social significance of scientific discovery*, Vol. 4. Detroit, MI: Gale. pp. 376–381.

Gide, C. (2005 [1912]). *Les institutions de progrès social*. Paris: Librairie de la Société du Recueil Sirey (In: F. Moulaert and O. Ailenei. Social economy, third sector and solidarity relations: a conceptual synthesis from history to present. *Urban Studies*, 42(11), p. 2040).

Gottlieb, A. (1999). God exists, philosophically. *New York Times*, July 18, 1999.

Hampton, J. (1999). The failure of Hobbes's social contract argument. In: C. Morris, ed., *The social contract theorists: critical essays on Hobbes, Locke and Rousseau*. New York: Rowman & Littlefield. pp. 41–58.

Harrison, P. (1992). Descartes on animals. *Philosophical Quarterly*, 42(167), pp. 219–227.

Harvey, G. (2005). *Animism: respecting the living world*. Cambridge, MA: Wakefield Press.

Hobbes, T. (1994 [1651]). *Leviathan*. Edwin Curley, ed. Indianapolis, IN: Hackett Publishing.

Kaufman, F. (2003). *Foundations of environmental philosophy*. New York: McGraw-Hill.

Kelly, J. (2005). *The Great Mortality: an intimate history of the Black Death, the most devastating plague of all time.* New York: HarperCollins.

Klever, W. (1996). Spinoza's life and works. In: D. Garrett, ed., *The Cambridge companion to Spinoza.* Cambridge, UK: Cambridge University Press. pp. 13–60.

Laland, K.N. and Brown, G.R. (2011). *Sense and nonsense: evolutionary perspectives on human behaviour.* Oxford: Oxford University Press.

Lange, F.A. (1877). *The history of materialism and a critique of its present importance,* Vol. 1. Boston: Houghton, Osgood & Co.

Manchester, W. (1992). *A world lit only by fire: the medieval mind and the Renaissance, portrait of an age.* Boston: Back Bay Books.

Mann, M. (1987). Ruling class strategies and citizenship. *Sociology,* 21(3), pp. 339–354.

Mason, P. (2015). *Postcapitalism: a guide to our future.* New York: Farrar, Straus and Giroux.

Mautner, T., ed. (2005). *The Penguin dictionary of philosophy.* 2nd edition. New York: Penguin Press.

Mill, J.S. (1848). *Principles of political economy.* Book IV Chapter VI. London: Longmans, Green & Co.

Mill, J.S. (1924 [1873]). *Autobiography of John Stuart Mill.* New York: Columbia University Press.

Moulaert, F. and Ailenei, O. (2005). Social economy, third sector and solidarity relations: a conceptual synthesis from history to present. *Urban Studies,* 42(11), pp. 2037–2053.

Nash, R.F. (1989). *The rights of nature: a history of environmental ethics.* Madison, WI: University of Wisconsin Press.

O'Brien, R. and Williams, M. (2013). *Global political economy: evolution and dynamics.* 4th edition. New York: Palgrave Macmillan.

Reeves, R. (2007). John Stuart Mill. *Salmagundi,* 153/154, pp. 47–59.

Ripstein, A. (1999). The general will. In: C.W. Morris, ed., *The social contract theorists: critical essays on Hobbes, Locke and Rousseau.* New York: Rowman & Littlefield. pp. 219–238.

Rosenthal, M.A. (2001). Tolerance as a virtue in Spinoza's ethics. *Journal of the History of Philosophy,* 39(4), pp. 535–557.

Rousseau, J.J. (1923 [1761]). *The social contract & discourses.* Translation by G. Cole. London: J.M. Dent & Sons.

Rousseau, J.J. (1992 [1755]). *Discourse on the origin and foundations of inequality among men.* Translation by D. Cress. Indianapolis, IN: Hackett Publishing.

Simmons, A.J. (1999). Locke's state of nature. In: C. Morris, ed., *The social contract theorists: critical essays on Hobbes, Locke and Rousseau.* New York: Rowman & Littlefield. pp. 97–120.

Spencer, H. (1864). *The principles of biology.* London: Williams & Northgate.

Spinoza, B. (1950 [1677]). *Ethics, demonstrated in geometrical order.* Translation by R. Elwes. London: Dent, E.P. Dutton & Co.

Spinoza, B. (1996 [1661]). Letter to Henry Oldenburg, September 1661, as per Klever, W. 1996. In: D. Garrett, ed., *The Cambridge companion to Spinoza.* Cambridge: Cambridge University Press. pp. 13–60.

Spinoza, B. (2007 [1670]). *Theologico-political treatise.* Israel, J., ed. Translation by M. Silverthorne and J. Israel. Cambridge, UK: Cambridge University Press.

Szűcs, E., Geers, R., Jezierski, T., Sossidou, E.N. and Broom, D.M. (2012). Animal welfare in different human cultures, traditions and religious faiths. *Asian-Australasian Journal of Animal Sciences*, 25(11), pp. 1499–1506.

Thacker, C. (1983). *The wildness pleases: the origins of romanticism*. London: Routledge.

Worster, D. (1994). *Nature's economy: a history of ecological ideas*. Cambridge, UK: Cambridge University Press.

2 Dimensions of environmentalism

Key points

- Environmental perspectives on the nonhuman world can range from biocentric to anthropocentric, from spiritual to material, and from ecocentric to egocentric.
- Environmental concepts of human relations span from individualistic to collective and parochial to global.
- Within its wide conceptual space, environmentalism is based on some fundamental human values.

A modern environmental problem

Take a stroll through any mainstream grocery store in the developed world and you'll find yourself surrounded by highly processed foods, beverages, cosmetics, hygiene products, and household cleaners. Choose a random selection of those items and scan the ingredients. Chances are good you'll see an ingredient that has become a major environmental issue: palm oil. Originally harvested in its native West Africa, palm is now grown around the tropical and sub-tropical world primarily for its oil, which is in global demand. Palm harvest supplies over a quarter of the world's vegetable oil, and about 80% of it comes from Malaysia and Indonesia. As an inexpensive alternative to other vegetable oils, palm production has increased dramatically in recent years, in part due to the push to reduce trans-fats in the diets of affluent people (who consume a lot of highly processed food). Trans-fats, formerly found in all sorts of processed foods, have been linked to heart disease and type 2 diabetes. Trans-fat free palm oil is marketed as a healthier substitute (Unnevehr and Jagmanaite, 2008; Pye, 2013).

Though it has been touted for health benefits, palm oil is not a great alternative to trans-fats, because it too is a rich source of saturated fats. However, it is cheap—perhaps the cheapest cooking oil in the world—and so it has been a major part of the response to the trans-fat scare. Global production of palm oil increased by 65% between 1995 and 2002, primarily driven by consumers in the US and Europe

(Pye, 2013: 1). Market demand has spurred plantation-style monoculture production on some 14 million hectares of tropical land. Much of this land is cleared tropical forest, home to some of the most biodiverse ecosystems on Earth. The pressure to clear more land is increasing, for palm oil is not only useful as a food additive. It is also a component of purportedly cleaner-burning fuels like biodiesel. By one estimate—assuming that demand continues to rise on the current trajectory—the global consumption of vegetable oils will nearly double by 2050, requiring an additional 12 million hectares of tropical palm plantation (Corley, 2009).

Does this qualify as an environmental problem? It certainly has the makings. The conversion of tropical forest to palm plantation means habitat loss for some iconic and highly threatened species, like the orangutan, Sumatran tiger and rhino, clouded leopard, and proboscis monkey. Millions of other plant, animal, and microbial species exist in tropical forests, which routinely show a marked loss of species richness when converted to palm plantation (Fitzherbert *et al.*, 2008). There are far more species in these forests than humans have named or even seen, and we certainly don't know how they all function or interact. We do understand something about how tropical forests function—enough to know that humans depend on such forests to store carbon, recycle nutrients, form soil, induce precipitation, and regulate climate. These alone are reasons for humans to curtail irresponsible palm harvest, but there are cultural reasons as well. Palm plantations often encroach on the land of indigenous peoples who have long depended on the forest for instrumental values like food, fuel, and fiber. Furthermore, many of these forests are considered sacred by the people that live in them. Displaced by plantations and deprived of their connections with the forest, indigenous people often end up working for a palm oil industry that has been accused of numerous human rights violations (Dewi, 2013).

Palm plantations are monocultures maintained by herbicides, insecticides, and fertilizers. These chemicals can contaminate the water sources on which local people depend. Forests are cleared for plantation by slash and burn techniques that can foul the air for months at a time. Deforestation exposes the soil to weathering, resulting in erosion and subsequent siltation of local aquatic ecosystems. In some areas the water table is lowered with drainage canals. The drained areas include ancient peatlands that, once dried, are burned to prepare the site for plantation. After palm is established and harvested, processing plants release a high-carbon effluent that can deplete the oxygen of rivers, lakes, and bays and result in the loss of aquatic life. The anaerobic decomposition of tons of organic waste releases methane—a potent greenhouse gas—into the atmosphere, just as the fires used to clear the next plantation site release carbon dioxide. Truly, the palm oil story goes far beyond qualifying as a single environmental problem. It is a bouquet of environmental problems (Jiwan, 2013).

There has been a broad response to the palm oil problem from environmental organizations, aimed variously at the mitigation of deforestation, climate change, and biodiversity loss. Environmental actions have included forest conservation projects, brand and end-product targeting, and lobbying governments on biofuel choices, all countered by industry discourse on corporate responsibility. It is tempting, but too simple to blame these problems only on the industries and the demand that drives them. The nations that host palm plantations and global development programs must also be held to account. Palm oil development was ramped up in Southeast Asia in the late 1970s as part of national development strategies with the support of the International Monetary Fund (IMF) and later expanded to global production by collaboration between national governments and transnational corporations. Palm development was touted as a means to alleviate poverty. Now, some four decades later, the industry seems to have created more harm than good for local peoples and ecosystems. Land use conflicts, heavy use of fire and agricultural chemicals, a lack of local investment, the use of migrant workers and associated labor conflicts, and abundant waste have troubled the industry at the local level, particularly for people that the development was initially intended to benefit (Pye, 2013).

Conceptual cartography

In this single example we see many aspects of environmentalism: resource utility, animal welfare, ecosystem function, human rights, the status of indigenous cultures, corporate and government regard for environmental and human health, the importance of sacred space, loss of biodiversity, pollution, and the abuse of both environment and the poor by the (often oblivious) affluent. These issues are complex, and it seems that many of the demands are not easily compatible. Should the lifestyles and sacred spaces of indigenous cultures be given precedence over agricultural production? Should nonhuman species outweigh human development? If so, which plants and animals are to be given the privilege? It is an issue of the wealthy and the poor, the human and nonhuman, the "natural" state and the "developed" state of the land. How are we to make sense of such complexity?

The palm oil dilemma illustrates some ancient questions of human conduct and some questions that have emerged only recently, with the onset of globalization. Essentially, though, they are the same concerns of human responsibility toward the nonhuman world and toward one another that we encountered in the previous chapter: materialism and spiritualism, mechanism and holism, utility and restraint, individual rights and the common good. These tensions, I have suggested, are the basis of all environmental problems. In this chapter I explore conflicting environmental perspectives and common environmental values. My purpose is to identify the boundaries of the movement—to map the conceptual space of modern environmentalism.

It could be argued that environmentalism has so many connotations that it defies definition. If you disagree, try to define it yourself. Does your definition have something to do with Earth's capacity for supporting life? Do you prioritize human life, or is your environmentalism one that seeks equal regard for all living things? What happens when the use of natural resources, which are critical to human life, has a negative effect on natural processes and ecological relationships that sustain nonhuman life? What if the "resource" is living organisms themselves, and the very act of using those living things diminishes or depletes them? If living or nonliving natural resources can be used without depletion, to what extent should humans be allowed to modify, manipulate, or change them? Are there states or arrangements of nature that should remain unchanged by humans? And what of the spiritual connection humans have with living and nonliving things? How should an environmentalist address spirituality, and according to whose spiritual view? How much of environmentalism is—or should be—about human treatment of other humans?

Our interactions with the world and with one another are loaded with such questions, and this is one reason that environmental worldviews are so diverse. Environmentalism means different things to different people, and different perspectives can result in different narratives (Box 2.1). Some of these differences amount to subtleties among people who are otherwise in agreement. In other cases, however, people who claim the title *environmentalist* hold views that are diametrically opposed, or nearly so. My goal, therefore, is not to develop a concise definition. Rather, I will present for consideration several conceptual dimensions of environmentalism by representing perspectives on opposite ends of the spectrum. This is an oversimplification, to be sure, for few ideas are linear and polar. Neither does it imply that the extremes are the only possible points of view, for most people probably fall somewhere in the middle. I characterize the extremes only to identify the boundaries of the ideology. My evaluation of the different dimensions will unfold throughout the rest of the book.

Here, then, are the dimensions that I will consider in this chapter: 1) Should environmentalism give priority to human well-being, or should the focus instead be on the equal protection of nonhuman life? 2) What role does spirituality play in environmentalism, particularly as people interact with and rely upon material aspects of the world? 3) To what extent should an environmentalist allow for human manipulation of nature? 4) Should environmentalism be more concerned with the promotion of individual rights or social responsibilities? 5) What is the proper scale and extent of our environmental responsibility?

Anthropocentrism and biocentrism

The question of whether humans are part of or separate from nature is an old debate, as we have seen, reaching back at least as far as Thomas Aquinas and Francis of Assisi. It is the debate of Cartesian human–nature dualism—with the machine-like view of nature and the ecological imperialism it engenders versus the organismal view of nature favored by Henry More. It is Darwin's paradox of the self-interested, life-and-death competition of nature in the midst of kinship, cooperation, and coexistence. It all comes down to a simple question: should humans place their own needs (and wants) above the needs of other species?

I noted in the previous chapter that my students routinely define environmental disasters as catastrophes that befall humans, particularly if the catastrophe was caused by humans. Admittedly, my students represent only a thin slice of society, and there are certainly other opinions. I will venture to observe, however, that

Box 2.1 Interrogating environmental narratives

The different ways in which people perceive and make sense of the world are represented by different environmental narratives. Cronon (1992) makes the case that cultural narratives reflect the discourse of a particular time, place, situation, and ideology, and that narrative can frame behavior. As an example, Cronon examines different narratives of the Dust Bowl in the American west of the 1930s. In one Dust Bowl narrative, human subjects are depicted as heroically battling the environmental obstacles of an inhospitable landscape. In another, settlers stubbornly force their way of life onto an ecosystem that can't support it. These and other narratives portray a variety of themes—human ascent, failure of the state, genocide, progress, hubris, natural limits, rugged individualism—all with regard to the same series of events.

Are all narratives equally valid? If they are not, how are we to know which narratives best represent reality? Cronon argues that environmental narratives should be constrained by three factors. First, they must conform to known facts about the past. Second, they must be consistent with scientific principles. Finally, environmental narratives must "confront contradictory evidence and counter-narratives" (Cronon, 1992: 1373) both to incorporate and to refute varied perspectives.

The many dimensions of environmentalism are narratives of their own, each representing a unique interpretation of the human relationship with the nonhuman world. Minteer and Pyne (2013) have traced the origins of two overarching narratives of American environmentalism, namely pragmatism and preservationism. They argue that these perspectives are not equally valid, specifically that the preservation narrative is inconsistent with the realities of ecological change. The traditional concept of pristine wilderness unfettered by human influence is less meaningful in the face of highly managed ecological systems that are manipulated according to human desires. Accordingly, Minteer and Pyne find the pragmatic narrative of conservation, utility, and management to be more meaningful.

Environmental narratives inform individual and collective action, and contradictory narratives can confound action. Part of the work of the environmentalist, then, is to interrogate narratives in the light of facts, principles, and evidence.

most people—even most environmentally minded people—in modern western affluent society are fundamentally anthropocentric. Others are repulsed by such a notion. For some people, regarding the human species as the highest priority is the *opposite* of environmentalism. But anthropocentrism and environmentalism are not incompatible. In fact, anthropocentrism undergirds many worldviews that are commonly associated with environmentalism. The utilitarian conservationist recommends wise use of resources for this and future generations (of humans); the ecosystem manager advocates for the protection of ecological relationships and processes (that benefit humans); the preservationist works to restrict encroachment on certain environments that are aesthetically pleasing or have cultural significance (for humans); the animal-rights activist works for humane (human-like) treatment of other species.

Since our attitudes and behaviors are all generated from the human perspective, it has been argued that they are *necessarily* anthropocentric. Undeniably, some human-centric behavior can be reprehensible. The philosopher Hayward (1997) allows that inflicting arbitrary suffering on nonhuman species—or rationalization that permits such treatment—is objectionable. Commodification of nature, as in livestock confinement facilities, clear cutting, ocean floor trawling, animal experimentation and the like, could certainly be construed as sources of undue suffering. The biocentrist might argue that such treatment of nonhuman species cheapens all life (Regan, 1985). But the simple fact that an action is done with human agency for human interests does not necessarily mean that it is misguided or immoral. Hayward suggests instead that the greatest criticism of anthropocentrism is that we don't do it well enough. In his words, "a cursory glance around the world would confirm that humans show a lamentable lack of interest in the well-being of other humans" (Hayward, 1997: 57). An anthropocentric environmentalism prioritizes human well-being.

A view from the other end of the debate holds that humans should not place themselves above other species at all, but rather that all species have equal value and therefore an equal right to exist (Guha and Martinez-Alier, 1997: 94–95). The philosopher Paul Taylor, for example, has argued that each individual organism is its own "teleological center of life, pursuing its own good in its own way" (Taylor, 1981: 207). As each living thing depends on other living things, none can be regarded as superior. Biocentrism sees intrinsic value, not just instrumental value, in all living things. It envisions a world in which humans restrict their own population, resource demands, and waste production in order to leave large expanses of Earth to other species. There is often a spiritual dimension to biocentrism bordering on or embracing pantheism—it recalls Spinoza's notion that there is spirit in all living things (and for some, even nonliving things). It holds that humans are part of and fully reliant upon a network with these other entities and should act accordingly. In one manifestation biocentrism leads to Gaianism—the notion that the Earth itself is an organism which maintains the conditions necessary for life (Lovelock, 1972; Lovelock and Margulis, 1974). Humans, in this view, are just one node of the complex network, albeit an important one. To the Gaian, anthropogenic stressors like global climate change are fluctuations that the complex system of Earth must fight to regulate.

The anthropocentric-to-biocentric dimension of environmentalism is a question of utility and morality (Nash, 1989: 92; Kaufman, 2003). Clearly, humans must use other species and nonliving resources in order to survive. Biocentrists insist that the value system of right and wrong by which we treat one another (or by which we should treat one another) be extended to nonhuman life.

Anthropocentrists do not. The disagreement, then, is the extent to which humans should treat the nonhuman environment as instrumentally or intrinsically valuable. Taylor (1981) attributes the prevailing western sense of human superiority to the value we place on rational thought, to the legacy of Cartesian dualism, and to the influence of Judeo-Christian theology. These claims to superiority, in Taylor's estimation, give people the false impression of preeminence over other forms of life on the planet. To Taylor, our hubris stems from a misunderstanding of our species' place in the universe. Curiously, the argument from the other side is also framed around misunderstanding. The evolutionary biologist Stephen Jay Gould has similarly argued that our sense of power over the natural world is a misconception. But Gould does not conclude that we should therefore regard all life as equal. Rather, he concludes that we should seek environmental solutions "for human needs at human scales," for "we have a legitimately parochial interest in our own lives, the happiness and prosperity of our children, the suffering of our fellows" (Gould, 1990). In other words, he suggests environmental action for anthropocentric reasons.

Some have pointed out that biocentrism is primarily a position of the wealthy. It is a question for those who are materially secure; in Roderick Nash's words, it is a debate for those with full stomachs (Nash, 1965: 343). In *Varieties of environmentalism*, Guha and Martinez-Alier (1997: 16) propose that we should speak of two environmentalisms: that of the poor Global South and that of the wealthy Global North. For billions of poor people the questions of equal rights for all species or protected wilderness areas or their role as one node in a vast, self-regulating complex of organisms are not central issues of daily life. Rather, questions of subsistence are at the forefront. Access to potable water, equitable distribution of land, a safe and reliable food supply, rights to local resources: these are the critical issues when one is living day-to-day on the brink of starvation. In less developed regions of the world, the argument goes, the "environmentalists" are not concerned with biocentrism. Rather, they are fighting for basic human rights against wealthier humans who seek to commandeer, manage, and extract resources or dispose of wastes in their home (Guha and Martinez-Alier, 1997: 12). In these situations the question is not so much one of species rights as it is of human rights— a kind of desperate anthropocentrism.

In the palm oil example we see the tussle between anthropocentrism and biocentrism. As noted, the tropical forests that are cleared for palm plantations are areas of incredible biological diversity, including some charismatic species that are in decline. For example, many of the environmental campaigns against unscrupulous palm oil harvest feature the orangutan, an intelligent, social ape that is clearly threatened by deforestation. To a biocentrist, the presence of the orangutan alone may be enough to demand that these forests be off-limits to human development. But of course the forests that support the orangutan also support unknown and unknowable numbers of other species, which in the biocentric view have an equal right to exist. Actually, *which* species deserve the right to exist is a bit of a conundrum for the strict biocentrist, for living things tend to eat, infect, out-compete, and parasitize one another. Many species are also harmful to humans (in that they cause disease or otherwise threaten human life) or they are necessarily beneficial (in that they produce food, fuel, or fiber). Why, then, is it imperative to extend rights to the orangutan, but not to species that the orangutan eats, to species that could be harmful to us, or to species that we consume? If the defense of other species only extends to those that humans find to be interesting, attractive, or unpalatable, isn't that just veiled anthropocentrism?

The philosopher James Sterba has responded to such criticism with a nuanced biocentrism (Sterba, 1998). Recognizing that different species have different life strategies and different interests, it may make more sense to speak of an *equitable*— rather than equal—co-existence. An understanding of the realities of ecological relationships might allow for behaviors of self-preservation, defense of one's own kind, and promotion of species and resources that one depends upon or cares about over other species or resources. We may, in Sterba's biocentrism, have an obligation to rectify undue stress or destruction that we have brought to bear on other species. Basic needs, in this perspective, are warranted, while frivolous wants are not. But it seems that even Sterba's biocentrism comes down to human attitudes and judgements.

The reality is that human interactions with their environment necessarily involve encroachment upon and judgement of other species. In most cases, the potential benefits to humans are given higher priority than the potential costs to the nonhuman world. The palm plantation industry, after all, was initiated with human development in mind. Development can bring jobs, infrastructure, education, health care, emergency services, and other amenities that the developed world takes for granted, and such infrastructure can ultimately reduce the need for environmental destruction. In Malaysia and Indonesia the well-intentioned development quickly became co-opted by corporate interests, and in too many cases the social development has been lacking. Still, some argue that a commodity like palm oil can be harvested sustainably and used to build human communities along with the protection of nonhuman species (Laurance *et al.*, 2010). Others reject even sustainable harvest and insist that we must see other species as something more than expendable masses of protoplasm. In a word, the strict biocentrist looks at a nonhuman organism and sees spirit.

Materialism and spiritualism

So you might be, on one extreme, an anthropocentrist who believes that natural resources and nonhuman species can and should be unconditionally used for human benefit. Or you might support the biocentric belief that the rights afforded to humans should be extended to all species. Probably you fall somewhere in between. For many people, such questions are closely connected to their perception of the universe—specifically to their view of spirituality. We have already encountered pantheism and animism, belief systems that understand nonhuman species, and even nonliving aspects of the environment, to have a spiritual essence or vitality, and therefore intrinsic value. In some cases, spiritual environmentalists take this farther to suggest that all living things (and sometimes nonliving as well) are interconnected by the same spirit. This blurs the boundary of self-identity, such that preservation of the environment is the same thing as self-preservation. In certain cultures the spirit of self is shared with a location—a mountain, a shoreline, a forest—thus conferring sanctity to that place. If the individual, the place, and nature are one and there is no distinct self, then material reductionism makes little sense. Instead, humans and their environment must be considered holistically, as one interdependent system. Some spiritualists thus identify strongly with the biocentric perspective, for equality among all species is consistent with the belief that each species hosts a supernatural energy. Spiritualism is not synonymous with biocentrism, however. Many monotheists, for example, believe that a deity created the world and all the species in it but created humans as the greatest species of all. As we have seen, the case can be made that this sort of spiritualism has enabled the use and abuse of the nonhuman world (Merchant, 2005: 65).

The romanticism of early modern Europe was drawn from the spiritualism of an earlier age, and it is because of romantic inspiration that spirituality is such a strong component of environmentalism today. But spirituality is not a European invention; it is a universal human characteristic. In non-western cultures, spiritualism can be indistinguishable from environmentalism. In the Amazon basin of Ecuador, for example, the peoples of the Cofran, Siona-Secoya, and Quichua tribes have been displaced by plantations for palm oil production. The culture of these tribes is closely integrated with the forest; theirs is an animistic existence that places intrinsic value on the organisms of the forest and in natural phenomena, which are believed to harbor spirits. Many tribal life stages and decisions are associated with these spirits, including the diagnosis and treatment of illness, the pursuit of game animals, the punishment of enemies, requests for beneficial weather conditions, and communion with the deceased (Wilbert, 1996). The palm industry has cleared much of the forest, thereby removing the native people from their spiritual connection. Theirs is a worldview that is not easily portable or malleable; it is this place, with its endemic plants, animals, and physical features that is their identity. Through spirituality, their culture is tied to the forest. When the forest is lost, the culture is lost (Ashley, 1987).

Spiritual environmentalism, then, does not separate the individual from the whole. Joanna Macy has described the boundary of the self as something that need not end at our skin, but rather as an inclusive consciousness that can extend to embrace all of nature (Macy, 1992). Spiritual environmentalism sees organism, culture, and cosmos as part of a great unity, with constituent entities bound together by an intangible force. Our existence is indivisible from the great web of life, and all beings share a common fate. This is an environmentalism of feeling and emotion, not of objective information. It suggests that people have the ability to find peace through mental communion with the whole of nature, and thereby to "effect a transformation of values that in turn leads to action to heal the planet" (Merchant, 2005: 136).

Spiritualism's many forms give it a rich cultural diversity to which this brief introduction does not do justice, but—for the purpose of identifying dimensions of environmentalism—we will leave it at that for the moment to consider the other end of the spectrum: materialism. The materialist sees a universe comprised of matter and energy only; there is no supernatural essence and no non-physical substance. As the materialistic saying goes, everything in biology can be described by chemistry, and everything in chemistry can be described by physics. This Baconian and Linnaean worldview holds that complex systems, like human societies and their environment, can be understood through a comprehension of their fundamental components. So, while a more holistic thinker might claim that a forest, a person, or a society is more than the sum of its parts, the materialist would say that it is *precisely* the sum of its parts. This is not to say that there can't be synergistic properties that emerge when parts are combined, as when sodium and chlorine combine to form salt, or when trees and indigenous humans combine to form a culture. Materialism only observes that the capacity for the new properties was in the components all along. In the words of biologist David Sloan Wilson, "the parts permit the properties of the whole but do not cause the properties of the whole" (Wilson, 2002: 67).

A material environmentalism (considered by some an oxymoron) rejects the notion of supernatural essence in the nonliving and the living, including humans. Instead, it is concerned with the physical principles of matter, energy transfer, and phase change. It holds that living things on Earth evolved by physical replication of molecules acted on by natural selection over billions of years, not by super-natural intervention. Organisms are containers of energy with the capacity to move, grow, sense their environment, and, most critically, to reproduce—hence, a primary reason for their existence is to make copies of themselves. What sort of environmental ethic could arise from such a worldview?

For its denial of the supernatural, materialism is sometimes conflated with consumerism—the idea that material possessions are all that exist, so we can therefore consume to excess. But materialism and consumerism are not the same thing. Indeed, a materialist may have a strong will for self-denial, conservation, and compassion. For example, it makes complete sense—even material sense—to live within our physical means, so that future generations of living things can have the opportunity to exist. Materialism does not preclude wonder, or appreciation of beauty, or a fascination with and respect for life. A materialistic environ-mentalism, then, is a quest for materially sustainable communities.

Some spiritualists rage at materialism as the source of all that is wrong with the world. To consider the Earth and its inhabitants as mere containers of energy is to deny that they are special or worthy of protection at all. If materialism is not synonymous with consumerism, it enables consumerism. Materialists, for their part, are not terribly convinced by the proposed alternatives to their worldview. For example, the Gaia hypothesis, noted previously, implies that the Earth is a "self-regulating cybernetic system" that some materialists consider to be "ill-defined, unparsimonious and unfalsifiable" (Kirchner, 1989: 223; Merchant, 2005: 106). Materialists have the same criticisms of monotheistic, pantheistic, and other supernatural views of creation. Such beliefs emphasize a life of harmony and balance with the universe and mystical connections with vital energies. They are a search for an overarching connection that links all things and which provides purpose or direction to existence. This is an understandable desire, for the material universe is a cold place. In the absence of demonstrable evidence of such a unifying force, however, spiritualistic or holistic principles will remain difficult for the materialist to accept, and may even be considered contrary to reality. Even so, the general tenets of compassion, frugality, and humility would seem to be desirable characteristics all along this spectrum.

As with all of these dimensions of environmentalism, most people live at neither at one extreme nor the other, and one's view may well change through the course of a lifetime. Wherever you find yourself, your view on the spiritual world is likely to have a profound influence on your version of environmentalism. In fact, it quickly takes us to our most basic existential beliefs. Do you believe that humans and all other creatures were born of Mother Earth, a living goddess who cares for and expects honor from her children? Do you believe that God made man from the clay of the Earth and set him above all other living things? Do you believe that humans and all other species evolved from common ancestors by natural selection over billions of years? How then does your belief system shape your attitude toward other species, nonliving things, and other humans?

Ecocentrism and egocentrism

A third dimension of environmentalism is well illustrated by the palm oil dilemma. The fundamental problem with palm oil isn't the use of the substance itself. Humans were harvesting and consuming it long before it became a global environmental issue. Rather, the problem is in the large-scale conversion of tropical forests into palm plantations. Such intensive (and extensive) alteration has displaced wildlife, disrupted ecological function, and disenfranchised humans—and these issues have brought the palm oil industry to the attention of the global environmental community. We may view this as a systematic change—the existing ecosystem of the tropical forest is being changed into a human-dominated system.

To what degree should environmentalism be concerned with human modification or manipulation of ecological systems? Or, stated differently, is there a *proper* state of natural structure and function with which humans should not interfere? This is sometimes referred to as the ecocentric versus egocentric question. An ecocentric approach places the priority on—and even grants moral status to—the structures, functions, and processes of the biosphere. Egocentrism is all about the end user (you and me): we want to achieve and maintain the structure, function, and process that benefits us (Callicott, 1987; Kaufman, 2003).

This dimension of environmentalism presupposes that ecological systems are entities worthy of consideration, but this notion is far from settled. Many environmentalisms see "natural systems as integrated, stable wholes that are either at or moving toward mature equilibrium states" (Sterba, 1998: 368). Ecological science, however, has since challenged this concept of ecosystems. Donald Worster neatly summarizes what is arguably now the prevailing scientific perspective: "Nature is fundamentally erratic, discontinuous and unpredictable. It is full of seemingly random events that elude models of how things are supposed to work" (Worster, 1990: 13). If this is the case, how are we to evaluate the ways in which we alter ecological systems?

Humans have been modifying their environment for millions of years, and many nonhuman species do the same. Beavers convert streams into ponds, alligators dig wallow pits, oysters construct beds, and ants move tons of soil to suit their needs. Plants, too, change their environment, sometimes to facilitate their own growth (by mobilizing soil nutrients, for example), and sometimes to inhibit the growth of competitors (by releasing allelopathic chemicals). But humans have far exceeded the reach of other species, and there is no environment on Earth that we have not modified—intentionally or otherwise. We are the ultimate ecological engineers.

In part, humans manipulate their environment for egocentric utility—to harvest, to extract, to exploit. In certain cases we modify nature simply to make it more useful or aesthetically pleasing for ourselves. We mow, we landscape, we favor beneficial organisms and even alter species to suit our needs. Another common reason for environmental modification is to maintain stability—at least in the short term. Ecological disturbances, such as fire, flood, storm surge, landslide, drought, and pest outbreak are disruptive to human life. In an effort to maintain stability we reduce forest fuel loads, manage pest populations and build flood walls, irrigation and drainage systems. The stability gained is ephemeral; in fact many such human modifications lead to larger problems elsewhere or later in time. These will be dealt with by future modifications, we assume. But in the short term we find stability to be beneficial. A case could even be made that extreme manipulation of certain aspects of our environment is done in part for environmental protection. Construction of artificial reefs, replacement of invasive species with native species, introduction of organisms for biological control, terracing of landscapes to prevent erosion, prescribed burning—all are cases of extreme, but well-intentioned, manipulation. While these may all be part of ecological conservation efforts, they are also clearly part of an egocentric agenda.

But is any modification of nature therefore acceptable, for any reason? Consider a hypothetical person who collects bird eggs on his daily rounds to feed himself and his family. Now imagine that he decides he can save time by holding the birds in a large pen, so that the eggs are all in one place every day. Over time he begins to breed the birds to select for their best qualities—larger eggs, hardiness, and greater egg production. He then improves the efficiency of production by clustering the birds into small, densely packed cages and feeding them a mixture of grain, cooked bird remains, and antibiotics. Eventually he learns to insert a gene from a fish into the birds' genome which allows the birds to tolerate temperature extremes, so their production does not decline in hot weather. I suspect that many people who consider themselves environmentalists would be fine with the place in which all of this started—gathering eggs from nests—but not fine with genetically modified birds in confinement facilities. Somewhere along the continuum, a line was crossed. But it is not easy to say where that line is.

The modification, manipulation, control, and domination of nature by humans does not just have implications for the nonhuman world. It is also related to human social issues, particularly as perceived through the lenses of utility and equity. Utilitarianism, particularly as advocated by Jeremy Bentham, is about consequences. It is about securing the greatest good for the greatest number of people. The utilitarian is thus egocentric, for manipulation of the nonhuman world is justified if it provides happiness for people that outweighs any adverse consequences for others. John Stuart Mill's philosophy tempers the utility by recognizing that the ecosystem has value as well, even though it is not as easily measured. Thus the consequences of our utility reach farther than the product that is brought to market. Kant would have us judge utility of nonhuman nature not on its outcomes, but on the motives behind the action. Which of those motives are right and pure, and how would we know? (Kaufman, 2003: 9–15).

In certain feminist lines of thought, manipulation of nature stems from a male-dominated society in which *control* is the goal—control of resources, of other species, and of other people. Proponents of this worldview point out that the domination of nature has been devastating to both society and environment, and that gender, racial, and ethnic bias have left some humans environmentally impoverished. They believe that a more egalitarian, equitable, community-oriented society would preserve both nature and the human race. I'll have more to say on this later, but for now it is worth noting that problems of human manipulation of their natural environment are inextricable from dilemmas of human society. Another way of saying this is that many human social problems have foundations in the utility, modification, and allocation of natural resources (Sturgeon, 2008 [1997]).

Some may insist that any human manipulation of living things or their habitat is out of the realm of true environmentalism altogether. This is the perspective of the preservationist—it is the "let it be" approach (Schmidtz, 1997: 328). Proponents of such pure ecocentrism may well acknowledge that Earth's ecosystems and nonhuman species have long been modified by humans but argue that such manipulation is not always for the betterment of either human or natural communities. This calls for restriction of human activity in reverence of the system: to leave some areas wild, to leave some resources unharvested, to leave some species to their own destiny, whatever that might be. It recalls the "balance and harmony of nature" that became popular with the romantic movement—the idea that "human encroachment spoils nature which, left to its own devices, will develop toward a state of integrity" (Sterba, 1998: 368).

Since it is not entirely clear that ecosystems are entities, it is even less clear that they have destinies (Cahen, 1988). Much as Darwin demonstrated that evolution does not progress toward a goal, modern ecologists have demonstrated that ecological succession has no goal. Some ecocentrists, in response, have allowed that the ecocentric goal is not the maintenance of a specific complement of species, but rather the preservation of ecological relationships within "normal" parameters (Callicott, 1996). Even if one finds this argument persuasive, the bounds of "normal" will be defined according to human desires. In fact, no modern ecosystem or nonhuman species is un-influenced by humans; all are either under some sort of human-derived stress or have a legacy of stress. This stress may be such that the processes of feeding, migration, reproduction, succession, and ecological function are severely hampered or arrested, and no amount of time or protection will result in restored function. Thus the preservationist approach may not result in any sort of desirable outcome, and intervention may ultimately be necessary.

Individualism and collectivism

Environmentalism is fundamentally intertwined with social systems, whether people are at the center of your worldview or not. Imagine that a fishing vessel is working the waters of the northern Pacific. This particular operation is less than scrupulous—it regularly ignores quota limits, it is sloppy with regard to by-catch of non-target species, and it has been known to encroach on marine sanctuaries. Does this rogue outfit pose an environmental dilemma? It does, and at many levels. Let's consider the biological problems in this example. A marine ecologist would point out that quota-based catch limits are set to protect the target fish species. Regular overharvest can quickly lead to a decline in that species, which will not necessarily have an easy or quick recovery. By-catch is another concern. Killing untold numbers of non-target species will certainly affect the ecosystem. Exactly how ecosystem function will change may be unclear, but it will almost certainly not have a positive effect on marine diversity. Additionally, marine sanctuaries are nurseries. They are intended, in part, to provide for the reproduction and main-tenance of harvestable species for future years and future generations. Illegal harvesting in these areas will further threaten the ocean ecosystem far beyond the borders of the sanctuary.

These are all solid environmental arguments against illegal fishing practices. While they are biological arguments, all are inextricably related to issues of human utility and equity. The exploitation of natural resources is often associated with the exploitation of people. Catch limits, for example, are set to ensure future harvest of the target species. Overharvest is unfair to upstanding fishing operations, who may suffer the economic consequences of fishery collapse. Ecological function, diversity and breeding grounds support populations of species desirable to other people. Disregard for regulation is thus unfair to current and future generations in need of the resource. Garrett Hardin famously identified this as a tragedy of the commons (Hardin, 1968). The point is that natural resources have limits, and one person's pursuit of a resource can infringe upon the desires of another. In such situations, value judgements must be made about which resources may be used and who may use them. Value judgements are products of social structure and cultural milieu—made according to the interests of people with the power to decide. Environmental dilemmas are therefore exercises in social negotiation.

In fact, it could be argued that environmental problems are questions of social responsibility. Environmentalism is closely associated with human societal structures like economic systems, political movements, and regulatory structure. Environmental justice is an entire field of inquiry and action based on societal aspects of environmental issues. Who is privileged and who is marginalized in certain societal structures? Who benefits from environmental "goods" (provisions, commodities, services, scenery, or recreation) and who suffers from environmental "bads" (pollution, degradation, blight, or waste)? Who profits and who is impoverished? Who has the capacity to influence change, and how much is that capacity dependent upon race, ethnicity, gender, and wealth? If we place social justice at the heart of environmentalism, responsibility toward the nonhuman world is situated within social responsibility.

The ends of this dimensional spectrum are represented by individual freedom and social control. Individual freedom of expression and behavior is certainly a great achievement of human civilization. The right to act according to one's own desires, however, can quickly lead to conflicts of interest. Many environmental problems are the consequence of contradictory attitudes about the status of nonhuman nature, the sanctity of places, and the human role as manipulator or member of the ecological community. Even where attitudes are similar, one person's right to resource use can be enacted to the detriment of another. Some have argued that the best solution to such dilemmas—indeed, the best sort of environmentalism—is that which recognizes individual property rights and enforces boundaries (Anderson and Leal, 2001). Where private rights are clearly defined, the reasoning goes, there are fewer disputes and resources are used in the most efficient manner possible. The opposing view holds that such individualist approaches "emphasize competition over wildlife resources for individual use and gain, whereas collectivist cultures would emphasize sharing of wildlife resources for collective benefit" (Manfredo and Dayer, 2004: 323). Private appropriation of resources may arguably lead to the most efficient yield, but it is by definition beholden only to individual demands. In socially mediated structures, by contrast, the utilization of resources is subject to the consent of all stakeholders.

Some environmentalists note that certain human social structures are amenable to collective decision-making, while others encourage individual freedom (Merchant, 2005: 43–45). Indigenous tribal cultures, for example, seem to offer a more egalitarian approach to resource use than cultures of global corporate capitalism. Egalitarian collectives—which some see as the ancient, ancestral social structure of our species—are not driven by the profit motive, but rather by social cohesion. The free market of capitalism, by contrast, circumvents interpersonal responsibility in favor of individual gain.

Another quick glimpse at the palm oil industry illustrates the point. Norman Jiwan has reviewed the social and ecological effects of the palm industry in Indonesia. In this case, private interests have acquired the right to convert forest to plantation, and in so doing have encroached upon traditional indigenous cultures. In addition to the ecological upheaval described at the beginning of the chapter, the situation has ensnared small landowners in predatory relationships with the industry. It has offered employment for low wages, diluted labor rights, and weakened safely regulation, while most of the profits are realized elsewhere (Jiwan, 2013). Individual rights and freedoms have thus proven beneficial for some but detrimental for others. In contrast, Koczberski and Curry (2005) describe smallholder palm oil production in Papua New Guinea as an interspersion of palm production, subsistence agriculture, and diverse cash crops that include forest products like fruits and nuts. This arrangement does not maximize the production of palm oil, but it does provide a measure of economic—and even biological—diversity. Furthermore, the system allows for social and kin-based networks to exist alongside land ownership and livelihood, and it thus provides a measure of social responsibility regarding resource use (Koh *et al.*, 2009). In this collective arrangement, the most efficient production of palm oil is not achieved, but local equity is.

Environmental equity is drawn from the social contract, as espoused by Hobbes, Locke, and Rousseau. In modern western society we have all sorts of written contracts, like a lease for use of land, a deed of ownership, or a permit to harvest. Still, many of our social contracts are unwritten; they pertain to the ways we treat others beyond that which is mandated by legal documents. And what kind of social agreements do we have? Is it the world according to Hobbes, in which all are motivated by self-interest, and only held in check by the force of law? Is it the moral world of Locke, in which our personal systems of ethics hold our greed at bay and protect the common good? Or do we see the normative social contracts of Rousseau promoting self-sacrifice for the benefit of all? The answer is that all three occur in the modern world. In the absence of social pressures, however, collective action can be undermined by individual freedom. Unchecked self-interest can become selfishness, and selfishness has a way of becoming full-blown greed (Pinker, 2003: 318–335).

Parochialism and globalism

Social responsibility is easier to achieve among those we know well and with whom we regularly interact—our families, co-workers, close friends, and acquaintances. Beyond these close circles the social pressures for reciprocal behavior are tenuous. Environmentalism thus includes an element of scale; that is, how should it be conceived in time and space? Representing the extremes of this conceptual axis are those who believe that environmental action is best accomplished on local scales or for the current generation and those who think more globally and intergenerationally.

Let's first consider spatial scale. As an environmentalist is it enough for me to focus only on my local environment and community, or must I also concern myself with other people in other environments? I know the phrase: think globally, act locally. Sage advice, that, because it is not easy to act globally. The idea behind the catchphrase is that all of our local actions add up to global effects, and global effects will determine our collective fate. So it makes some sense, both practically and philosophically, to act locally. And since local behaviors constitute global effects, the two are not really opposite ends of the spectrum at all, but different scales of the same effort.

Still, there are those who insist that environmentalism is—or should be—primarily a local phenomenon. There is some logic to this attitude. Ecological regions are unique, and so too are the organisms they support, the resources they offer, and the environmental problems they present. Sociocultural context also occurs on the small scale. Therefore, the argument goes, environmental solutions are best tailored to specific people in specific places. Nolon's (2002) article "In praise of parochialism" makes the case that grass-roots movements and local regulations are more nimble and flexible mechanisms of environmental action than federal policies, particularly with regard to land use decisions. Thus, issues like habitat conservation, infrastructure development, aquifer protection, floodplain maintenance, and erosion prevention are best addressed at the local level. In certain ways parochialism even offers ecological advantages to species conservation, since it promotes the protection of endemic diversity with local investment (Hunter and Hutchinson, 1994). Nolon summarizes the case for parochial environmentalism:

> Because citizens at the local level are directly affected by environmental problems and have a great stake in the success of efforts at every level of government, there is a strong incentive to resolve land use and environmental problems collaboratively, rather than confrontationally.
>
> (Nolon, 2002: 365)

And yet, parochialism has a negative connotation for some environmental scholars. Many of our greatest problems are biospheric, for one, and thus seemingly beyond the reach of local authority. More critically, a parochial focus can lead to narrow-minded isolation, promoting local concerns in ignorance of—or at the expense of—other people in other places. Local communities around the world differ by demographic characteristics and accordingly have different needs. It has been hypothesized, for example, that postindustrial communities experience both objective environmental problems and subjective environmental values in different ways than preindustrial communities (Brechin, 1999). Thus the desire of one demographic to reduce dietary trans-fat can infringe upon the desire of another to exist within a forest. This sort of demographic divergence can have all sorts of ecological implications. For instance, a number of scholars have demonstrated that a reliance on local autonomy regarding land use can hamper global habitat conservation efforts, via misallocation of funds and short-sighted management schemes (Hunter and Hutchinson, 1994; Pouzols *et al.*, 2014).

In a similar way we may consider the timescale of environmentalism. Some argue for the short-term view: this has been called temporal parochialism. The idea is that resources should be used to the maximum benefit of the present time. As the American forester Gifford Pinchot famously suggested, "the development of our natural resources and the fullest use of them for the present generation is the first duty of this generation" (Pinchot, 1910: 44). The rationale, as adopted by some modern environmentalists, is that maximizing current production and development—and thereby alleviating poverty—is the best thing we can do for future generations. Scholars Sharon Beder and Wilfred Beckerman have further argued that the needs of future generations are uncertain, given unforeseeable sociocultural and technological changes, and that intergenerational needs can therefore be discounted (Beckerman, 1994; Beder, 2000). Others hold that no amount of current economic development can offset environmental degradation that impairs the relationships and processes which sustain life on the planet. In this sense, the very *reason* for protecting or preserving other species or resources is for the enjoyment and use of future generations of humans. Some arguments in favor of restraining our current impact on the environment are that we do not know the function of all species, and thus should err on the side of caution in protecting every bit of diversity we can; that it is precisely because we cannot foresee the needs of future generations that we should maintain the greatest range of options; and that future technologies will likely depend on a natural resource base, just as our current technologies do (Ott, 2003).

The temporal and spatial scales of environmentalism are analogous to the expanding circle of ethics described by Singer (1981: 111–126). Just as the biocentrism pushes us to extend human rights to nonhuman species and spiritual environmentalism extends sanctity to places and objects, global and intergenerational environmentalism extend ethical considerations to people we will likely never meet. All of these expanded circles call on our capacity for sacrifice or restraint with no immediate personal benefit. This is a critical question for human morality. If an action on your part would keep your sibling from getting ill or prevent your neighbor's house from burning down, you would certainly act. Indeed, you'd have a moral responsibility to act. What if the problem is far away in space or time, the effects of your action are negligible, and the action itself will diminish your own prospects? Is your action still morally imperative?

Many dimensions, core values

In these various dimensions we begin to see the conceptual space of environmentalism, and it is a large space indeed. Clearly, a single definition of environmentalism that transcends sociocultural boundaries and worldviews is elusive. Moreover, the breadth of possible definitions is disconcerting: one who cuts trees for a living may have just as much a claim to the title *environmentalist* as one who risks his life to prevent trees from being cut. This, I suspect, causes some people to avoid the label altogether. What, then, is the *right* sort of environmentalism? This question is difficult to answer, for all of the conflicting viewpoints noted above have valid points. A central goal of this book is to resolve these dimensions.

While this exercise of exploring the conflicts of environmentalism may be frustrating, it is not without merit. Through it we can identify some fundamental reasons that an individual or group might be invested in the protection, preservation, or conservation of the world around them. There are common—if conflicting— themes to what we value, even among extreme environmental positions. From the various dimensions described above I draw six major environmental values:

- Utility—We use the world around us, including other species and nonliving material, to secure sustenance, to achieve happiness, and to minimize suffering.

This includes things that we harvest directly as well as functions (like pollination, nutrient cycling, waste decomposition, etc.) and experiences of cultural significance. The environmental argument for utility is concerned with meeting our own needs, but it is also an argument for conservation. It is a plea to better understand and protect natural resources for current and future human use.

- Stability—Humans rely on the security and provisional aspects of nature but are also at odds with its destructive potential. Anthropogenic destabilization of nature is perceived as a threat to human security, so some environmental work is aimed at preserving the stability of landscapes, resources, ecosystems, and natural processes. Whether stability is an intrinsic characteristic of nature or whether management is required to achieve it is a matter of debate.
- Equity—This is an argument for fair share and fair treatment. It includes those who work for fair treatment among species and those who seek fair treatment among humans, particularly in terms of gender, race, ethnicity, and income. It includes the notion that people of all cultures and all generations deserve access to basic environmental rights and privileges.
- Beauty—Nature is appealing to humans, both in its own right and in the art, literature, and performance it inspires. Beauty here is intended in the broadest sense as that which is profound, moving, and emotional in a way that is neither religious nor moral but may be connected to both. For many people, human domination of nature destroys this beauty and is grounds for protest.
- Sanctity—Certain aspects of nature are sacred to some people and some cultures. They evoke feelings of a connection to a higher power or powers, to unseen spirits, or to other organisms and objects in the universe. Human encroachment upon or manipulation of sacred landscapes, species, or relationships can be an affront to these spiritual connections.
- Morality—This is the overarching sense that the defense of the nonhuman world for any of the above reasons is the right thing to do; it is the way people ought to behave.

These principles are what prompt any sort of environmentalist to protect, manipulate, remediate, or restore our world. These are the ideals and imperatives that form environmental mindsets and that drive environmental actions. The task of environmentalism, I believe, is to recognize and reconcile these values.

Bibliography

Anderson, T. and Leal, D. (2001). *Free market environmentalism*, 2nd edition. New York: Palgrave Macmillan.

Ashley, J.M. (1987). *The social and environmental effects of the palm-oil industry in the Oriente of Ecuador*. Research Paper Series No. 19, Latin American Institute. Albuquerque, NM: University of New Mexico.

Beckerman, W. (1994). Sustainable development: is it a useful concept? *Environmental Values*, 3(3), pp. 191–209.

Beder, S. (2000). Costing the Earth: equity, sustainable development and environmental economics. *New Zealand Journal of Environmental Law*, 4, pp. 227–243.

Brechin, S.R. (1999). Objective problems, subjective values, and global environmentalism: evaluating the postmaterialist argument and challenging a new explanation. *Social Science Quarterly*, 80(4), pp. 793–809.

Cahen, H. (1988). Against the moral considerability of ecosystems. *Environmental Ethics*, 10(3), pp. 195–216.

Callicott, J.B. (1987). The conceptual foundations of the land ethic. In: J.B. Callicott, ed., *Companion to A Sand County almanac: interpretive and critical essays.* Madison: University of Wisconsin Press. pp. 173–181.

Callicott, J.B. (1996). Do deconstructive ecology and sociobiology undermine Leopold's land ethic? *Environmental Ethics*, 18(4), pp. 353–372.

Corley, R.H.V. (2009). How much palm oil do we need? *Environmental Science and Policy*, 12, pp. 134–139.

Cronon, W. (1992). A place for stories: nature, history, and narrative. *Journal of American History*, 78(4), pp. 1347–1376.

Dewi, O. (2013). Reconciling development, conservation and social justice in West Kalimantan. In: O. Pye and J. Bhattacharya, eds., *The palm oil controversy in Southeast Asia: a transnational perspective.* Singapore: Institute of Southeast Asian Studies. pp. 164–178.

Fitzherbert, E.B., Struebig, M.J., Morel, A., Danielsen, F., Brühl, C.A., Donald, P.F. and Phalan, B. (2008). How will oil palm expansion affect biodiversity? *Trends in Ecology & Evolution*, 23(10), pp. 538–545.

Gould, S.J. (1990). The golden rule: a proper scale for our environmental crisis. *Natural History*, 9(90), pp. 24–30.

Guha, R. and Martinez-Alier, J. (1997). *Varieties of environmentalism: essays north and south.* London: Routledge.

Hardin, G. (1968). The tragedy of the commons. *Science*, 162(3859), pp. 1243–1248.

Hayward, T. (1997). Anthropocentrism: a misunderstood problem. *Environmental Values*, 6(1), pp. 49–63.

Hunter, M.L. and Hutchinson, A. (1994). The virtues and shortcomings of parochialism: conserving species that are locally rare, but globally common. *Conservation Biology*, 8(4), pp. 1163–1165.

Jiwan, N. (2013). The political ecology of the Indonesian palm oil industry. In: O. Pye and J. Bhattacharya, eds., *The palm oil controversy in Southeast Asia: a transnational perspective.* Singapore: Institute of Southeast Asian Studies. pp. 59–65.

Kaufman, F. (2003). *Foundations of environmental philosophy.* New York: McGraw-Hill.

Kirchner, J.W. (1989). The Gaia hypothesis: can it be tested? *Reviews of Geophysics*, 27(2), pp. 223–235.

Koczberski, G. and Curry, G.N. (2005). Making a living: land pressures and changing livelihood strategies among oil palm settlers in Papua New Guinea. *Agricultural Systems*, 85(3), pp. 324–339.

Koh, L.P., Levang, P. and Ghazoul, J. (2009). Designer landscapes for sustainable biofuels. *Trends in Ecology & Evolution*, 24(8), pp. 431–438.

Laurance, W.F., Koh, L.P., Butler, R., Sodhi, N.S., Bradshaw, C.J., Neidel, J.D. and Vega, J.M. (2010). Improving the performance of the Roundtable on Sustainable Palm Oil for nature conservation. *Conservation Biology*, 24(2), pp. 377–381.

Lovelock, J.E. (1972). Gaia as seen through the atmosphere. *Atmospheric Environment*, 6(8), pp. 579–580.

Lovelock, J.E. and L. Margulis. (1974). Atmospheric homeostasis by and for the biosphere: the Gaia hypothesis. *Tellus*, 26, pp. 2–10.

Macy, J. (1992). Deep ecology work: toward the healing of self and world. *Human Potential Magazine*, 17(1), pp. 10–31.

Manfredo, M.J. and Dayer, A.A. (2004). Concepts for exploring the social aspects of human–wildlife conflict in a global context. *Human Dimensions of Wildlife*, 9(4), pp. 317–328.

Merchant, C. (2005). *Radical ecology: the search for a livable world*. New York: Routledge.

Minteer, B.A. and Pyne, S.J. (2013). Restoring the narrative of American environmentalism. *Restoration Ecology*, 21(1), pp. 6–11.

Nash, R.F. (1965). *Wilderness and the American mind*. New Haven, CT: Yale University Press.

Nash, R.F. (1989). *The rights of nature: a history of environmental ethics*. Madison, WI: University of Wisconsin Press.

Nolon, J.R. (2002). In praise of parochialism: the advent of local environmental law. *Pace Environmental Law Review*, 23(3), pp. 705–755.

Ott, K. (2003). The case for strong sustainability. In: K. Ott, ed., *Greifswald's environmental ethics: from the work of the Michael Otto professorship at Ernst Arndt University 1997–2002*. Greifswald: Steinbecker Verlag Ulrich Rose. pp. 59–64.

Pinchot, G. (1910). *The fight for conservation*. New York: Doubleday, Page & Co.

Pinker, S. (2003). *The blank slate: the modern denial of human nature*. New York: Penguin.

Pouzols, F.M., Toivonen, T., Di Minin, E., Kukkala, A.S., Kullberg, P., Kuusterä, J., Lehtomäki, J., Tenkanen, H., Verburg, P.H. and Moilanen, A. (2014). Global protected area expansion is compromised by projected land-use and parochialism. *Nature*, 516(7531), pp. 383–386.

Pye, O. (2013). Introduction. In: O. Pye and J. Bhattacharya, eds., *The palm oil controversy in Southeast Asia: a transnational perspective*. Singapore: Institute of Southeast Asian Studies. pp. 1–18.

Regan, T. (1985). The case for animal rights. In: P. Singer, ed., *In defence of animals*. Chichester, UK: Wiley. pp. 13–26.

Schmidtz, D. (1997). When preservationism doesn't preserve. *Environmental Values*, 6(3), pp. 327–339.

Singer, P. (1981). *The expanding circle*. Oxford: Clarendon Press.

Sterba, J.P. (1998). A biocentrist strikes back. *Environmental Ethics*, 20(4), pp. 361–376.

Sturgeon, N. (2008 [1997]). Ecofeminist movements. In: C. Merchant, ed., *Ecology*, 2nd edition. Amherst, NY: Humanity Books. pp. 237–249.

Taylor, P.W. (1981). The ethics of respect for nature. *Environmental Ethics*, 3(3), pp. 197–218.

Unnevehr, L.J. and Jagmanaite, E. (2008). Getting rid of trans fats in the US diet: policies, incentives and progress. *Food Policy*, 33(6), pp. 497–503.

Wilbert, J., ed. (1996). Siona-Secoya. *Encyclopedia of world cultures*, Vol. 7. Boston: G.K. Hall.

Wilson, D.S. (2002). *Darwin's cathedral: evolution, religion, and the nature of society*. Chicago: University of Chicago Press.

Worster, D. (1990). The ecology of order and chaos. *Environmental History Review*, 14(1/2), pp. 1–18.

3 Many ecologies

Key points

- Ecology encompasses many worldviews that represent different ways of understanding the cosmos.
- Objective, subjective, and intuitive ecological perspectives differ in their consideration of evidence, dualism, and holism.
- Integral ecology is an effort to reconcile different ecological perspectives.

The tragic history of human thought is simply the history of a struggle between reason and life—reason bent on rationalizing life and forcing it to submit to the inevitable, to mortality; life bent on vitalizing reason and forcing it to serve as a support for its own vital desires.

Material reason vs. essence of living

So observed the Spanish philosopher Miguel de Unamuno in 1913 (de Unamuno, 1954 [1913]: 115; Richards, 2008: 453). He was not writing about the human relationship with the natural world, but he may as well have been. Environmentalism is of the same struggle. It is both a recognition of life's material limits and an effort to be more fully alive.

This mental burden—the price of self-awareness—has long been borne by members of our species. For ages the realities of life's limitations have been tempered by the promise of a vitality beyond our fleeting existence. However, rational science of the "age of reason" challenged the notion of the supernatural (Worster, 1994: 29). Evolutionary theory was just one of many new ideas to question certain long-held notions of the universe, but it was particularly disruptive. Darwin's view of life, according to one contemporary author, "had come into the theological world like a plough into an ant-hill," and "those thus rudely awakened from their old comfort and repose had swarmed forth angry and confused" (White, 1894; Richards, 2008: 383). The confusion was—and is—about the understanding of the universe and our place in it.

What this means, both in Darwin's time and today, is that many people lead conflicted lives, caught up in the mental struggle between the harsh realities and ideal possibilities of existence. As a case in point I turn to a friend of Darwin's, the German biologist Ernst Haeckel. Haeckel (1834–1919) is the perfect place to begin a chapter on ecology, not only because he coined the term but also because his intellectual breadth and disparate thought portend the state of ecology today.

Haeckel was a great popularizer of Darwinian evolution—in some ways a louder voice than that of Darwin himself—but unlike Darwin he could be cantankerous and rude in his argumentation (Richards, 2008). He was absurdly talented: an accomplished artist, marine biologist, groundbreaking embryologist, physician, author of hundreds of published manuscripts, and discoverer of thousands of new species. But it is Haeckel's internal conflict that I find to be most fascinating. He was, for instance, both a materialist and a romantic spiritualist. In Haeckel's perspective the living and nonliving, the mind and body, the natural world and the spiritual were all of one substance; and yet these material leanings were linked in his mind to the spirit of harmonious nature, an essence that humans might reach beyond their physical limits. He was, in this sense, both a monist (one who denies dualities of mind/body or human/nature) and a pantheist, much in the line of Spinoza. Further, while he was an ardent champion of natural selection, he was also a progressivist—meaning that he saw the process of evolution as an advancement toward perfection. Herein lies one of several reasons that Haeckel's reputation has suffered over the years. Progressive evolution applied to the whole world means that "the lower, less perfect forms will continually be eliminated; the higher, more perfect will be preserved; and these latter will produce again a still greater number of yet more perfect forms" (Haeckel, 1864; Richards, 2008: 97). All well and good—and arguably not so different than Darwin's message—until applied to human ethnicity and social structure. Haeckel's progressive evolution has been tied, perhaps unfairly, to the eugenics movement, to racism and even to Nazism. But this takes us beyond the man. Ernst Haeckel was, in the words of biographer Robert Richards, a man of both "the deeply feeling spirit and the aggressively rational mind" (2008: 454). How, then, could his view of the environment—his ecology—be any different?

Modern ecology spans the conceptual breadth of Haeckel's imagination. Ecology encompasses not only ways of studying our environment, but also ways of conceptualizing and idealizing it. It extends from an evaluation of what the natural world is to a declaration of what it ought to be. This diversity of thought is directly related to the ambiguities of existence we have encountered in the previous chapters. What is the nature of our relationship to the nonhuman world and to one another? To what extent do we have responsibility toward these other entities? What is our role in this great web of life, and how can we come to know it better?

In this chapter I break the many fields of ecology down into different ways of knowing—different approaches to understanding the cosmos. There is danger in such classification, for it implies boundaries that do not exist and it forces the lumping and splitting of thoughts that sometimes resist lumping and splitting. I will classify nonetheless, for it is the best way to make sense of diversity. I will also refrain from attempting an exhaustive list of the various ecologies, which is probably an impossible task, for new ones would emerge before I finish listing the old ones. Instead, I will loosely follow the lead of previous authors (Guattari, 2008 [1989]; Merchant, 2005) and focus on general categories—scientific ecology, social ecology, and two approaches to spiritual ecology—as well as an attempt to integrate them all. My purpose is to show the various ways in which we try to make sense of ourselves and this place we call home.

Scientific ecology

The science of ecology is the study of the distribution, abundance, function, and interaction of living things with each other and with their nonliving environment. An ecologist, by this definition, might study competition among two plant species in a drought-prone environment. Such a study might postulate reasons why one species grows and reproduces better than the other in times of stress—perhaps it acquires nutrients more efficiently or conserves water more effectively. The scientific ecologist's job is to test these ideas in the field, in the greenhouse, in the lab, or with simulations, to analyze the results, and to draw conclusions based on the evidence. Already, then, we can make some observations about this natural science-based definition of ecology. First, it concerns relationships among species or individual organisms. It is less about the proper role of humans, though human actions can certainly alter or influence other species (humans may have a role in causing the drought stress on the plants, for example). Second, it is materialistic; that is, it is not about the spiritual or aesthetic values that humans place upon other organisms. It concerns the physical, chemical, and biological status of organisms, alone or in populations, communities, and ecosystems. Third, it at least attempts to be objective; that is, it seeks to eliminate emotion, personification, and human value judgement from its conclusions. Accordingly, scientific ecology has traditionally not engaged in social commentary—though this is becoming more common, as we shall see (Fromm, 2009: 101).

A primary focus of scientific ecology has long been the interaction of organisms and environmental conditions in the nonhuman world. This makes the field sound homogeneous, but actually many natural scientists consider themselves to be ecologists. For example, advances in genetics and molecular biology have launched entire fields of research in molecular ecology and conservation genetics. Such ecologists might work to determine the phylogeny of closely related species, to understand hybridization between meta-populations of a species, to relate diversity of species to diversity of biochemical function, or to link organismal behavior with gene expression. Closely related are physiological ecologists, who relate organismal function to environmental conditions. Behavioral ecologists study the interaction of organisms with others in instances of mating, brood rearing, migration, competition, feeding, territorial disputes, and so on; evolutionary ecologists are interested in how such interactions came to be. Population ecologists consider the dynamics of groups of a single species, while community ecologists consider many populations at once, and paleo-ecologists consider the same thing but of communities that existed in the distant past. Ecosystem ecologists add abiotic factors like water availability, fire frequency, or nutrient concentration to the study of biological communities. Landscape ecologists consider many eco-systems at once over large parts of the Earth's surface, and there are even global ecologists who model whole-Earth processes to answer questions of planetary import. Ernst Haeckel, were he alive today, might marvel at how ultra-specialized the science of ecology has become!

Certain principles of scientific ecology are well established. Modern species, for example, have common ancestors, and have diverged over evolutionary time by the Darwinian process of natural selection. Species fill functional niches within ecosystems and thereby affect other species and the abiotic nutrient and energy cycles in which they exist. Living things rely intimately on each other, not only in a familial or social sense but also as parasites, predators, mutual symbionts, sca-vengers, and decomposers. Subject to abiotic conditions and pressure from other organisms, cohorts of species can be loosely grouped together in communities and ecosystems. These units are ever-changing in response to succession, stress, and disturbance. Stress (chronic limiting factors for growth) and disturbance (periodic environmental upheavals) are natural features of the world. For example, living things are often limited by water or nutrient stress, salinity, pH, temperature, or by disturbance events like fire, flood, treefall, or upwelling (Spieles, 2010: 57–58).

Part of the goal of scientific ecology is simply to understand the world in which we live and the organisms that share it with us. But it would be incorrect to claim that all this work is for pure knowledge alone. Ecological research is often con-ducted for the modification or manipulation of organisms and environments to achieve some desirable end—some form of utility. Thus, scientific ecological research is applied to agriculture (agroecology), ecosystem modification (restor-ation ecology), human health (medical ecology), optimizing the built environ-ment (industrial ecology), and even to the introduction and augmentation of nature in human-dominated landscapes (urban and reconciliation ecology). No doubt I have omitted some important fields of scientific ecology and their appli-cations, but the point is clear: we have invested much in the effort to understand the science of ecological relationships and, in many cases, to use the knowledge gained for some form of benefit for at least some segment of human society.

Such applications of ecological science have clear ties to utilitarianism, and hence to mechanism and materialism. Modern scientific ecology is, for the most part, a rational attempt to understand the fundamental components of the natural world. In this sense it is of the Linnaean school, in which natural objects (including living things) are isolatable, analyzable, quantifiable, and subject to categorization—and often, to technological innovation, manipulation, and even exploitation (Worster, 1994). Scientific ecology is also an evolutionary ecology in which Darwinian selection is accepted as fact. This too colors the application of science, for in Darwinian evolution there is no apparent purpose or direction to life.

Some snort with derision at this sort of ecology, rejecting it as reductionist positivism that does not consider the whole but rather minces relationships into basic parts that can then be exploited. Indeed, scientific ecology can be used to this end, but the criticism hardly represents the entire discipline. On the contrary, scientific ecologists have long recognized that organisms are interrelated with other organisms and with their abiotic surroundings. This is called systems ecology, and it is the field that gave us the concept of the ecosystem (and the inspiration for many other branches of ecological thought). But systems ecology is itself a conceptual battleground, for it straddles the fence between the components and the aggregate. Systems ecology recognizes the interrelation between organisms, for instance, but it is not universally accepted that all constituent organisms are therefore of equal importance. Nor does it imply that an ecological system has an ideal stable state toward which it is naturally drawn. Nonetheless, some see a holism in systems ecology, a way of recognizing the *proper* condition of the natural world and the *proper* character for natural and human components. Others see it as just another form of reductionism, isolating mathematically described processes as a "machine" that one may then manipulate (Merchant, 2005: 110).

Scientific ecology strives to be based on logic and reason. Even so, it can't avoid being influenced (and even biased) by its psychological, social, cultural, and political context, if only in the selection of what is studied and what questions are asked. Scientific inquiry itself is a social construct. The exclusion of human emotions, judgements, beliefs systems, and biases is no easy task. Of course there are biases, frauds, self-serving agendas, and flat-out incorrect conclusions. The scientific processes of randomization, replication, evaluation, and the interrogation of peer review attempt to minimize subjectivity and to reject false inferences. There are rules for methods of questioning, evaluating, concluding, and decision-making. Evidence is required for claims, even though evidence is sometimes ambiguous or contradictory. Revelation, intuition, and tradition do not constitute evidence. Interestingly, it is this very reliance on logic and reason that, to some, equate scientific ecology with the manipulation and domination of nature. To those of this opinion, the rigid reason and despiritualization of the scientific method lead inexorably to the ability to predict, control, harness, and exploit nature. Consequently other ways of knowing and acting are trivialized. The overwhelming devotion of modern western affluent society to scientific ecology, according to some, has spurred the abuse of the nonhuman world that is leading us to global environmental catastrophe (Merchant, 2005: 41–61).

As I have noted, it is not quite true to state that scientific ecology provides no commentary on human social dilemmas. In a growing body of scientific ecology, human activity is expressly considered, both for the stress it exerts on natural ecological systems and for the ecological services (ES) on which humans depend (Ehrlich and Ehrlich, 1981; Millennium Ecosystem Assessment, 2003). These include services of utility or provision, as with the harvest of food, fuel, and fiber; services of function, like pollination, water purification, and carbon storage; and cultural services, like recreation, aesthetic appeal, and spiritual connection (Box 3.1). Ecological stress and disturbance can alter ecological structure and function, thereby limiting ecological service.

Humans have a way of changing stress and disturbance regimes. Intentionally or unintentionally, we alter ecological parameters like soil salinity and nutrient availability, water temperature, fire frequency, and flood intensity. Drainage, irrigation, habitat fragmentation, acidification, fire prevention, and biomass

Box 3.1 Ecosystem services and cultural values

Ecosystem services (ES) are those aspects of the nonhuman world that directly benefit humans. This concept provides a means of identifying human priorities, and in so doing it represents an attempt to integrate different ecological perspectives. As defined by the Millennium Ecosystem Assessment (2003), ES include not only tangible products and processes of the nonhuman world but also intangible qualities of cultural significance. Herein lies a difficulty, for material products and processes are easily quantifiable while cultural benefits are not.

Scholars Kai Chan *et al.* (2012) contend that the ES model can marginalize cultural values. They propose a nuanced model, one that differentiates between tangible services and intangible values while recognizing their intimate connection. For example, cultural values like recreation, education, aesthetic appreciation, inspiration, tradition, ceremony, heritage, and identity are inseparable from the physical condition of ecological systems but are themselves social and conceptual constructs. Such intangible values are culture- and even individual-specific and not readily generalizable. These, the authors argue, cannot be understood through economic valuation. Rather, they must be approached with a broader set of methodological tools. Qualitative approaches, particularly those that provide narratives of what people value about their ecological surroundings, can be used to better inform an assessment of ES. Ideally, cultural values should be included along with economic valuation in environmental decision-making.

In this sense, the different ecological perspectives are not irreconcilable. Objective assessments of applied scientific ecology, subjective concerns of social ecology, and the intuitive sense of spiritual ecologies all fall within the same triangle of individual, other, and nonhuman. Different ways of knowing the world and our place in it, while they may appear to be incompatible, should be incorporated into a common environmentalism.

harvest are thus all examples of anthropogenic pressures on ecosystems, communities, species, and biological functions. Furthermore, we introduce the stress of invasive species into ecosystems even as we overharvest or otherwise jeopardize species that were previously dominant. There is even a whole new class of chemical stressors: those synthesized by humans. Pesticides, fossil fuel emissions, plastics, chlorofluorocarbons, industrial and biomedical effluents, genetically modified organisms—all are novel stressors on ecological systems, and many are the topic of scientific ecological research. Here is where scientific ecologists *are* providing social commentary. These anthropogenic stressors alter ecological relationships, often to the detriment of some species and to the advantage of others (Spieles, 2010: 66–68).

Many scientific ecologists study the effects of such stressors on the ways in which humans interact with their environment. Cumulative stressors and altered disturbance regimes can change ecosystems in unexpected ways. Changes that are at first subtle can accumulate until a critical threshold is reached, at which point the ecosystem can shift into a new state, with new dominant organisms and processes. This has been well documented in many systems, such as lakes that shift from a clear to algal-dominated condition, as hard coral reefs give way to algae, and in forests that come to be dominated by grass and herbaceous vegetation (Scheffer *et al.*, 2001). Such shifts are not easily reversible, and they often diminish the efficacy of ecological services, whether it be the pollination of crops by insects, the transformation of wastes by microorganisms, the production of edible protein in the oceans, or the regulation of climate in the atmosphere. Thus, we have a feedback cycle: human activity is altering the capacity of ecosystems to support human needs. The perception of this as a looming crisis has prompted some scientific ecologists to wade into the social waters.

Human social behavior itself may be studied from an ecological perspective. The field of sociobiology, synthesized by E.O. Wilson in 1975, extends the study of animal behavior to the human animal (E.O. Wilson, 1975). Sociobiology has given rise to a number of related fields, including human behavioral ecology, memetics, evolutionary psychology, and gene-culture coevolution (or dual inheritance theory). These fields straddle the natural and social sciences in different ways, but essentially they all seek the same end: to better understand why humans in their social organizations behave as they do (Laland and Brown, 2011).

Social ecology

Adding humans to the notion of ecology—not just as another organism, but as *people*, with thoughts, behaviors, and sociocultural constructs—does not exclude reason and logic, but it does complicate things. This is the study of human relationships with the natural world, with one another, and with the built environment.

Social ecology has been described as an "archipelago of disciplines that only partially communicate with each other," where "one man's heresy is another man's commonplace" (D.S. Wilson, 2002: 83–84). However divided, the different intellectual realms do share a common paradigm. According to Marina Fischer-Kowalski and Weisz (2016: 3):

> they look at natural and social systems as systems in their own right that interact with one another, they believe causality between these systems works in both directions, and they search for less destructive and more sustainable ways in which the two systems can interact.

Many such scholars and activists offer a critique of social, political, and economic systems as they pertain to environmental problems. But social ecologists hardly speak with one voice, and even these basic characterizations are inadequate. At the risk of offending those I omit—and offending all by lumping them together—I will briefly consider the perspectives of a few different islands of the archipelago.

In some cases, social ecology is a response to scientific ecology's careful exclusion of social and cultural bias. It is in this sense the *study* of social and cultural bias. This perspective is well represented by political ecology. Political ecology is an emerging field that encompasses many sub-disciplines, but in general it considers the relationships of political and economic systems, race and ethnicity, gender, and cultural norms with resource use, environmental protection, and conflict. Political ecologists often work with local or regional cases of resource use and misuse in the context of socially derived power, privilege, and marginalization. Further, political ecologists seek to interrogate environmental actions by situating them within political, economic, sociocultural, and historical context (Perreault *et al.*, 2015).

As an example of a political ecology issue, consider the establishment of a nature reserve in a developing nation. What political, economic, and environmental conditions gave rise to the establishment of the nature reserve? Who will have access to it, and for what purpose? Will extraction of resources be allowed, and if so by whom? How will it be regulated? What sorts of indigenous use of the environment occurred there traditionally, and is such use still allowed in the reserve? Should spiritual values be considered differently than material values? Who benefits from the reserve, and who is marginalized? These are questions of ecological service, as a scientific ecologist might study, but in a sociocultural context they become questions of power and justice.

Political ecology as a field is so diverse and interdisciplinary that it is hard to generalize. In many instances, it is descriptive and analytical rather than judgemental. In this sense, it examines social contracts among stakeholders of an environmental resource or problem and evaluates the effectiveness (or failure) of governmental regulation, moral obligation, and civic responsibility in multicultural juxtaposition. In other cases, political ecology trends toward moral imperatives—forthcoming with values, criticisms, and priorities, the point of which is "not to merely understand the world, but to change it" (Bridge *et al.*, 2015: 8).

A criticism of political ecology is that it often approaches environmental issues with a predetermined notion that environmental outcomes are always politically determined. Hence the field focuses on the political games afoot with "little or no attention to actually demonstrating environmental effects" (Vayda and Walters, 1999: 169–170). While it is in theory a field that brings sociocultural evidence together with scientific evidence, critics claim that the scientific evidence is too often lacking. Further, some political ecology work is effectively promoting—and is intended to promote—a particular political agenda, especially the idea that local control over resources is inherently more environmentally sustainable than remote control. Too often there is scant evidence that this is indeed the case. These criticisms essentially call for political ecology to be more scientific—to exclude biases and judgements in the formulation and analysis of questions, particularly the bias that sociocultural factors are always paramount (Vayda and Walters, 1999).

As we depart from the island of political ecology we encounter some ecologies that are less fields of inquiry and more social critiques. The American sociologist Murray Bookchin (1921–2006) proposed a social ecology that favors the holistic, cooperative aspects of scientific ecology over the hierarchical, competitive, appropriative aspects. Bookchin's work holds that foraging human societies were once egalitarian, non-hierarchical communities that lived in harmony with one another and the land. Whether this vision is accurate, mythical, or a representation of a world with a much lower population density is debatable (Fromm, 2009: 73). In any case, such a society is not now our prevalent mode of existence. To Bookchin, the domination that characterizes extractive and synthetic societies has driven the exploitation of the Earth (Bookchin, 1989). Ecological problems, in this light, are problems of how people treat one another. Scarcity and deprivation are *symptoms* of dominance and oppression.

In Bookchin's perspective, human societies can be said to exhibit the attributes of ecological communities, including such characteristics as mutualism and parasitism. We might think of social mutualism as a participatory, reciprocal, communally beneficial decision-making relationship among parties. Social parasitism, by contrast, is the domination of one group by another, as in the manipulation and exploitation of land, resources, or labor. Bookchin asserts that sociocultural evolution has trended toward exploitative relationships, and that such relationships threaten our tenuous ES. Social systems, in other words, are linked to ecological systems: just as ecological stress diminishes ecosystem function, social stress diminishes socioecological function (Light, 1998: 7–8). It follows, then, that perceived harms to natural communities will not be resolved without social reform. Bookchin places the need for reform squarely on the political economy of capitalism: "it was not until organic community relations, feudal or peasant in form, dissolved into market relationships that the planet itself was reduced to a resource for exploitation. This centuries-long tendency finds its most exacerbating development in modern capitalism" (Bookchin, 1985: 89–98). Such human institutions, in Bookchin's way of thinking, have corrupted the evolutionary development of cooperation (Bookchin, 1980: 59; 1986: 42–60).

Bookchin's divisive character and theses have invited many criticisms (Watson, 1996; Light, 1998). I will note just a few. First, his work suggests a directionality of evolution, from an idealized nature toward an idealized human society. It is unclear that a cooperative, non-hierarchical nature ever existed, and it is increasingly clear that biological evolution does not proceed directionally. Second, Bookchin seems to recognize the cooperative characteristics of natural communities and human relationships while downplaying competition and conflict. In this sense, he acknowledges only part of the Darwinian model. Finally, Bookchin's ecology tends to moralize evolution, to see it as a process that would generate the righteous but for the interference of human institutions (Albrecht, 1998: 96–99; Kovel, 1998: 48; Rudy, 1998: 277–290).

Social ecologists have done a fine job of evaluating each other's fields, so I will offer commentary only on the ways of knowing we have encountered so far. In scientific ecology, the standard is testable assertions and objective evidence, obtained by repeatable, observable, verifiable experimental results. The results might be open to interpretation, but they ideally provide the same data regardless of who considers them. Such evidence could support or refute a claim that agricultural herbicides have a detrimental effect on nearby plant populations, for instance. Political ecology and comparable realms of social ecology often demand similar evidence, but here objectivity is more challenging since humans are part of the systems in question. Does agriculture have an adverse effect on the nearby indigenous culture? It may, but there may also be benefits, and the effects may vary according to individual perspective. It would take some observation, some interviewing, and some understanding of indigenous socioecological, economic, and cultural systems to fathom the potential and actual consequences of different actions. The results are subjective, or rather *intersubjective*; they are the interaction between different points of view. Clearly, scientific ecologists have an easier job than social ecologists. Plants are easier to understand than people.

As we progress on our tour of ecologies, we will become further removed from objective evidence-based arguments and closer to subjective and intuitive ways of knowing. This is not meant as a criticism, only as a recognition that certain versions of ecology see objective rationality as a precursor to manipulation and exploitation and therefore reject it as the best means of acquiring knowledge.

Socio-spiritual ecologies

We now travel to an ecology of a very different sort. Deep ecology is a branch of ecological philosophy that aims to reach, well, *deeper* than the understanding of resources, stressors, and associated efforts to conserve and protect. Deep ecology holds that such efforts are necessary but not enough; we need to move beyond these "shallow" notions to understand humans as intrinsically connected with, equal with, and cooperative with other species and resources. Environmental problems, to a deep ecologist, have their foundation in the way people conceive their relationship with the nonhuman world. Depending on the version, deep ecology also includes several recommendations that are primarily aimed at human societies but that mirror the same attitudes proposed for human–nature relationships: encouraging societies that are less fragmented, more interdependent, and less driven by oppression and centralization (Naess, 1973: 95–110). Rather than simply reforming the ways in which we use resources and dispose of waste, deep ecology seeks to revolutionize human society and its relationship with the Earth; it is a shift from humans-and-nature to humans-in-nature (Devall, 1980).

To some, deep ecology has a strong spiritual imperative: a God-Human-Nature complex, innate and inseparable. In this sense it stresses that humans are not separate from (nor in control of) nature but that humans and nature are one and the same. Pushed to the extreme, the God-Human-Nature complex encompasses all organisms and inorganic surroundings of Earth into one self-regulating superorganism. We have seen this already, manifested as the Gaia hypothesis. Based on ancestral wisdom of wonder and respect for creation, spiritual deep ecology emphasizes the rights of all species to "pursue their own evolutionary destinies"

(Devall, 1980: 299). For some deep ecologists there are particular action steps associated with the principles: ceasing human manipulation of "stable natural processes," reduction in human production of goods, technology, and industry, reduction of the human population growth rate and energy consumption, return to hunter/gatherer/gardening culture, spiritual development, and vast areas of Earth prohibited from extensive human encroachment (Devall, 1980: 158). In sum, deep ecology is a call for a holistic consciousness. To characterize it according to the environmental dimensions of the previous chapter we would say that it is biocentric, spiritual, and relational.

Deep ecology has its share of critics as well. One line of criticism observes that the biocentric, relational worldview promoted by deep ecology is just another human political ideal projected onto the environment, one assumed to be superior without critique or analysis (Merchant 2005: 109–110). It has also been attacked as anti-feminist, ignoring the historic male domination over both women and nature and imposing a new domination in the limitation of reproductive rights. But the greatest problem with deep ecology may be that it ignores much of what we know about evolutionary ecology. While it strives to recognize an equality between all species, it fails to acknowledge that species rarely exist in peaceful cooperation. Rather, competition, suffering, and death are the drivers of evolution. It is premised upon a romanticized nature of balance and harmony, and it overlooks the struggle for existence not only in nonhuman nature but also among billions of people. The biocentrism at the heart of deep ecology, as others have argued, is absurd, for living things feed on other living things. Further, it proposes a grand holism that embraces the good of existence but omits the bad. In imagining that the universe is ideally designed for human self-actualization, it is more than a little teleological (Fromm, 2009).

Ecofeminism shares some views with both deep ecology and Bookchin's ecology, but it places much of the blame for both societal and ecological ills on "the domination of both women and nature by men" (Merchant, 2008: 24). It is a social and political movement with a variety of goals, depending on author; these include an end to militarism, the cessation of domination, oppression, and discrimination of all sorts, economic liberation, procreative freedom, and decentralization. Like many of the viewpoints I review in this book, ecofeminism is diverse (Merchant, 2005: 198). Some ecofeminists advocate a rational scientific individualism—just one that includes women as equals—while others reject scientific rationalism as the tool of domination. Others seek societal change that fully recognizes women's role in production and reproduction. Still others see ecofeminism as an interconnection between women and nature that should be the basis for society, while some believe ecofeminism to be a "denunciation of a presupposed relationship between women and nature" (Lauwers, 2017: 108). If there is a common ecofeminist perspective, it is that real change can only be brought about by the end to relationships based on domination. Vandana Shiva, for example, has advocated for a feminist ecology that recognizes the intrinsic worth of and democratic relationship among all species, peoples, and cultures (Shiva, 2006: 9–11).

There is in some ecofeminist writing a strong spirituality, including a sense of ancient feminine connection with nature (Merchant, 2005: 202). It sees nature as a goddess, and the Earth as Mother. There is a sense of loss in this impression: that ancestral human societies, once more peaceful, egalitarian and connected under the guidance of the ancient feminine, were co-opted by male domination during the agricultural revolution. Women and environment have since suffered under the same exploitation. The spiritual ecofeminist movement urges a recon-nection of nature and culture, of the spiritual with the material. A well-reasoned protection of nature is not enough, in this view. In fact reason and protection themselves may be regarded as acts of control and domination. Rather, the spir-itual ecofeminist vision seems to argue that if human societies could be restruc-tured to be more relational, caring, and interconnected, environmental health would follow (Merchant, 2005: 193–222).

An ancient precedent for a better society based on an inherent feminine con-nection with nature is difficult to reconcile with evolutionary history. As we will see in the following chapters, there likely were indeed times of more egalitarian human interactions in our collective past, but it is not at all clear that these societies were more environmentally benevolent. The claim to a greater feminine connection with nature would seem to be at odds with the assertion that an egalitarian society was once better and that it should be the goal now; rather, it seems to be a call for a matriarchal society. The appeal to the sacred feminine goddess or Mother Earth takes us into psycho-spiritual ecology, the merits and limitations of which will be discussed below. Lauwers (2017: 108) argues that this perspective is not representative of ecofeminism at all, but is instead a mis-understanding of a movement that is aimed at promoting "a better understanding and respect for living things." Lauwers acknowledges that "the intertwining of social, philosophical and spiritual writings turned [ecofeminism] into a difficult-to-grasp movement" (2017: 110).

Psycho-spiritual ecologies

My penchant for categorizing gets me in trouble, as it places an artificial boundary at an arbitrary point on a continuum. You are fairly warned, then, that some of what I label as psycho-spiritual ecology could well fit in the previous section and vice versa. This is an ecology of the mind; indeed, in some manifestations it exists entirely within the human mind. It is a search for understanding of the human place in the universe. In one conception, it is the notion that the human spirit is inherently connected with nature, for in nature we find the highest expression of the soul, the closest connection with the divine. It is the feeling that we *are* our connections, and the greatest self-actualization—the deepest connections with our inner selves—draws on the deepest connections with the natural world. While this attitude intimates a deep reverence for nature, it plays out along the whole range of human–nature relationships. Some spiritual ecologists literally worship the Earth as a god or goddess who gives and maintains the proper conditions for life. Some believe there is a supernatural essence penetrating every aspect of the universe, from the stars over our heads to the rocks at our feet. Others embrace a nature-as-brother-or-sister kindred spirit to humans, while still others see mental connection with nature as a means of being closer to the one God. Some spiritual ecologists see themselves as beings created in God's image, thus having dominion over nature. Spirituality, it seems, can place a person in many different cosmic positions (Spretnak, 1986; Macy, 1992: 331–337).

While spiritual ecology is not always religious, it has clear ties to many religious traditions. Some of these are tied to ancient ritual and custom, while others are re-invigorations of animism or pantheism. In modern spiritual ecology we see many romantic ideals, including the notion of grandeur in nature, the peaceful balance and harmony in pristine wilderness, the restorative effects of mystical communion with the nonhuman world, and the corruptive influence of human society. There is, in this perspective, a unity in nature that humans once shared and to which we can return by transcending the material world (Thacker, 1983: 23).

A body of scholarly work in spiritual ecology revolves around the spirit of place. To philosopher Michael Northcott, there is an instinctive human connection with places, and much of our social strife and environmental problems are attributable to the way we treat—or mistreat—our places. Private, corporate, or state ownership of land for production, cultural homogenization of landscapes, the loss of historic and prehistoric human marks on the land, and general disconnection with the land (especially among children) have left us in a state of *placelessness*, which is harmful to human, social, and environmental health. Connection with place can be as much about the built environment as the natural environment; to Northcott it is when we treat places as interchangeable sites of production and habitation that they lose their sanctity. Northcott rejects the idea of setting aside large wilderness areas, and instead advocates the reconnection of land and livelihood in a local economy of place. This would promote not only health, but also morality, for in Northcott's view morality has been disconnected from the spatial context in which he believes morals emerged. Our connection with the spirit of place, in this view, is a connection with the right way to live; it is a moral geography (Northcott, 2015: 144, 152, 158).

A very different spiritual ecology is presented by Félix Guattari. His view, which he calls mental ecology, advocates maintaining a subjective heterogeneity, a singular personality, in the face of a homogenizing and mass-marketed capitalism. It calls for us to abandon scientific methods and models and instead to embrace aesthetic paradigms, for "it is artists who provide us with the most profound insights into the human condition" (Guattari, 2008 [1989]: 8). This is an ecology of the human consciousness, of inventing and reinventing one's own mind, and as such it is quite far removed from the ecology of the natural environment in which humans physically find themselves. As to how this might help us alter the environmentally destructive actions of the human race, Guattari calls for consensus through dissensus—extensive rejection of the dominant social structures in favor of "individual competence as a social force, for the development of a new, egalitarian, decentralized, participatory democracy, oriented towards an environmentally sustainable way of living" Guattari (2008 [1989]: 10).

Curiously, Guattari's mental ecology is an atheistic spiritual ecology, for he sees the need for a materialist ethic which recognizes mortality and the limits of physical existence. As an atheistic spiritualism that calls for materialistic grounding amid a rejection of science, this is truly a unique point of view.

Some central questions of spiritual ecology consider the human–nature relationship: does nature have meaning beyond human mental constructs? How do we perceive beauty in nature? Must we understand nature in the scientific sense and sociocultural context to appreciate it, or is it through engagement, immersion, and emotional connection that we best experience our world? Spiritual ecologists also wrestle with perceptions of nature versus reality. Is it through connection with a pristine, unspoiled natural ideal—a nature of harmony, stability, balance, and order—that humans find a higher spirituality, or must humans fully embrace disorder, discordance, and imbalance as well? And what do we mean by nature anyway? If humans are a part of nature, are the built environment, societal structures, and human expressions themselves things that should be embraced in the quest for spiritual clarity?

There are no clear actions associated with this sort of ecology. It is, in fact, not altogether apparent that the questions it poses can be answered in any objective way (though of course this is not the goal). Rather, this is an introspective ecology of intuitive realities. It is an exercise in "developing our consciences, of knowing self in the context of the bigger body and, as far as we can, discerning our membership role within it" (Maiteny, 2015: 136). This sort of ecology may not always be practically applicable to specific environmental dilemmas. Its value, rather, is that it provides a nature of the imagination. This, some spiritual ecologists contend, is what binds humans to the nonhuman world and to one another (Guattari, 2008 [1989]: 8).

Integral ecology

These various views of ecology have all arisen in response to common desires: to understand the structure and function of the nonhuman world, to discern factors driving the human relationships with one another and with the Earth, and to demonstrate ways in which anthropogenic stress can be lessened and the Earth's capacity to support life strengthened. From these points of origin the views diverge to span the wide dimensions of environmentalism, from the material to the spiritual, the biocentric to the anthropocentric, the interventionist to the preservationist, and from individualist to collectivist.

Can the ecologies be reconciled into a concerted approach to environmental problem solving? An attempt to do just this is called integral ecology. Integral ecology is not clearly defined, but in general it is the view that everything in the universe is interconnected, and that study of the individual parts of the whole cannot lead us to understanding. Rather it is the whole that must be considered at once (Pope Francis, 2015). In one conception, it is really systems ecology inclusive of social systems and of the "perception, experience, intentionality, and awareness" within each interconnected member (Esbjörn-Hargens, 2005: 23). It thus considers the behavior, experience, and culture of each component of the global system. The argument is that it is impossible to know ecosystem or organism unless one incorporates the shared experience of culture into that view. It is, in this sense, a call to find mutual understanding by empathetically inhabiting the perspectives of other organisms (Esbjörn-Hargens, 2005: 6).

Integral ecology speaks (in at least one version) of the intrinsic good in every organism and of the harmony of the interconnected whole, arguing that strained sociocultural relationships can harm the environment and vice versa (Pope Francis, 2015: 140). It insists that our biological and sociocultural needs (and problems) are interconnected. Consequently, it calls for protection not only of species and ecological relationships, but also of social bonds and cultural traditions. In cases where any of these are compromised or lost, harmony intended by the Creator is lost. In short, integral ecology proposes a common ground between scientific, social, and spiritual ecology.

Is this sort of integral ecology a Rosetta stone? Is it the fundamental worldview that can reconcile the dimensions of environmentalism? I believe that it is not, for three reasons. These irreconcilable differences are: 1) the manner in which the different ecologies consider evidence and ways of knowing; 2) the different considerations of dualism; and 3) the different views of progression and holism.

First, the admirable attempt at ecological integration promotes a path to knowledge that is incompatible with the various realms of ecology. Scientific ecology (and some social ecology) is premised on sensory experience and objective reasoning. Certain realms of social ecology, as we have seen, contend that truth is a subjective (and intersubjective) matter of construction, and therefore dependent on both perceiver and context. Integral ecology (at least as described above) promotes the notion that the way in which ecological relationships ought to work, or what courses of action, if any, should be taken, is knowable from individual thoughts or preferences, intuition, and/or spiritual revelations. The scientific reaction to this should be clear: these are unmeasurable, untestable, and prone to disagreement. The way I imagine the perspective of another organism, for instance, is likely different from the way you would, and we have no good way to determine whose vision is best. Similarly, the social ecologist might have difficulty with an approach that projects human characteristics onto nonhuman entities. It seems, though, that understanding the fundamental principles of ecological structure and process is not even really a goal of integral ecology. According to Sean Esbjörn-Hargens, "integral ecologists affirm the ultimate mystery of all phenomena as a way of preventing attachment to conceptualizations of reality" (Esbjörn-Hargens, 2005: 36). One may just as well appeal to the unknowable mind of a higher power (as some proponents of integral ecology do) and admit that "ours is not to reason why."[1] For evidence-based approaches to knowledge, this is entirely unacceptable.

Second, integral ecology does not seem to reconcile the various views of Cartesian dualism in the different ecologies. I find it interesting that scientific, social, and spiritual ecology share a rejection of the dualism of human and nature, though for quite different reasons (each hotly contested by the others).

The material scientist sees humans as just another organism, made of the same matter and energy and evolved from the same origins as other species. Some social ecologists see the interconnection of human and natural systems, accusing the material scientist of separating the human from the nonhuman world while themselves seeing no dualism. Spiritual ecologists (at least some spiritual ecologists) see the essence of both human and nature as being of the same substance, holding that this essence is created and bound by nonmaterial energy—contrary to many scientific and social ecological perspectives. As to Descartes' mind/body dualism, it is rejected by material scientists, who see both the mental and the spiritual as manifestations of neurophysiology—in other words, as part of the physical world. Certain social ecologists would agree, while spiritual ecologists find living (and sometimes nonliving) things to have a vital energy that is different from the physical; it is an essence that communes with an overarching Spirit in the creator, the giver of life, or Mother Earth. The spiritualist is therefore looked at with suspicion by the materialist, who sees this as clear dualism. Descartes would be amused to see that his conjecture is still such a hot item. I'm not convinced that integral ecology settles the matter, for it seems to run the gamut from mechanical systems ecology to the mental ecology of the spiritual overlord.

Third, integral ecology (again, of the sort I have presented here) seems to hold the view that there is a *correct* version of the natural environment. In the more secular integral ecology it is a nature in which all organisms, cultures, and individual psyches are self-actualized. In the more religious integral ecology it is the idea that the deity or deities intend for a harmonious natural state, and that it is the human task to achieve this state. Again, it is the materialists who have difficulty with either view. While there are some holistic ecologists who speak of ascendancy toward ecological harmony and natural balance, it is not at all clear that such things exist. To the contrary, evidence suggests that organisms and ecological systems respond independently to environmental contingencies—including to the selective pressures brought about by humans—and that natural harmony exists only in the human mind.

In my estimation, then, we can add integral ecology to the list of ecologies on which well-meaning environmentalists will disagree. But I do not introduce it here simply to tear it down. It does provide an excellent lens through which we can see both the human qualities that are needed for an effective environmentalism and the human characteristics that get in the way. From my perspective, integral ecology correctly notes that environmental problems are issues of sociocultural context and conceptual construct. It also suggests that environmental problems occur at the intersection of ecological relationships and social relationships.

While I take issue with the ideas of integral ecology described here, I believe there is an integrative thread that winds through our different philosophical perspectives, our contradictory environmental dimensions, and our many ecologies. It explains why we are both the cause of and the potential solution for environmental problems and why we have such difficulty in coming to consensus on the best course of action. To see it clearly, we will need to take a journey through our own evolutionary history.

Note

1 From Tennyson, "The charge of the Light Brigade," 1854.

Bibliography

Albrecht, G.A. (1998). Ethics and directionality in nature. In: A. Light, ed., *Social ecology after Bookchin*. New York: Guilford Press. pp. 92–113.
Bookchin, M. (1980). *Toward an ecological society*. Montreal: Black Rose Books.
Bookchin, M. (1985). Ecology and revolutionary thought. *Antipode*, 17(2–3), pp. 89–98.
Bookchin, M. (1986). *The modern crisis*. Philadelphia: New Society.
Bookchin, M. (1989). *Remaking society*. Montreal: Black Rose Books.
Bridge, G., McCarthy, J. and T. Perreault. (2015). Editors' introduction. In: T. Perreault, G. Bridge and J. McCarthy, eds., *The Routledge handbook of political ecology*. London: Routledge, pp. 3–18.
Chan, K.M., Satterfield, T. and Goldstein, J. (2012). Rethinking ecosystem services to better address and navigate cultural values. *Ecological Economics*, 74, pp. 8–18.
de Unamuno, M. (1954 [1913]). *Tragic sense of life*. Translation by J. Flitch. New York: Dover.
Devall, B. (1980). The deep ecology movement. *Natural Resources Journal*, 20, pp. 299–313.
Ehrlich, P.R. and Ehrlich, A. (1981). *Extinction: the causes and consequences of the disappearance of species*. New York: Random House.
Esbjörn-Hargens, S. (2005). Integral ecology: the what, who and how of environmental phenomena: an ecology of perspectives. *World Futures*, 61, pp. 5–49.
Fischer-Kowalski, M. and Weisz, H. (2016). The archipelago of social ecology and the island of the Vienna school. In: H. Haberl, M. Fischer-Kowalski, F. Krausmann, and V. Winiwarter, eds., *Social ecology: society–nature relations across time and space*. New York: Springer. pp. 3–28.
Fromm, H. (2009). *The nature of being human: from environmentalism to consciousness*. Baltimore: Johns Hopkins University Press.
Guattari, F. (2008 [1989]). *The three ecologies*. Translation by I. Pindar and P. Sutton. London: Athlone.
Haeckel, E. (1864). On Darwin's evolutionary theory. As per Richards, R.J. (2008). *The tragic sense of life: Ernst Haeckel and the struggle over evolutionary thought*. Chicago: University of Chicago Press.
Kovel, J. (1998). Negating Bookchin. In: A. Light, ed., *Social ecology after Bookchin*. New York: Guilford Press. pp. 27–57.
Laland, K.N. and Brown, G.R. (2011). *Sense and nonsense: evolutionary perspectives on human behaviour*. Oxford: Oxford University Press.
Lauwers, M. (2017). Ecofeminism. In: A. Chone, I. Hajek and P. Hamman, eds., *Rethinking nature: challenging disciplinary boundaries*. London: Routledge. pp. 106–113.
Light, A., ed. (1998). *Social ecology after Bookchin*. New York: Guilford Press.
Macy, J. (1992). Deep ecology work: toward the healing of self and world. *Human Potential Magazine*, 17(1), pp. 10–31.
Maiteny, P. (2015). Trees of knowledge, death and possible life: ancestral warnings of ecosystemic holocaust, its psycho-spiritual causes, and clues to resolution. *Self & Society*, 43(2), pp. 128–137.
Merchant, C. (2005). *Radical ecology: the search for a livable world*. New York: Routledge.

Merchant, C., ed. (2008). *Ecology*. 2nd edition. Amherst, NY: Humanity Books.

Millennium Ecosystem Assessment. (2003). *Ecosystems and human well-being: a framework for assessment*. Washington, DC: Island Press.

Naess, A. (1973). The shallow and the deep, long-range ecology movement: a summary. *Inquiry*, 16(1–4), pp. 95–100.

Northcott, M.S. (2015). *Place, ecology and the sacred: the moral geography of sustainable communities*. New York: Bloomsbury Press.

Perreault, T., Bridge, G. and McCarthy, J. eds. (2015). *The Routledge handbook of political ecology*. London: Routledge.

Pope Francis. (2015). *Laudato si': on care for our common home* [Encyclical].

Richards, R.J. (2008). *The tragic sense of life: Ernst Haeckel and the struggle over evolutionary thought*. Chicago: University of Chicago Press.

Rudy, A.P. (1998). Ecology and anthropology in the work of Murray Bookchin: problems of theory and evidence. In: A. Light, ed, *Social ecology after Bookchin*. New York: Guilford Press. pp. 265–297.

Scheffer, M., Carpenter, S., Foley, J.A., Folke, C. and Walker, B. (2001). Catastrophic shifts in ecosystems. *Nature*, 413(6856), pp. 591–596.

Shiva, V. (2006). *Earth democracy: justice, sustainability and peace*. London: Zed Books.

Spieles, D.J. (2010). *Protected land: disturbance, stress, and American ecosystem management*. New York: Springer.

Spretnak, C. (1986). *The spiritual dimension of green politics*. Rochester, VT: Bear & Company.

Thacker, C. (1983). *The wildness pleases: the origins of romanticism*. London: Routledge.

Vayda, A.P. and Walters, B.B. (1999). Against political ecology. *Human Ecology*, 27(1), pp. 167–179.

Watson, D. (1996). *Beyond Bookchin: preface for a future social ecology*. Brooklyn, NY: Autonomedia.

White, A.D. (1894). *A history of the warfare of science with theology in Christendom*. Vol I. New York: D. Appleton.

Wilson, D.S. (2002). *Darwin's cathedral: evolution, religion, and the nature of society*. Chicago: University of Chicago Press.

Wilson, E.O. (1975). *Sociobiology, the new synthesis*. Cambridge, MA: Belknap.

Worster, D. (1994). *Nature's economy: a history of ecological ideas*. Cambridge, UK: Cambridge University Press.

Part 2
Evolutionary context

4   Sociobiological evolution

Key points

- Our species has evolved characteristics that are prerequisite for an environmental ethic.
- Cooperative reciprocity and mental scenario building are products of sociobiological evolution.
- Normative cultural codes are products of sociocultural evolution.

What sort of creatures are we to have such wide-ranging views on the world and ways of knowing our place in it? How is it that the human understanding of environment spans from the material to the spiritual, from anthropocentric to biocentric, from humans as ecological engineers to humans as just another node in the great web of life? There is a single but complicated answer: we are products of evolution.

We have seen that environmentalism and ecology have no simple definition. It is unsurprising, then, that there are many different sorts of evolution. To evolve, after all, simply means to change. Everything changes. So we could discuss the cosmologic evolution of galaxies, stars, and solar systems, or we could consider the physical and chemical evolution of matter and energy since the Big Bang. As entertaining as these would be, more central to the topic of this book is the evolution of our species and its social groups. Following convention, I will use the term biological evolution to refer primarily to natural selection as it acts on individual organisms and species. The term sociobiological evolution refers to behavioral selection that has effects within and among populations of social species. Sociocultural evolution refers to learned behavior that is acquired by imitation, communication, and education, not strictly by genetic inheritance.

In this chapter I explore these types of evolution as they apply to early humans for two reasons. First, they provide insight with which we can make sense of the modern varieties of environmentalism and ecology discussed in the previous two chapters. Second, the origins of human instincts and social systems illuminate the structural, economic, ecological, spiritual, aesthetic, and psychological problems of environmentalism that we face today. These are the focus of the rest of the book.

Precursors of environmentalism

What is it about our species that gives us the capacity for environmentalism? I suggest that certain traits—all part of our common evolutionary history—are prerequisite for the emergence of an environmental ethic in human individuals and cultures. These characteristics did not arise in response to environmental concerns, but rather as survival mechanisms in a very different set of living conditions than we encounter today.

In my view, there are three such qualities. The first is cooperative reciprocity. This is really the combination of two skills that I define in the broadest sense: cooperation—the ability to work together toward a common goal—and reciprocity—a process of exchange for mutual benefit (Bowles and Gintis, 2011: 2, 93). Environmentalism is a reach beyond individual needs and the protection of one's immediate family to consider the welfare of other individuals and even other species. It means limiting one's own ecological impact (at potentially a personal expense) in concert with and for the advantage of others (who are probably competitors). Understanding our environmental ethic, then, will require an understanding of the evolutionary basis for cooperative reciprocity.

The second prerequisite skill for environmentalism is also a combination—something I'll call time-shifting scenario building. This is drawn from sociobiologist Alexander's (1989) concept of scenario building and what psychologist Suddendorf (2013: 90–96) calls mental time travel. The "time-shifting" is the ability to recall the past and look to the future—a critical environmental skill, for how else would we be able to perceive or project environmental concerns? Scenario building is the ability to imagine different situations, to mentally simulate one's own actions (or a group's collective action), and to predict potential outcomes. Together, time-shifting and scenario building give humans the capacity to build mental models of past success and failure and to imagine future opportunities and threats. Time-shifting scenario building is enhanced when combined with cooperative reciprocity; together, they provide not only for group planning but also for *empathy*—the ability to consider a scenario from the perspective of another. The cooperative act of sharing mental models is an important part of how people today—and perhaps throughout the history of our species—approach environmental problems. In combination, these skills also support collective behavior alteration in the pursuit of some common good which could not be achieved alone (Alexander, 1989; Suddendorf, 2013).

A third prerequisite for environmentalism is a common cultural code (Singer, 1981: 152). This is a behavioral guideline; it is a system for evaluating our social and environmental surroundings. The understanding of right and wrong, the sacred and the profane, the beautiful and the ugly, the useful and the detrimental is deeply etched into human culture. Such value systems give humans a normative basis to judge their own actions and those of others. Together with cooperative reciprocity and time-shifting scenario building, cultural norms provide for the complex ideas and behaviors of environmentalism.

To what extent can cooperation, reciprocity, scenario building, and socio-cultural norms be attributed to biological evolution? To what extent are they culturally derived? This is a version of the nature versus nurture question or, put another way, a question of our two inheritances (Henrich and McElreath, 2007). The first of our inheritances is our genetic endowment, the product of biological evolution. The second is our learned behavior, that which we acquire by imitation and education through sociocultural evolution. Both play a role in making us human, and together they inform our complex and sometimes contradictory thoughts and actions. The goal of this chapter is to provide a theoretical back-ground for our combined evolutionary heritage. In particular, I'll explore some conflicts of human nature to provide insight on why we think about the environment as we do. But before we get there we'll have to go back to our humble beginnings.

Evolution by natural selection

The modern understanding of biological evolution is only slightly nuanced from that described by Charles Darwin and Alfred Russel Wallace over 150 years ago (Darwin and Wallace, 1858). The underlying themes are variation, chance, competition, selection, and inheritance. Here is the short version: living things tend to produce more offspring than can be supported by their environment. Not all of those offspring will survive. And while they may be related, they are not all identical—there is variation in the individual traits of a given species. Some traits give some individuals a statistical survival advantage in certain environmental conditions. Advantageous traits are contingent upon environmental conditions, and those conditions can and do change; hence that which constitutes an advantage today may be a liability tomorrow. In any case, many individuals competing for limited resources means that some will have more success than others. The most successful will have the best opportunity to pass their genes on to the next generation (a concept not fully understood in Darwin and Wallace's time). In this way, the gene frequency of a given population gradually changes, and associated traits change accordingly.

Darwin and Wallace showed with this mechanism that species are far from immutable—that species are in fact malleable. Subjected to a changing world, species change in response. The environmental conditions in which the compe-tition for life unfolds are known as selection pressures, and the process is called natural selection. A dramatic change in selection pressure can effect a dramatic change in the appearance, behavior, or function of species over geologic time, while long periods of relatively stable conditions can result in little biological change. In certain cases, sub-populations may be subjected to different selection pressures when they are separated in time or space (via chance events) or genetic compatibility (via mutation), or as they come to harbor individuals with new traits (also via mutation). This can result in divergence, and ultimately speciation—the advent of new species. The process is the basis for the branching tree of life by which modern species (and even extinct species) can be traced back to a common ancestor. What it means is that all life is related at some level: oak trees and dandelions, whales and pythons, humans and mushrooms. The thought is (still!) a terrifying sacrilege for some and a thrilling insight for others (Darwin and Wallace, 1858; Darwin 1859).

Some have pointed out that the whole process is rather selfish, and that the selfish unit is the individual gene, or perhaps the genome of an individual (Dawkins, 1976). Imagine that you are one of 10,000 salamander eggs that hatch in a small pond. Your first need is nourishment, and that goes to the biggest, strongest, and quickest. There is no sharing here, and some of your siblings and cousins will starve (in fact some may eat one another). As you try to find enough to eat, you must evade predators. This challenge rewards the best camouflaged, the stealthy, and the lucky. More will die, but each salamander that is preyed upon is one less competitor for you. Now the day comes to emerge from the pond and seek terrestrial habitat (which is also coveted by other species). The first to shelter, those fortunate enough to escape predation and environmental hazards, and the most adept at feeding will survive; many others will die. Still more will perish during the terrestrial phase of life due to parasites, pathogens, predators, or climatic changes. Finally, it is time to return to the pond, another perilous journey. The competition for the best locations to deposit eggs, the frenzy to fertilize those eggs, and the best immunity and nutrition will determine whose offspring make up the next generation. There are far more losers than winners. In the parlance of evolution, if you pass your genes on to the next generation you've been *selected for*, and if not you've been *selected against*.

There is coordination here, and even a basic sort of cooperation. After all, the salamanders arrive at the same pond at the same time for the same purpose. Even so, it is hard to argue that this is anything beyond an individual struggle for existence. Human lives are far different than those of salamanders, of course, but we have at least one characteristic in common with these distant relatives. We too are driven to compete with others to maintain or enhance our own prospects.

The "selfish" act of individuals competing to pass on their genes is the only apparent goal of evolution. There is no lofty endpoint toward which life strives, no ideal state that, once achieved, will signal the end for a need to change. Humans have long imagined (and some imagine still) that our species is the epitome of life on Earth, and that all other species are but links on the Aristotelian great chain of being below our own. This was the perspective of most of humanity until very recently. Paleontologist Robert Broom (1866–1951) represented the sentiments of his era when he proclaimed in 1933 that, with the appearance of our own species, "there was no further need for evolution" (Broom, 1933; Tudge, 1996: 80). But today, overwhelming evidence from the fossil record, from comparative anatomy, physiology, and especially from molecular genetics disproves the hierarchical "chain of being" concept. Instead it supports the branching tree metaphor, meaning that—speaking evolutionarily—*Homo sapiens* occupies just one of many twigs, no more evolved than any other species with which we share the planet. It is an important point, and it emphasizes that no organism or species intends to evolve in any particular direction (at least in the sense of biological evolution). Individuals either successfully pass on their genes or they do not. It is a lonely view of life, and one that is subject to much suffering and death.

Individualism, cooperation, and reciprocity

The description above is a basic view of our *primary* inheritance: our genetic legacy as acted upon by natural selection for billions of years. So what does this have to do with environmentalism? Well, if human character and behavior were formed through trait-by-trait natural selection alone, an environmental ethic would be hard to explain. Environmentalism can take many forms, but in general it involves concern for the well-being of other people and other species on Earth. Evolution by natural selection, at least as described so far, seems to be fixated on the individual drive to procreate, not on common well-being. It is hard to see how cooperation, reciprocity, time-shifting scenario building, and a code of conduct arose from simple life-or-death selection.

Consider another example, this one a bit closer to the human condition than salamanders: a troop of apes. Perhaps this troop is of the lineage that gave rise to modern chimpanzees, bonobos, and humans; it is the common hominid ancestor that geneticists tell us existed about six to seven million years ago (Suddendorf, 2013: 19). We can infer some general characteristics of these creatures from archeological evidence and comparative study of modern primates. It is likely, for example, that this troop consists of a few dozen individuals that occasionally and temporarily fuse with neighboring troops, with which they co-exist, compete, and co-mingle. Within groups, mating is typically polygynous, and even when mating rights are established there is rampant cheating. Resources and territory are commonly defended by cooperative action of group members. Care of the young is likewise a cooperative venture, supported by extensive social bonding within the group. Within-group bonding may have conferred upon this troop the basic elements of culture—such as common and unique foraging and grooming patterns, distinctive actions and reactions to stimuli, and shared territory (Whiten, 2011; Pandit *et al.*, 2016). Furthermore, it is plausible that apes like these exhibited many of the basic instincts, emotions, and desires that we experience today. Six million years is but an instant in geologic time, meaning that modern humans and ancestral apes share nearly their entire evolutionary history. So perhaps we can see something of ourselves in them (Maryanski and Turner, 1992: 18–19; Massey, 2002: 1–4).

One thing that we can glean from this brief sketch of our distant ancestors is that they must not always act in their own immediate best interest—though not for lack of the selfish drive of competition. These apes are, after all, not so different than salamanders. Their biological imperative is to survive, to mate, and to produce offspring. On the other hand, they are quite different than salamanders; their lives are not completely selfish, for they are social creatures—they protect, provide for, and share resources with those in their group. Social bonding facilitates—and is facilitated by—mutual responsibilities, long-term associations, and common purposes that constrain selfish behavior. In this way, social organization is a check on the competitive instinct, and in certain instances it can reach beyond mere cooperation. There is exchange of material, thought, and action happening here. There is reciprocation (Massey, 2002: 3).

It is worth pausing for a moment to consider social structure in general. In *Sociobiology* E.O. Wilson (1975: 379–380) highlights four "pinnacles" of advanced social structure and behavior that have evolved among Earth's living things. The first, colonial invertebrates (like corals and bryozoans), are the most primitive but also the most socially perfect, with constituent organisms highly specialized into castes that serve the colony. Their coordination and cohesion is so nearly complete that the colony effectively functions as a single organism. Individuals essentially devote their entire lives to the collective (in fact, it hardly makes sense to think of them as individuals). The second example is the social insects—also magnificently successful and specialized into castes that serve the whole, but with more individuality than corals (as seen in worker bees that venture forth to search for food and to bring that information back to the collective, or in the occasional struggle for egg-laying dominance within the hive). Third are the social primates, like our common ape ancestors, which have more individuality still. We can find hierarchy in primate societies, as well as cooperative care, defense, and foraging. But there is also the opportunity for upward mobility (challenging the alpha) and even innovation. For example, modern primates have been observed to invent means of washing food, luring termites out of a mound, and separating grain from the stalk, all of which have been imitated by curious onlookers. This shows an individuality unseen in more "perfect" social animals. In some cases primate individuality may even take the form of selfishness that appears to run counter to the common good (McGrew, 2004).

And then there is human society, which Wilson places in a category all by itself. Human societies have collective structures of hierarchy, specialization, and even castes, but individuality is in some ways paramount, such that the needs and desires of the individual can and do eclipse the collective good. Even ostensibly cooperative behavior can be part of complex social arrangements that are ultimately selfish. I might, for example, do something for the good of others as a not-so-subtle way of enhancing my own reputation and standing among my peers. On the other hand, the success of one's social group is important to one's own success, so it behooves the individual to be a cooperative group member. There is, in short, a tension between individual desires and the expectation for service to the group (E.O. Wilson, 1975: 380–382).

This basic conflict is at the heart of a great deal of human tribulation. It touches all the positives of innovation, expression, devotion, and compassion, all the negatives of aggression, domination, and oppression, and the many conditionals of competition and collaboration. Consider, for example, the seven deadly sins of Christian lore: pride, envy, sloth, greed, lust, gluttony, and wrath. These are acts of the individual seeking satisfaction for himself over the well-being of the group. Virtue, by contrast, is represented by the four cardinal virtues of prudence, justice, temperance, and courage—things that make you a good group member. Similar notions of virtue and vice are ubiquitous in human cultures. The words may differ, but the sentiment is ingrained: selfishness is bad behavior, and cooperation is good (E.O. Wilson, 2012: 241–254). Modern environmentalism revolves around this tension, and we will return to it often.

But back to our group of ancestral apes. Is it reasonable to attribute their social characteristics and behaviors to natural selection? Yes, and no. Yes, in the sense that natural selection is the predominant driver of biological evolution. These apes are part of a twig on the branching tree, just like the salamanders. Their characteristics were selected for over billions of years because they increased the likelihood that individuals with those characteristics would successfully reproduce in a given set of environmental conditions. No, in the sense that it is probably not this simple. Some characteristics, it seems, are inherited together, such that higher-order complexes of traits may include some advantageous features and others that are somewhat incidental. An example of this from our own ancient lineage is the shape and position of the human pelvis (Gruss and Schmitt, 2015). As it became advantageous for our ancestors to move out of the trees and traverse on land, the theory goes, a more upright posture was selected for, necessitating a narrower pelvis. There were survival advantages associated with an upright, bipedal posture, but the narrow pelvis that came with it played havoc with childbirth and necessitated the birth of small, younger, and more helpless infants—the most immature at birth in the animal kingdom (Dutton, 2009: 140). This necessitated longer periods of infant care, mate cooperation, and social protection—again, advantages in some respects, but also potential disadvantages to individual survival and procreation (Harari, 2015: 10). So, is it fair to say that natural selection resulted in cooperative protection of infants? It is, but the story is more complicated than single trait selection.

Some traits serve no functional purpose other than attracting or competing for a mate. This is sexual selection, and it explains such ostentatious displays as enormous racks of antlers, brilliantly colored feathers, and elaborate courtship behaviors (D.S Wilson, 1975: 318). These and similar characteristics are advertisements, pure and simple. They proclaim to potential mates that the bearer is fit and healthy—and in some cases proclaim that she or he has excess energy to devote to the advertisement itself. Such showy displays can be energetically costly and potentially dangerous, as they could just as easily attract a predator as a mate. Well, not *just* as easily, for if the showy feathers or large rack of antlers became *maladaptive* they would quickly be selected against and become less showy or smaller over time. The benefits of attracting a mate must outweigh the costs of the trait, at least according to the rules of natural selection. Among social organisms, sexual selection is locked in an ongoing struggle against the benefits of group cooperation. Interestingly, some environmentally related modern human behaviors such as ostentatious display of generosity (as a show of excess and beneficence) and waste (as a show of excess to the extreme) have been proposed as examples of sexual selection (Dutton, 2009: 153–156).

Other traits are inherited though they have no apparent selective or sexual advantage. Gould and Lewontin (1979) have called these spandrels, after the odd triangle that is incidentally created on either side of an arch. Spandrels can arise as a by-product of selection as long as they are not disadvantageous, and they have no purpose (though purpose and advantage can arise later). The color of blood is a spandrel. It is a by-product of the iron in erythrocytes—which is critical to our survival—but the color itself confers no survival advantage. Other traits are ambiguous in their purpose (or lack thereof). Some modern apes, for example, have been known to beat on trees and fallen logs simply to listen to the sounds, which can entertain a troop for some time. How did this behavior arise? We don't know. Perhaps it evolved with a specific purpose that confers a real survival advantage, say as a communication mechanism within the group. Or, perhaps it is a spandrel. Careful listening would have conferred an advantage in a species that relies on hoots, screeches, and cries of the forest to indicate danger. The ability to smack trees might have provided an advantage in finding tasty insects that dwell within. The combination—thumping trees to create pleasing sounds—may be a by-product of these other adaptive traits. Interestingly, spandrels can acquire advantage over time. For example, I can imagine that thumping on trees and hollow logs to produce pleasing sounds may have over time become a social bonding mechanism among apes. Perhaps those apes that are socially connected with other apes have a better chance of surviving to reproduce (Arcadi *et al.*, 1998).

The upshot of all this is that, while natural selection is indeed the best explanation we have for the evolution of species, it would be incorrect to state that the characteristics of a species are only driven by the selfish desire to pass one's genes to the next generation. In fact, there are other aspects of selection that allow for the evolution of complex behaviors and traits, and these might be useful in the quest to understand the origins of environmentalism. Cooperation among individuals, for example, is a complex behavior that apparently provided our ancient ancestors with an evolutionary advantage.

To advance this understanding further we'll next explore the evolution of reciprocity and altruism. This is critical, for environmentally sensitive behavior requires more than cooperation. Often, it involves sacrifice that may or may not confer an immediate gain: I voluntarily decrease my own consumption or reduce my waste production so that (in the extreme case) others may prosper at my expense, or (more commonly) others may prosper along with me, which thereby increases future competition for me and my descendants. How can we explain such behavior?

Reciprocity and altruism

Do humans exhibit truly altruistic behavior? The academic jury is still far from settled on the question, but there are some theories that might lead us down the path. One is kin selection (Hamilton, 1964). This notion arises from a conundrum of evolution by natural selection: the existence of organisms which, through sterility and/or status, have a reduced chance of reproduction in favor of enhanced reproduction for a close relative. In this way a worker bee, for instance, devotes her life to the promotion of reproduction for her sisters. But this is not really altruism.

True, the sacrificial individual is giving up or reducing her chance of procreation, but the action is done to increase the overall chance that her genes will be passed on to the next generation. It does not violate the evolutionary imperative to selfishly do everything possible to pass on one's genes, for the genes of close relatives are a large fraction of one's own genome. In theory, promoting procreation for a large number of kin is as good as seeking one's own procreation. It may be, as some have argued, just an elaborate form of selfishness. Still, it is a form of reciprocal behavior—meaning that it confers a benefit to both parties. In our hypothetical troop of ancestral apes we can imagine kin selection at work: warning calls from sentries who thereby put themselves at great risk for their kin, food sharing among relatives that might decrease the nutrition of a given individual, care for another individual's child, or assistance given by some to close relatives in need. All of these behaviors, of course, are characteristics of humans as well, though the extent to which they can be attributed to kin selection is debated (Kurzban *et al.*, 2015).

More controversial is cooperative reciprocity among non-kin—the concept of group selection (D.S. Wilson, 1975). Simply stated, this is the notion that more effective cooperation, communication, or connection at the group level (a population that reaches beyond close relatives) might confer upon some groups a survival advantage, such that individuals of certain groups have a reproductive advantage over individuals of other groups. This is not such a far cry from kin selection, especially given that kin are not always easily discernible, so that "kin"-supporting behaviors might well be inclusive of non-kin. It is, however, closer to true altruism, for (in theory) individuals would be compromising or sacrificing themselves for the good of the group, kin or not. The extension of self-sacrificial behavior to groups beyond kin is problematic to some scholars. In our group of apes, for instance, which might include members that are not close relatives, there would have to be an individual trait, coded for by genes, that is disadvantageous to the individual but good for the group—think of it as an "altruistic genotype." For one group to prosper better than others because of altruism, there would need to be a preponderance of individuals with this altruistic genotype. However, in every generation the altruistic individuals would be at a reproductive *disadvantage* versus the "selfish" individuals. Thus, selection pressure would quickly cause the group to lose its altruists over time. This would seem to defeat the idea of group selection (Pinker, 2012).

Others have argued that if the external pressures (e.g. group-to-group competition or environmental stressors) were great enough to be frequently lethal to groups with a low level of altruistic individuals, then the "altruistic genotype" could provide a selective advantage and altruistic behavior could thrive within a group. Adding credence to this is evidence that the late Pleistocene was a time of extraordinarily unstable climate, perhaps providing the environmental stress that might have selected for groups with a high degree of altruism. Another recent hypothesis proposes that within-group social pressures were very strong in early hominids, such that cheaters and free-loaders were routinely punished or ostracized while altruistic behavior was favored. Our ancestral apes, in this scenario, could have had an advantage over other groups if they had many cooperative individuals in the midst of frequent warfare, rapid climate upheaval, or chronic and fierce competition for limited food (Richerson and Boyd, 2005: 133–134; Bowles, 2009; Boehm, 2012: 17). Still another idea is that group selection occurs through the variation of cultural rather than genetic traits. In this case it is learned behavior—and conformation to the dominant culture—that confers the benefits of cooperative reciprocity and discourages dissension (Boyd and Richerson, 1988; Laland and Brown, 2011: 262–266).

None of these scenarios imply that group selection is driven by unrestrained altruism. Rather, they suggest that cooperative reciprocity can provide an advantage beyond the circle of kin, and that the benefit need not always bring direct or tangible advantages to the players. Indeed, the benefits may in certain circumstances be indirect or delayed (D.S. Wilson and Sober, 1994; Pinker, 2003: 259). For instance, the benefit to one's sacrifice for the group could be a matter of reputation: the giver realizes no immediate return, but is raised in esteem in the eyes of the other group members, which may confer future benefits contingent upon some future need (Bowles and Gintis, 2011: 31; Boehm, 2012: 50). Status within the group further complicates reciprocity. As David Graeber has pointed out, social exchange can be unequal when it occurs among unequals. Differences in need, ability, or hierarchy, for example, mean that reciprocity is not always direct or in-kind, but rather an exchange that takes place within the social context of "mutual expectations and responsibilities" (Graeber, 2011: 94–110, 102).

In these sorts of arrangements human relationships become complicated, for one must interpret, calculate, and remember who has done what for whom and why. Therefore, the reasons for social actions are not always clear. Certain human actions may be truly altruistic, but this can be difficult to discern, even for the actor. In any case, it is our social interactions—and mechanisms of social control—that provide for group cohesion, and group cohesion appears to confer a long-term survival advantage to participating individuals (D.S. Wilson, 2002: 17–19). Cooperative reciprocity is in this sense an important characteristic of human societies. At the same time, it hints at a darker aspect of human nature, for cohesion *within* groups sets the stage for competition *among* groups. Laland and Brown (2011: 265) state this succinctly: "In truth, group selection does not favor altruistic individuals so much as 'selfish' groups."

Reciprocity, mutualism, and parasitism

It is useful to distinguish between behavior that is *selfish* and that which is done in *self-interest*. Truly selfish acts aren't about reciprocity; they are all take and no give. An individual acting selfishly would simply take the meat and run, or stifle the cry of alarm and slink off into the jungle, leaving others unaware of the lurking predator. It is zero sum, with a winner (the selfish individual) and a loser (the one robbed or abandoned). The self-interest of reciprocal behavior is different—it is non-zero sum, or what we commonly call a win–win scenario. You do well because I do well, and I do well because you do well (Smith, 1976 [1759]; Collins and Barkdull, 1995).

Of course, the self-interest of reciprocity raises the possibility of cheaters—those who will accept favor in the guise of a mutually beneficial arrangement but never return the favor. These free-loaders are truly selfish, and they could seriously undermine the supposed adaptive advantage of reciprocity, since they would have greater fitness than the honest individual in the long term. Several hypotheses have been advanced to explain the existence of reciprocity despite the apparent advantages of cheating (Bowles and Gintis, 2011: 4). One is the idea, noted above, that early hominid groups developed efficient systems of punishing or even killing free-loaders and cheaters. A second is that groups developed elaborate social systems of normalization, such that encouragement of reciprocity and banishment of cheaters became the way of the group. Third, in the face of extreme competition from other groups, those with a high degree of cooperative reciprocity tended to be better competitors over time. These three ideas are entirely compatible, of course, and it is possible that the first two hypotheses set norms that were maintained because they were successful by way of the third hypothesis. In any case, norms of acceptable group behavior are strongly encoded into human social dynamics. Be it for the shame of punishment or the reward of group acceptance, we know that there is a fine line between selfish behavior and self-interest. The economist Adam Smith (1723–1790) postulated that we judge our own actions through the eyes of an imaginary "impartial spectator" who watches our behavior—think of this as a mental judge or jury who knows the line and sees when we cross it. It is, in this perspective, our social conscience that keeps most of us, most of the time, from acting in pure selfishness (Smith, 1976 [1759]: 137; Collins and Barkdull, 1995).

If we broaden the sense of reciprocal behavior it leads us to symbiotic relationships that occur among species. It is likely that every organism on the planet has some sort of symbiotic relationship with other organisms. In the process of being selected for or against, living or dying, and reproducing or not, species evolve in response to one another. In some cases it is a predator–prey arms race: bats evolve echolocation to find and catch moths in mid-flight; those moths that survive have better maneuverability and pass on traits of elusive flight; bats that have better honed echolocation are able to catch evasive moths; moths that have the ability to emit confusing ultrasonic chirps can misdirect the bats; bats that can better distinguish between real and false signals have better success (Miller and Surlykke, 2001). The organisms themselves are selection pressures driving the evolution of both species. In other cases it is a parasite–host relationship that develops, as when a wasp evolves to overcome plant defenses and lay its eggs inside leaf tissue. Sometimes the relationship has no effect on the host and so is called a commensalism, as with fire birds hitching a ride on the back of a rhinoceros and grabbing a meal from the insects that are startled to flight by the lumbering beast. Even in this case, the bird has evolved to rely on the rhino and its habits, so this too is a case of co-evolution. But the most interesting types of co-evolution for our discussion are the mutualisms—those interconnections that benefit both species at once.

Mutualistic relationships are common and ancient. Sometimes the trade is nutrient for nutrient, as in the mutualism between mycorrhizal fungi (which provide phosphorus to the plant) and plants (which provide organic carbon to the fungus). In other situations habitat, shelter, food, protection, grooming, camouflage, or similar commodities may be part of the trade. These relationships are thought to have originated, as you might expect, through natural selection. Species A gleans a resource from species B in a way that does not harm species B. This resource gives species A a great advantage in survival and reproduction. Individuals of species A that are best able to attract and maintain connection with species B have the greatest advantage. Species B individuals that are most receptive to the "gift" offered by certain individuals of species A have an advantage also, and disproportionately survive and reproduce. And so it goes.

Some mutualisms are obligate, meaning that the two species have evolved to rely on one another so specifically and so completely that they can no longer exist apart. The mitochondria and chloroplasts in eukaryotic cells are thought to be obligate symbionts that once, ages ago, lived separately as prokaryotic cells. Now they are inseparable from their symbiotic partner. Other, and perhaps most, mutualisms are facultative and temporary. Mutualisms present an interesting piece to the puzzle of the origins of environmentalism, because they widen the circle more than kin selection or even group selection. In mutualism we see a reason why a species might protect, conserve, and even promote members of other species, and potentially even the habitat in which those other species live. There is also a potential dark side to this arrangement, for mutualisms are essentially an evolutionary means of outcompeting other species. Furthermore, mutualisms do not always remain mutually beneficial. Some symbionts cheat, and if they can get away with it (meaning that they can maintain the relationship and still take but no longer give), the mutualism can become a commensalism, and the commensalism a parasitism (Boucher, 1988). This too might be instructive in our quest to understand environmentalism.

To this point we have considered the sociobiological origins of cooperation and reciprocity, both of which are apparently ancient. They are present in social animals and particularly notable in our closest primate relatives, suggesting that these are adaptations that have long provided selective advantage in our lineage. As a behavioral and psychological interface between our competitive individualism and our tendency for social cohesion, they are a critical aspect of our genetic inheritance.

My second prerequisite for the development of environmentalism, the capacity for time-shifting scenario building, is not as evident in our nearest primate relatives (or in any other animals) and so is more distinctly human.

Early hominid sociobiology

Depending on when exactly you place the label "hominid" on our lineage (recall that our evolutionary line diverged from that of our closest primate relative about six million years ago), something like 99.9% of human history has occurred as foragers in nomadic hunter-gatherer societies (Suddendorf, 2013: 19; Harari, 2015: 77). Anthropological study of modern human foragers, along with modern primatology, can provide us with some clues to the lives of our ancient ancestors around the time of human divergence. These proto-human foragers were probably similar to the ape-like ancestor in their small, mobile, low-density populations and in the cooperative care and defense among kin. Diets were likely opportunistic and omnivorous, relying as much or more on gathered plant material as on animal flesh. Humans (and hominid relatives) apparently maintained low population densities for millions of years for reasons that are not entirely clear. Some theories are that low caloric diets, long periods of nursing, and a physically demanding lifestyle reduce fertility, and/or that infanticide is commonly used to reduce the number of mouths to feed. In any case, there was almost certainly a high mortality rate, at least in comparison with modern human societies; by some estimates only about 50% of newborns would survive to adulthood. In these respects, our distant ancestors may have resembled many other primate species (Zihlman, 1978: 4–20; Johnson and Earle, 2000: 55–56; Richerson and Boyd, 2005: 227; Suddendorf, 2013: 227).

But some important differences emerged in early humans that set our species apart. For one, early human groups differed from other primates in their habitat. The move from woodland to savanna provided new opportunities, but also new selection pressures. Habitat characteristics likely drove some major evolutionary change in our species, including the upright, bipedal posture, the use of hands and eventually tools, and the birth of infants at prematurity, necessitating prolonged and cooperative care. The shift to the savanna seems to have been accompanied by an increase in dietary meat and soft plants. Evidence points to the active hunting of small to very large animals, along with competitive scavenging, both of which imply within-group cooperation. Indeed, the extent of social cooperation— particularly among unrelated individuals for non-procreative purposes—is a notable feature of our species. Some scholars have theorized that the evolutionary advantages of complex social relationships played an important role in the amplification of human cognitive capacity (Box 4.1; Zihlman, 1978; Burkart et al., 2009; Apicella et al., 2012; E.O. Wilson, 2012: 199–204).

We have seen that one prerequisite for environmentalism, cooperative reciprocity, was likely well established within—if not necessarily among—groups of our foraging ancestors. To what extent was the second prerequisite of time-shifting scenario building present in these early humans, and can we say that it was an adaptive result of natural selection? There is disagreement on these questions. The sociobiological view is that these characteristics are genetically derived, and that they all arose in early human societies because they conferred some survival advantage to individuals. Alternate views include that these human qualities are spandrel characteristics that arose as by-products of other adaptive traits, or that they are incidental properties of selected traits, not the direct result of genetic change themselves but useful qualities that emerged from the complexity of the whole. But spandrels and emergent properties are still derived from natural selection and could still result in selectable, adaptive advantage. Others argue that these traits are too complex to have arisen from natural selection; they must be learned behaviors that were transmitted through the group by means of invention

Box 4.1 Ecological and social cognition

Human cognitive development is among the most remarkable features of biological evolution. Of the primates that lived six million years ago, a subset emerged to become our species and its close relatives—organisms with the mental capacity to transform the world. The reasons for this evolutionary leap are debated. One leading hypothesis is that increasingly complex social interactions drove the expansion of intelligence. According to this idea, the management of social stress, the advantages of cooperative learning, and the intricacies of social competition selected for greater cognitive capacity. Increased cognitive ability in turn leads to greater social complexity in terms of hierarchy, differentiation, reciprocity, appraisal, deception, and empathy.

A competing hypothesis is that environmental complexities selected for the cognitive ability to navigate an increasingly unpredictable and competitive world. In this perspective the rapidly changing demand for technical expertise fueled the cognitive explosion. Of course, an unsatisfactory aspect of this hypothesis is that all primate species were presumably exposed to similarly complex environmental conditions. A unique evolutionary leap would require a unique ecological environment. Still, it is possible that the transition from woodland to savanna could have resulted in cognitive evolution driven by ecological expertise.

These two hypotheses are not mutually exclusive. Sterelny (2007) has proposed a hybrid model in which the ecological expertise of survival is itself a socially cooperative venture. Practical experience and mental models, shared as collective and intergenerational intelligence, conceivably allowed for both ecological survival and social complexity. Indeed, Sterelny suggests that coordinated ecological activity among early hominin foragers is inseparable from complex social activity. Thus the great leap of intelligence, according to this hypothesis, is the result of intertwined social and ecological selection pressures. The implication is that the way members of our species interact with their environment has long been tied to the way we interrelate with one another.

and imitation; in short, by sociocultural evolution (Richerson and Boyd, 2005: 203–210).

While we don't have a lot of evidence for the emergence of mental time shifting and scenario building (since they tend not to fossilize well), the onset of tool use provides an intriguing clue. The oldest tool artifacts that have been found are thought to have been created about 2.6 million years ago (Roebroecks and Villa, 2011; Suddendorf, 2013: 246–247). It is not the crafting of various tools itself, though that is of course an important aspect of behavioral evolution. Many other animals use tools, such as chimpanzees' use of twigs to fish termites out of their nests. But these uses are generally in the moment, meaning they use on-hand materials for an immediate task. The difference in human evolution is the conceptualization and construction of a tool that might in the future be applied to a problem or situation that one has encountered in the past (or that one imagines). At some point in our prehistory the practice of creating such premeditated tools began, and as we don't see such tool use in our close primate relatives, it seems to be uniquely human (with a possible allowance for some now-extinct hominid cousins). The significance is this: the act of creating a tool that is not for immediate use implies a memory of a past scenario—perhaps a hunt or butchering—in which the tools at hand were inadequate. It also implies future scenario building: what will I do when that situation comes again? How can I best prepare for it? Such thoughts show advanced skills of abstract imagination (Massey, 2002: 4; Heft, 2015: 254–255). The point, for this discussion, is that such skills are transferrable to environmental questions or scenarios. *I remember that last season we were hungry, and game was hard to find. How could we act differently this year to find enough to eat?* I'm not claiming that the earliest tool users had an environmental conscience, only that they had developed a critical mental capacity that would later (perhaps much later) allow for environmental conceptualization.

Mental model building is really about consciousness, which is not yet fully understood. Neuroscientists Graziano and Kastner (2011) have theorized that consciousness evolved in response to increasing information-processing demands on the brain. As sensory perception evolved, according to the theory, so did centralized coordination of sensory information. Graziano and Kastner call the most basic centralized coordination *overt* attention—the ability to focus on objects of interest. This is common to all vertebrates. The vertebrate brain apparently does this by creating a simulation model of the object of attention and comparing actual perception to the model. According to Graziano and Kastner, the next step in neurological evolution is the cerebral cortex, a center of *covert* attention. This means that you don't need to directly perceive something for your cortex to call it to attention; it is "virtual movement of deep processing" (Graziano, 2016). Covert attention, too, creates simulation models of the world, constantly updated by perception but also influenced by emotion, rationality, and memory to imagine different scenarios of self, world, and others. This theory of consciousness, if accurate, begins to explain our ability to evaluate, envision, and innovate. It also might explain our propensity for mind–body and human–nature dualism (Massey, 2002: 15–21).

It is easy to see how the ability to consider mental models might have conferred a survival advantage to our ancestors. An interesting corollary is that the development of language may have amplified the time-shifting scenario building in groups of early hominids (Suddendorf, 2013: 99–100). The reasoning is similar to that of premeditated tool use. Many animals communicate, but language is far more advanced. Archeological analysis of skull structure provides evidence that language may have arisen by 70,000 years ago—though it is conceivable that gesture-based sign languages evolved even earlier (E.O. Wilson, 2012: 225–235). The capacity for both language and mental model building are closely tied and genetically derived, for while tool making and grammar are teachable and subject to imitation, the *conceptualization* of future tools and the *acquisition* of language are not. The ability to communicate complex thoughts and ideas would have allowed the sharing and rehearsing of mental scenarios and therefore greatly increased their power (Dutton, 2009: 152). Imagine that it is not just one tool maker wondering how that last hunt could have gone better, but several in a group discussion, sharing and analyzing mental models together. The biologist Colin Tudge has called this the collective intelligence (Tudge, 1996: 251). Clearly, development and refinement of a collective intelligence would have been a critical skill as groups of humans began to consider their own existence and share knowledge intergenerationally. It may also mark the birth of fiction, as the collective intelligence conjured hypothetical futures and developed folk accounts of the past (Dutton, 2009: 116).

Another potential benefit of shared mental models is the emergence of a capacity for empathy (Boehm, 2012: 185). Cooperative reciprocity combined with scenario building allows individuals to put themselves mentally in the position of others (perhaps even other species). Empathetic impulses can quite literally mimic the feelings that the observer imagines are being experienced by the observed; the effect of such "mirror neurons" has been documented in humans and other primates (Fabbri-Destro and Rizzolatti, 2008). The evolution of an ability to apply mental scenarios to others—and to imagine one's self in the place of the other—may mark the beginning of compassion, a critical precursor for environmental and social responsibility. Of course, responsibility thinking is complex, and the ability to hypothesize and empathize with others is not the same as behaving with virtue and righteousness. But the skill of mental scenario building is at the foundation of both (Bloom, 2016: 62–68).

So far, I have attributed the prerequisites for environmentalism primarily to Darwinian selection of adaptive traits. There is broad agreement that cooperation and reciprocity have a genetic basis. Time-shifting scenario building is more distinctly human, and circumstantial evidence suggests that it arose much later in human development, possibly as part of the mental leap that allowed for tool use and language development. It too has a genetic basis. But these prerequisite skills are not enough for an environmental conscience. Part of environmentalism is learned behavior—it is conveyed by invention, imitation, communication, and education. In short, it is an element of culture.

Sociobiology and sociocultural evolution

Cooperative reciprocity occurs within a unique group context. An acceptable behavior in one group might be cause for punishment in another. Likewise, mental scenarios and collective intelligence are group specific. We might say that collective intelligence adds cultural character—and cultural pressure—to the social group. In turn, the sociocultural norms of the group are the basis for individual values. From norms and values, it is a short trip to morality.

To what extent are social norms and values genetically derived, and to what extent are they learned or imitated? This question has been the subject of much debate, ranging from those who insist on a genetic basis for human culture to those who maintain that culture is entirely learned. In one view, it is the gene, or a cohort of genes, that control behavior, and in the other it is the unit of culture called the meme, or a cohort of memes, that are the essence of learned or imitated behavior. The two views are not mutually exclusive, of course; a blended perspective is that biological and cultural characteristics have co-evolved in humans (Richerson and Boyd, 2005: 12).

To explore this relationship it is useful to resurrect a rival theory of Darwinian evolution. The French naturalist Jean-Baptiste Lamarck (1744–1829) supported the notion that evolution occurs by the inheritance of characteristics that individuals acquire during their lifetime. These traits would stand a better chance of being passed on to the next generation if they were used, and would fall away if they were not. The result, to Lamarck, was an evolution of increasing complexity as influenced by the local environment. This theory, widely subscribed to in the 19th century (even by Darwin, for a time), was eventually discredited by later-day Darwinists, who showed that only genetic traits are heritable. As Kronfeldner (2007) explains, the Darwinian system of natural selection is *variational*, in that traits change over time because of selection pressures on population variation, while the Lamarckian system is *transformational*, in that individuals and population can take on new characteristics without selection.

Today, there is wide agreement that biological evolution proceeds according to Darwinian variational selection. But cultural evolution is different. Acquired cultural traits (things we learn or perceive or imitate) can indeed be passed on to others, even to subsequent generations. Such learned behaviors can certainly be transformational. We can even see the Lamarckian notion of use and disuse: if a cultural meme is popular, it gets passed on; if not, it will die out. Cultural transmission is therefore in some sense analogous to Lamarckian evolution. Even so, some of our behaviors are genetically inherited. The ability to learn by observing, for example, is not something that we need to be taught. Presumably, this skill is common in our species because it was selected for over generations of variation, and able learners had a survival advantage. Cultural transmission is in this sense a product of Darwinian evolution (Gould, 1979; Laland and Brown, 2011: 228–229).

Both genes and memes can be selected over time—by biological natural selection and by the selection for and against ideas, which we might call cultural selection. Like natural selection, cultural selection tends to favor ideas that work (solve a problem, fill a need, capture interest, provide comfort) in a given place and time. Often (as with natural selection) there are competing ideas that might co-exist temporarily but not indefinitely; sooner or later, some memes win and get passed on, while others fade away. Ideas that work tend to remain in the culture until confronted with ideas that present an (apparently) better way, or at least a different way. Cultural selection presents some important points to consider. First, societal change is cumulative, meaning that it is built upon its own history, with certain elements dragged along for the ride. It is also short-sighted, meaning that choices are often made to meet a current need, without much regard for long-term consequences. Third, it is specific to a particular set of contingencies for that time and place. Hence different cultures adopt different memes.

We need a nuanced view of "ideas that work" for cultural selection (Richerson and Boyd, 2005). In natural selection this is quite clear: does the adaptation increase the odds that an individual will survive and reproduce? Not so with cultural selection. While some sociocultural adaptations are innovations related to survival, such as provision for subsistence, shelter, or security, other ideas are "selected" (or maintained) not because they provide a survival advantage per se, but because they provide a basis for normalizing human relations and encouraging group continuity. This is more about group acceptance and common ideology than direct questions of survival. Another difference is that ideas can rapidly spread from person to person, group to group, while genes cannot; but ideas are also at times more resistant to change. Sociocultural evolution can therefore be both more rapid and more recalcitrant than natural selection. Finally—and this is a big difference from natural selection—memes can be maladaptive and still be selected again and again. Just ask anyone who insists on riding a motorcycle without a helmet.

The ability to pass on ideas or behaviors through culture is not exclusively human. Those tree-thumping chimpanzees, for example, have also been observed throwing rocks at trees for reasons unknown (Kuhl *et al.*, 2016). The behavior— described as "ritualized" by the authors—seems to involve the accumulation of rocks, a hoot of vocalization, the banging of a rock against a tree, and then a hurled projectile. There is no apparent survival advantage provided by this action, and no obvious benefit to personal procreation or group security. It seems to be just an innovative behavior. The interesting thing is that it has caught on, and other chimps, having observed a rock thrower, give it a try themselves. Now, whether such behavior can be considered *culture* is debatable, and whether the act of throwing rocks represents an adaptive advantage is also debatable. In any case, it is plausible that *culture-forming behavior* evolved because it enhances survival (E.O. Wilson, 2012: 28; Hodgson, 2015: 69).

If our behaviors are a combination of genetic and cultural inheritance, how does sociocultural evolution work in humans? One idea goes like this (Henrich and McElreath, 2003; E.O. Wilson, 2012: 191–224). All healthy humans have the same basic genetic endowment that is a sort of framework on which sociocultural learning happens. This framework has aspects that vary from the rigidly ingrained to the flexible. Blushing in embarrassment, for example, is a part of our genetic framework that is highly innate; it is present in all humans and does not have to be taught. In fact, it is autonomic: you can't help but blush when embarrassed. Other instincts are deeply ingrained but possible to overcome. The incest taboo, for example, is ingrained but not autonomic; it is occasionally overcome, as seen in historic European monarchies. Other behaviors are clearly learned but also strongly ingrained, like our habit of wearing clothing and attending to personal hygiene. Sure, you could stop combing your hair and run around naked, but this could be socially awkward. Some behaviors are at the far end of learned-and-not-ingrained, like the use of slang and fashion accessories. In this sense, certain behaviors are instinctual while other behaviors are channeled, but not completely determined, by our genetic inheritance (Laland and Brown, 2011: 59). The capacity to acquire bits of culture (memes) through imitation is itself an ancient part of our genetic framework; these instincts are not subject to short-term change. Other behaviors have varying degrees of malleability, and as they are subject to historical and geographic contingencies they are variable within and among cultures. It is this genetic framework—innate foundation plus the cognitive abilities of learning through social interaction—that drives cultural evolution (Pinker, 2003: 39).

Our instinctual and learned behaviors work together quite seamlessly. For example, humans are great imitators. We are quick to read the expressions and behaviors of other humans. We interpret social cues, we conform, we judge, we feel acceptance and shame (E.O. Wilson, 2012: 214). Much of this ingrained social analysis is about seeking approval, whether we choose to admit it or not. Imagine wearing a T-shirt to a formal occasion, or mispronouncing a common word at a job interview, or smelling strongly of urine in a crowded elevator. These would all be situations of great embarrassment: there are cultural norms of the ways you are supposed to look, sound, and smell, and deviating from these invites disapproval. So we read expressions and learn to imitate. True, there are always those who seek to be different. I have noticed among college students that some will suddenly change their hair color to pink, or pierce a body part, or get a tattoo. Interestingly, though, they tend to rebel by imitation—take a close look at those with colored hair, or piercings, or tattoos and you'll see remarkable similarities. The point is that these situations involve both the highly innate skills of social interpretation and the highly cultural norms of acceptance.

Within this structure (according to the theory), culture evolves through invention and innovation followed by imitation and diffusion (Henrich and McElreath, 2003: 129–131; Hodgson, 2015: 317–318). As cultural evolution does not often have the specter of life or death, it is subject to error and bias in ways that natural selection is not. There is no requirement, for example, that memes be copied precisely; in fact they often are not. Think of this as the occasional cultural mutation (Richerson and Boyd, 2005, 69). Repetition of a meme increases the chance that it will be absorbed, at least temporarily, into culture; we tend to conform to frequency. There is also no requirement that the meme be true. In fact, memes that are patently false but that capture the imagination tend to stick, and stick quite stubbornly, particularly if they are easy to remember. The lousy advice to "feed a cold and starve a fever" was published by English lexicographer John Withals in 1574 and repeated for well over 400 years in the Anglo-American world, notably by my grandmother (Fischetti, 2014). Other memes emerge not because they are true but because they facilitate the learning of adaptive characteristics. Association of a dangerous animal with a story of an evil spirit is a good example.

There are also contextual biases to cultural selection, meaning that memes are not equally shared or given equal value. Information from perceived prestigious or successful individuals, for instance, may be more easily incorporated into culture than information from lesser members, whether it is better information or not. Marketing agencies know this, and hence we have celebrity spokespersons. Why should it matter whether LeBron James recommends one beverage over another? It does, because he is a celebrity and the viewing audience places high value on his opinions. Individuals also have the propensity to conform—to go with the majority of their group—when conflicting information is present, even though the group trend may be less useful in terms of individual success. In short, cultural transmission of memes is biased and error prone, and the farther we are from innate, survival-based information, the more latitude for drift (Henrich and McElreath, 2003).

There is an evolutionary basis to cultural bias. Stories that are untrue but recall common group myths are social bonding agents. Fanciful legends may teach lessons of survival or group norms. Rituals that are nonsensical may nonetheless have great value in social navigation. Likewise, it makes sense that our ancient ancestors, struggling for survival on the savanna, would have strong reasons for imitating the behavior of a particularly esteemed or successful group member. Mimicking the actions of the successful may confer success upon the imitator. It also makes survival sense that, when in doubt, one should go with the majority, for group approval and acceptance might be far more important than the behavior itself (Henrich and McElreath, 2003).

Combine these biases of sociocultural meme transmission together with the more "hard wired" social instincts we inherit, like the rules of mate selection, the importance of kin, and the tendency for self-interest amid group pressure for reciprocity, and you've got a picture of the complicated human system of social interaction. In the perspective of sociologist Douglas Massey, sociocultural norms arise from "interactions between social structure and the emotional brain, and particularly . . . how families and communities act to create implicit memories that link behaviors, places, objects, experiences and thoughts to subjective emotional states, thus shaping future rational behavior" (Massey, 2002: 21). In this sense, sociocultural codes are as diverse as our species itself. Most pertinent to this discussion, however, is that social cues can be a force for tempering individualistic behavior in favor of service to the group—they can be the impetus for the "responsibility" thinking of our social contracts. Maryanski and Turner (1992) have called this a social cage. It is an apt metaphor, for these unwritten rules can hold us together in our social order—at least at the level of the small group—despite our tendency toward self-interest. An important point, though, is that sociocultural norms can and do change. As we will see in the next chapter, human sociocultural environments have evolved dramatically since our days on the prehistoric savanna. While certain rigid aspects of our sociocultural codes have been persistent, other cultural characteristics have been reimagined over and over again.

Evolutionary basis for environmentalism

At the beginning of this chapter I posed a question: What sort of creatures are we that we have such wide-ranging views on the world and our place in it? This brief trip through evolutionary history offers an answer. We are products of evolution, and evolution has resulted in some specific and at times conflicting worldviews that we all hold. We are self-interested egoists and nepotists. Whether we admit it or not, we tend to think first of ourselves. We readily (but selectively) cooperate with others, particularly when we benefit in return. We are terrific mental modelers who can imagine and share new prospects and new socioecological arrangements. These instincts all play out within cultural context, which can be both an avenue and a barrier to change.

It seems that biological and cultural evolution have provided us with both the prerequisite skills of environmentalism and the mental and social conflicts that confound those skills. The individual, kin, and group instincts are strong—and often contradictory—selection pressures. There is conflict of utility and equity: we are biologically driven to use our surroundings to our own advantage, and yet we have an instinct for reciprocity. Thus we face a social stress: to commandeer or to share? At another level we have the ability to imagine ourselves as the other, and yet our empathy is tested by cultural difference and parochialism. Indeed, we tend to focus our empathy on those most similar to us, evoking feelings that are most familiar to us (Bloom, 2016: 87–95). Thus a second stress: who is the other, and how are we to treat him or her? We face further conflict when our cultural code urges the transformation of the nonhuman world while simultaneously cherishing that which we perceive to be beautiful, vital, and sacred. Thus a third stress: to manipulate or to protect? All told, it seems that our evolutionary past has primed us for environmental anxiety.

Given our conflicted character, it is easy to see how we are troubled by modern societal issues. But we can also see in ourselves the building blocks of an environmental ethic. Our ancient instinct for cooperative reciprocity urges us toward social cohesion. Time-shifting mental scenario building promotes foresight, idealism, and compassion. Social norms and mental constructs have allowed our species to develop morality, aesthetic appreciation, and spirituality. The development of language spurred the transmission of these ideas, taking them from genetic foundations to the elements of modern culture. These qualities alone do not get us to environmentalism—they merely provide us with a species that is poised for just such a notion. The impetus for emergence of an environmental ethic is not found among these early humans. For that, we must turn to the evolution of human societies.

Bibliography

Alexander, R.D. (1989). Evolution of the human psyche. In: P. Mellars and C. Stringer, eds., *The human revolution*. Edinburgh: Edinburgh University Press. pp. 455–513.

Apicella, C.L., Marlowe, F.W., Fowler, J.H. and Christakis, N.A. (2012). Social networks and cooperation in hunter-gatherers. *Nature*, 481(7382), pp. 497–501.

Arcadi, A.C., Robert, D. and Boesch, C. (1998). Buttress drumming by wild chimpanzees: temporal patterning, phrase integration into loud calls, and preliminary evidence for individual distinctiveness. *Primates*, 39(4), pp. 505–518.

Bloom, P. (2016). *Against empathy: the case for rational compassion.* New York: Random House.

Boehm, C. (2012). *Moral origins: the evolution of virtue, altruism and shame.* New York: Basic Books.

Boucher, D.H., ed. (1988). *The biology of mutualism: ecology and evolution.* Oxford, UK: Oxford University Press.

Bowles, S. (2009). Did warfare among ancestral hunter-gatherers affect the evolution of human social behaviors? *Science,* 324(5932), pp. 1293–1298.

Bowles, S. and Gintis, H. (2011). *A cooperative species: human reciprocity and its evolution.* Princeton, NJ: Princeton University Press.

Boyd, R. and Richerson, P.J. (1988). An evolutionary model of social learning: the effects of spatial and temporal variation. In: T. Zentall and B. Galef, eds., *Social learning: psychological and biological perspectives.* Hillsdale, NJ: Lawrence Erlbaum. pp. 29–48.

Broom, R. (1933). *The coming of man: was it accident or design?* London: H.F. & G. Witherby.

Burkart, J.M., Hrdy, S.B. and Van Schaik, C.P. (2009). Cooperative breeding and human cognitive evolution. *Evolutionary Anthropology: Issues, News, and Reviews,* 18(5), pp. 175–186.

Collins, D. and Barkdull, J. (1995). Capitalism, environmentalism and mediating structures. *Environmental Ethics,* 17(3), pp. 227–244.

Darwin, C. (1859). *On the origin of species by means of natural selection, or the preservation of favoured races in the struggle for life.* London: John Murray.

Darwin, C. and Wallace, A. (1858). On the tendency of species to form varieties; and on the perpetuation of varieties and species by natural means of selection. *Zoological Journal of the Linnean Society,* 3(9), pp. 45–62.

Dawkins, R. (1976). *The selfish gene.* Oxford: Oxford University Press.

Dutton, D. (2009). *The art instinct: beauty, pleasure and human evolution.* New York: Bloomsbury Press.

Fabbri-Destro, M. and Rizzolatti, G. (2008). Mirror neurons and mirror systems in monkeys and humans. *Physiology,* 23(3), pp. 171–179.

Fischetti, M. (2014). Fact or fiction: feed a cold, starve a fever. *Scientific American,* January 3, 2014, p. 6.

Gould, S.J. (1979). Shades of Lamarck. *Natural History,* 88, pp. 22–28.

Gould, S.J. and Lewontin, R.C. (1979). The spandrels of San Marco and the panglossian paradigm: a critique of the adaptationist programme. *Proceedings of the Royal Society of London, Series B, Biological Sciences,* 205(1161), pp. 581–598.

Graeber, D. (2011). *Debt: the first 5,000 years.* Brooklyn: Melville House.

Graziano, M.S. (2016). A new theory explains how consciousness evolved. *The Atlantic,* June 6, 2016.

Graziano, M.S. and Kastner, S. (2011). Human consciousness and its relationship to social neuroscience: a novel hypothesis. *Cognitive Neuroscience,* 2(2), pp. 98–113.

Gruss, L.T. and Schmitt, D. (2015). The evolution of the human pelvis: changing adaptations to bipedalism, obstetrics and thermoregulation. *Philosophical Transactions of the Royal Society B,* 370(1663), p. 20140063.

Hamilton, W.D. (1964). The genetical evolution of social behaviour. *Journal of Theoretical Biology,* 7(1), pp. 17–52.

Harari, Y.N. (2015). *Sapiens: a brief history of humankind.* New York: Random House.

Heft, H. (2015). Evolution of human cognition. In: J. Wright, ed., *International encyclopedia of the social & behavioral sciences,* 2nd edition. Amsterdam: Elsevier. pp. 254–255.

Henrich, J. and McElreath, R. (2003). The evolution of cultural evolution. *Evolutionary Anthropology*, 12(3), pp. 123–135.

Henrich, J. and McElreath, R. (2007). Dual-inheritance theory: the evolution of human cultural capacities and cultural evolution. In: L. Barrett and R. Dunbar, eds., *Oxford handbook of evolutionary psychology*. Oxford: Oxford University Press. pp. 555–570.

Hodgson, G.M. (2015). *Conceptualizing capitalism: institutions, evolution, future*. Chicago: University of Chicago Press.

Johnson, A.W. and Earle, T. (2000). *The evolution of human societies: from foraging group to agrarian state*. Stanford, CA: Stanford University Press.

Kronfeldner, M. (2007). Is cultural evolution Lamarckian? *Biology and Philosophy*, 22(4), pp. 494–498.

Kuhl, H.S., Kalan, A.K., Arandjelovic, M., Aubert, F., D'Auvergne, L., Goedmakers, A., Jones, S., Kehoe, L., Regnaut, S., *et al.* (2016). Chimpanzee accumulative stone throwing. *Scientific Reports*, 6, p. 22219.

Kurzban, R., Burton-Chellew, M.N. and West, S.A. (2015). The evolution of altruism in humans. *Annual Review of Psychology*, 66, pp. 575–599.

Laland, K.N. and Brown, G.R. (2011). *Sense and nonsense: evolutionary perspectives on human behaviour*. Oxford: Oxford University Press.

Maryanski, A. and Turner, J.H. (1992). *The social cage: human nature and the evolution of society*. Stanford, CA: Stanford University Press.

Massey, D.S. (2002). A brief history of human society: the origin and role of emotion in social life. *American Sociological Review*, 67(1), pp. 1–29.

McGrew, W.C. (2004). *The cultured chimpanzee: reflections on cultural primatology*. Cambridge, UK: Cambridge University Press.

Miller, L.A. and Surlykke, A. (2001). How some insects detect and avoid being eaten by bats. *Bioscience*, 51(7), pp. 570–581.

Pandit, S.A., Pradhan, G.R., Balashov, H. and Van Schaik, C.P. (2016). The conditions favoring between-community raiding in chimpanzees, bonobos, and human foragers. *Human Nature*, 27(2), pp. 141–159.

Pinker, S. (2003). *The blank slate: the modern denial of human nature*. New York: Penguin.

Pinker, S. (2012). The false allure of group selection. *Edge*, June 18, 2012.

Richerson, P.J. and Boyd, R. (2005). *Not by genes alone: how culture transformed human evolution*. Chicago: University of Chicago Press.

Roebroecks, W. and Villa, P. (2011). On the earliest evidence for the habitual use of fire in Europe. *Proceedings of the National Academy of Science*, 108(13), pp. 5209–5214.

Singer, P. (1981). *The expanding circle*. Oxford: Clarendon Press.

Smith, A. (1976 [1759]). *The theory of moral sentiments, or an essay towards an analysis of the principles by which men naturally judge concerning the conduct and character, first of their neighbours and afterwards of themselves*. Indianapolis, IN: Liberty Press.

Sterelny, K. (2007). Social intelligence, human intelligence and niche construction. *Philosophical Transactions of the Royal Society of London B: Biological Sciences*, 362 (1480), pp. 719–730.

Suddendorf, T. (2013). *The gap: the science of what separates us from the other animals*. New York: Basic Books.

Tudge, C. (1996). *The time before history: 5 million years of human impact*. New York: Scribner.

Whiten, A. (2011). The scope of culture in chimpanzees, humans and ancestral apes. *Philosophical Transactions of the Royal Society B: Biological Sciences*, 366(1567), pp. 997–1007.

Wilson, D.S. (1975). A theory of group selection. *Proceedings of the National Academy of Sciences*, 72(1), pp. 143–146.

Wilson, D.S. (2002). *Darwin's cathedral: evolution, religion, and the nature of society*. Chicago: University of Chicago Press.

Wilson, D.S. and Sober, E. (1994). Reintroducing group selection to the human behavioral sciences. *Behavioral and Brain Sciences*, 17(4), pp. 585–608.

Wilson, E.O. (1975). *Sociobiology, the new synthesis*. Cambridge, MA: Belknap.

Wilson, E.O. (2012). *The social conquest of Earth*. New York: Liveright.

Zihlman, A.L. (1978). Women in evolution, part II: subsistence and social organization among early hominids. *Signs: Journal of Women in Culture and Society*, 4(1), pp. 4–20.

5   Sociocultural evolution

Key points

- Sociocultural evolution has changed the ways in which people interact with each other and with their environment.
- As the capacity for environmental change has intensified, social and ecological connections have become more distant.
- Affluent societies are less dependent on cooperative reciprocity; this can hamper global environmental action.

In the evolution of cooperative reciprocity, time-shifting scenario building, and cultural codes we have seen how humans acquired the social tools of survival. These skills are the result of biological and cultural selection; they are products of micro-evolution. However, sociocultural evolution on the macroscopic scale has triggered the impulse to care for the Earth. In this chapter we will explore the sociocultural conflict surrounding human interaction with other species, other people, and natural resources. While particular aspects of human relationships are culture-specific, they are drawn from a common evolutionary inheritance: the conflict of self-interest in the midst of kin and group, the simultaneous mistrust of and compassion for others, the propensity for shared mental models, and the biologically-and-culturally defined ethical imperatives. Add to all of this an emerging capacity for human-derived environmental change, and you have the ingredients for environmentalism.

Beyond the bottleneck

By approximately 100,000 years ago our ancestors were anatomically modern, and probably behaviorally modern or nearly so. They had spread beyond Africa to Eurasia in small foraging bands. Life was probably not easy, but it was about to get much more difficult. About 70,000 years ago, human populations apparently went into a decline that nearly drove the species—our species—to extinction. At the narrowest point in this population bottleneck our lineage may have been reduced to about 10,000 individuals (Ambrose, 1998). No one is quite sure why this happened, but there are some hypotheses. It could have been epidemic disease, although this seems unlikely, for human population densities were very low even before the bottleneck. It could have been a result of the dispersal within and beyond Africa, as various small populations became isolated, genetically homogenous, and easily extirpated. It could have been climate related, for the bottleneck occurred smack in the middle of the last ice age. The most intriguing—though disputed—candidate is a volcanic winter, caused by the eruption of Mt Toba in Indonesia about 73,000 years ago. This eruption was about 40 times larger than the greatest historic eruption ever recorded, and its effects were potentially great enough to alter the global climate (Ambrose, 1998; Rampino and Ambrose, 2000; Lane *et al.*, 2013). Perhaps the decline was due to all of the above. Whatever the reason, it seems that our species was nearly eliminated before human civilization got started.

While it is alarming for us to imagine, it would not have been such an odd thing if our species had been driven to extinction 70,000 years ago. Many of our close cousins went extinct (in fact they all did). By one estimate over 20 hominid species have gone extinct over the last six million years, and four of those died out in just the past few hundred thousand years (Suddendorf, 2013: 238). We don't know any more about the demise of those species than we do about the near-demise of our own, though there is some speculation that *Homo sapiens* may have played a role in the extinction of one or more of its relatives. One thing that we know for certain is that there is only a single species left on this branch of the evolutionary tree. That species has been remarkably mobile and adaptable: after the bottleneck, humans colonized about 75% of the Earth's land surface in about 1% of the time since our evolutionary split with chimpanzees (Gamble, 2007: 212).

Given that there are now over 7.5 billion humans, it is nearly unfathomable that we were once reduced to 10,000. That's the size of a small town. But our ancestors at the time of the bottleneck didn't know that their species was in global crisis. They just lived as best they could among kin and clan, some surviving to give rise to the next generation, and others not. Of course, they weren't all together in one place—they were scattered about in small bands, with some probably living in geographic refuges that offered shelter from the harsh climate. The distribution is significant. Spatial patterns of post-bottleneck recovery are an important factor in the development of human diversity, as the different bands dispersed and began their own lineages, some of which survive to the present day. The cultural diversity that emerged from geographic isolation came to be self-reinforcing, as cultural differences themselves are mechanisms of social isolation (Rindos, 1984: 59; Ambrose, 1998).

The various ways in which members of our species have lived for the past 70,000 years is the topic of this chapter. In particular, I am interested in how people of different societal arrangements influenced their environment—a subject for which there is some evidence—and how their environment may have influenced them, a matter that is more speculative. We are not entirely ignorant of the mental state of our ancestors, however, and so we will bring their evolutionary legacy of cooperative reciprocity, time-shifting scenario building, and cultural normative systems to bear on the social structures and environments in which they lived. Beginning with foragers who emerged from the bottleneck, then moving to more sedentary agriculturalists and pastoralists, then to the age of extraction, and finally to global society, I will consider three aspects of humans and their environment. First, how do people in these different societal structures relate to one another? Second, how does each social structure effect environmental change? Finally, how does each sociocultural milieu influence people's perception of their natural surroundings? The point of this exercise is to better understand how sociocultural evolution has altered relationships among people and with the nonhuman world.

The research on which I base this narrative is primarily drawn from anthropological and historical study of human societies. There are limitations to such ethnographic research (Richerson and Boyd, 2005: 225). Every society is subject to constraints and opportunities of local geography, climate, and resource availability, and thus each develops in its own way and at its own rate. This makes generalization a perilous journey. There are, however, patterns of change that are common to most societies as they grow, intensify, integrate, and stratify. What this means is that we have a variety of modern societies that can be compared and cautiously extrapolated back in time (using our unique human talents for time shifting and scenario building). Together with artifacts and evidence of past environmental conditions, we can construct basic models of past societies. The models will necessarily be painted with broad strokes, and I will not attempt to explain all variation within and among different cultures (Johnson and Earle, 2000: 45, 87).

As we consider some landmarks of human sociocultural evolution, I want to be careful not to portray it as a linear and universal progression from primitive to civilized. Humans that emerged from the bottleneck migrated to different environments, and the pace and direction of their cultural evolution varied accordingly. In large part this was due to the biogeographic region in which they existed—what sorts of hazards and resources, how many and which nonhuman species were present, how hospitable and how variable the climate. This geographic endowment has had a profound and varied influence on genetic and cultural inheritance. Thus, just like the evolution of species, it is best to think of evolving human cultures as a branching tree, not as a ladder of progress.

I will explore five main ways that human societies interact with local ecologies, loosely following the demographic transition model proposed in 1929 by the American demographer Warren Thompson (1887–1973) and, with some nuance, widely accepted today (Thompson, 1929). Other scholars have defined different stages of human social evolution based on their political structure; here, I will consider each in terms of their relationship with the environment. First, I will consider the foragers—small bands of hunter-gatherers that survived the bottleneck and spread around the world, even present today. Second, I will follow the branch of human society that domesticated plants and animals and developed a relatively sedentary agricultural society. The third branch represents societies that have grown to extract resources from the Earth in large quantities and over extensive areas. Finally, I will consider human societies that are post-industrial, affluent, and reliant on synthetic products, in juxtaposition with those in abject poverty. In each of these branches, I will highlight some features of group structure and the potential for environmental change before considering environmental values.

Foraging societies

Small bands of humans—or human-like primates—have been surviving on this planet as foragers for millions of years. In recent centuries anthropologists have discovered that a small number of these foraging societies still exist, mostly secluded in hard-to-reach places that are isolated from global upheaval. They are known variously as traditional cultures, indigenous peoples, and hunter-gatherers. For simplicity I will use the term foragers to denote people whose way of life primarily consists of direct contact with the nonhuman world. Undeniably, foraging cultures differ widely by ecoregion. Still, there are commonalities among such societies that may be instructive.

One common—and instructive—indicator of forager social structure is provided by the way they distribute food. Forager diets vary from plant-based to meat-based depending on geography, but it has been hypothesized that hunting (and the ensuing dissemination of meat) may have been a driving force for the sociocultural dynamics of reciprocity described in the last chapter. Modern foraging societies commonly exhibit formal, even ritualized, allocation of food among group members, especially in times of scarcity (Diamond, 2012: 301). Food distribution is an example of how social pressures make foragers largely egalitarian with regard to group resource use and decision-making. Resources are distributed through a system of "vigilant sharing," and selfishness is checked by the group assessment of fairness and indebtedness (Wilkinson and Pickett, 2010: 207). This single behavior provides a glimpse of how selfish behavior is countered by the coercive norms and traditional obligations of the group. Cooperation occurs within the social structure of reciprocation (Maryanski and Turner, 1992: 86–87; Hodgson, 2015: 241).

Romanticized conceptualizations of foraging societies have long been popular, but recent anthropological work has challenged the idea of the "noble savage."[1] Images of peoples at one with nature, without a trace of violence and immune to selfishness have not held up well to research-demonstrated violence, warfare, jealousy, possession, and exploitation (Pinker, 2003: 56–58). Modern foragers have been shown to judge others at least in part by their physical appearance, prowess, and status, not as unconditional equals (Apicella *et al.*, 2012). This is not to say that cooperative reciprocity, mutualism, empathy, and kindness are myths of foragers, only that foragers ancient and modern are subject to the same emotions, biases, and behavioral tendencies as humans in other social settings. In the words of David Sloan Wilson: "Hunter-gatherers are egalitarian, not because they lack selfish impulses, but because selfish impulses are effectively controlled by other members of the group" (D.S. Wilson, 2002: 21). The system of mutual support and mutual sanction effectively counters individual desires. It is characterized by direct and personal exchange, not only of goods but also of services and sentiments. Social proximity facilitates collective behavior. In economic perspective this society is the sum collection of its social currencies: individual debts, credits, responsibilities, and expectations (Graeber, 2011: 100, 130, 136).

Out-of-group relationships are quite different. The tribal nature of foraging societies is driven by homophily (the tendency to associate with similar others) and by territoriality. Diamond (2012: 38–53) describes the interaction of modern foraging tribes with neighboring groups in ways that range from friendly to warlike. Nearby neighbors can be partners for trade, a source of exchange for youths who have reached marriageable age, and potentially strategic allies. Friendly tribes also occasionally share common resources. Barter for raw materials or constructed goods among allies is done by direct, face-to-face exchange, as is conflict resolution. In certain cases other tribes may be truly seen as *others*—enemies of lesser worth, to be driven away or killed if they encroach. Warfare is fairly common in modern foraging groups, for reasons as varied as stolen goods, commandeered land, kidnapped children or wives, matters of prestige or honor, and scarcity of resources. Notably, war also takes the form of direct, face-to-face confrontation, as do the subsequent peace negotiations. But the important point here is that the cooperative, cohesive character of forager groups is accompanied by—and perhaps driven by—external rivalry (Apicella *et al.*, 2012; Diamond, 2012; Hodgson, 2015: 241–242).

Forager social structure can be generalized around some common attributes. The people of these small groups tend to be strongly bonded to one another. For each member there is intense social pressure to follow the ways of the group. This, along with the bleak prospects of defection, creates considerable incentive for within-group participation and facilitates collective action. There is less incentive—and even tangible risk—for individuals to explore connections with other groups. The basic character of foraging groups, then, is one of strong intragroup *bonding* but weak intergroup *bridging*. Culturally driven intragroup bonding—and the cooperation it engenders—has been hypothesized by a number of scholars as a key element of group selection (Pretty, 2003; Siegel, 2009; Sieferle, 2011; Apicella *et al.*, 2012).

Foragers and environmental change

Ancient foragers certainly had the capacity to alter their environment (Johnson and Earle, 2000). Most obviously, they were an important part of their local food web. By some reckoning early humans existed as scavengers, feasting on kills made by larger predators while cooperatively fending off other scavengers. But humans quickly learned to make their own kills and developed toolkits for this purpose. Simple weapons and butchering tools gave way to increasingly specialized technology, including knives, projectile points and spears, and eventually tools like the atlatl, barbed harpoon, and fish gorge. Modern foragers even use plant-extracted poisons to stun and harvest fish. Early humans began to make a considerably greater trophic impact as cooperative hunters stalking large game. Fifty thousand years ago there were more than 150 genera of megafauna on Earth. Over the next 40,000 years about two-thirds of those genera went extinct. While climate change and associated vegetation shifts seem to have played a role, growing evidence implicates humans as a major driver of extinction. This is particularly true in areas where humans arrived as an invasive species, i.e. beyond Africa and into northern Eurasia, Australia, and the Americas. The idea is that early humans had co-evolved with megafauna in Africa and central Europe (where there were fewer extinctions), whereas megafauna elsewhere were unaccustomed to humans and therefore easy prey. If humans did indeed play a role in driving large herbivores to extinction during this period, they undeniably had major effects on the surrounding ecosystems (Johnson and Earle, 2000: 83–84; Barnosky et al., 2004).

The earliest mark of humans as agents of environmental change may well have been the use of fire. Early hominids (including those in our own lineage and some close relatives) likely took advantage of natural fire—started by lightning or volcanic activity—in the renewal of vegetation and as a means of collecting animal carcasses, nicely charred and ready to eat. By one theory this was an important beginning to the practice of cooking meat, which made it more easily digestible and freer of parasites and pathogens (benefits that would not have been understood, but benefits nonetheless). Controlled fire use came later, and it revolutionized the upright ape's capacity for environmental change. Archeological discoveries of prehistoric fireplaces provide evidence that fire was regularly in controlled use by 300,000 to 400,000 years ago (Roebroecks and Villa, 2011). These were places for cooking, as burnt bones indicate, but also likely places of warmth, protection, companionship, and communication. Fireplaces were likely sites of shared mental models—and hence the birthplace of human culture. Eventually, fire would be used for so much more: to manipulate vegetation, to drive game, to manufacture tools, to signal friends, and to make war on foes (Tudge, 1996: 259–261; E.O. Wilson, 2012: 47–48).

How much the early masters of fire changed their landscape is unclear. At minimum, early humans likely changed the seasonality of ignitions, and anthropogenic fire would become a major ecological force in Eurasia, Australia, and North America, effectively establishing some of the great grasslands of the modern world (Bowman et al., 2011). Evidence from Australia suggests that modern Aboriginal fire use is quite sophisticated (and has been for a long time). Specific temporal and spatial burning has shaped the Australian landscape and altered species distribution, biodiversity, game and seed availability, and patterns of ecological succession. Foraging humans, in short, have long had the ability to "construct their own ecosystems" (Bird et al., 2008: 14799).

With fire, tools, and a taste for meat our ancient ancestors thus emerged from Africa as a species that could consciously and drastically alter its landscape. Scholars have long debated whether humans are part of or separate from nature. If ever there was a time when humans crossed the line and became something new, it was this time.

In these foraging groups we see human sociocultural instincts and behaviors that are still present today. Foraging individuals were (and are) reliant on one another for survival, thus cooperative reciprocity and associated rules of intragroup interaction are paramount. Social identity—the propensity to self-identify with a group in contrast to other groups—has been identified as a human characteristic in many different cultures and settings (Hogg, 2016). Innovations and inventions, like the growing toolkit, knowledge of medicinal species, hunting techniques, and use of fire, were (and are) learned, imitated, and socially ingrained. We may also assume that culture grows along with innovation in the form of stories, ceremonies, rituals, artistic expressions, and behavioral norms. None of this happens intentionally. Rather, it emerges as a series of evolutionary solutions to problems and opportunities, with the greatest problem being how to best survive harsh conditions in the face of competition. The forager lifestyle is in this sense an evolutionary improvisation. Its development brought all the advantages of human society, but it also represented a trade-off—giving up some control of self-interest by trusting in the reciprocation of others (Lerro, 2000: 43–49).

Forager environmental values

How can we characterize the environmental values of foraging humans? In my estimation, the overarching theme is that the communal and reciprocal existence of foraging societies is *inclusive of the nonhuman*. An animistic perspective of the universe means that one's spirit exists on the same plane as the spirits of all other entities. Thus the "social currencies" among group members are extended to the cosmos (Graeber, 2011: 130). In this social structure it makes little sense to speak of environmental values—utility, stability, equity, beauty, sanctity, and morality—as separate ideas. They occur in one seamless existence. For example, it is clear that human foragers utilize products of nature, as they live in daily reliance upon the world around them. It also makes sense that utility is subject to stability: regular migration patterns, predictable seasonal changes, and reliable features of the landscape provide renewal and life that exemplify beauty. Sanctity is inseparable from this relationship—it manifests in cultures of sacred ground, appeals to the spiritual essence of living and nonliving things, nature-based perception of creation and afterlife, and rituals for the well-being of both individual and group. Cooperative reciprocity is the moral code of the group, as it defines one's responsibilities to others and to the nonhuman. In short, relationships among self, group, and environment are more than *attributes* of foraging culture—they *are* foraging culture (Johnson and Earle, 2000; Lerro, 2000; Diamond, 2012).

I will note two corollaries to this view of foraging society. The first is an internal struggle of individualism amid social control, and the second is a broader consequence of strong group identity.

The philosopher Dutton (2009) sees traces of the individual-versus-group conflict in early human appreciation and expression of artistic beauty. On one hand, the sense of the beautiful may have played a communal bonding role, particularly as elements of nature were represented, ceremonialized, and ritualized. On the other hand, there is a strong role of sexual selection here, in that expression, adornment, and performance are weapons in the battle to secure a mate.

In other words, the individualism in our ancestors is apparent in their aesthetics. Much has been made, for example, of Ötzi, the 5300-year-old ice man discovered in the Alps in 1991. Ötzi was well appointed in tailored clothes, accessories, and tattoos that exceed function and imply fashion. Naturally, we don't know if Ötzi's adornments were elements of sexual selection, spirituality, personal aesthetics, all three, or something else altogether. In any case, Dutton proposes that the beauty of nature expressed as art "derives from a universal human psychology" that reaches back to the late Pleistocene (2009: 30). Dutton's argument, however, is that even in this expression of beauty we can see the conflict of *good for us* versus *good for me*.

In the same way we can see potential conflict in the forager sense of place. Intimate connection with environmental surroundings leads to a situation in which the inhabited territory is considered *ours*: our ceremonial grounds, our waters, our herd. This is not the same as modern ideas of possession and ownership in the developed world, but is rather a sense of belonging with one's surroundings. By contrast, everything beyond the forager's locale may be characterized as another place, an unknown realm inhabited by others, and even seen as the dwelling place of unfriendly spirits (Northcott, 2015: 19). Such tribal territoriality engenders xenophobia. Group-to-group dynamics are often competitive, combative, or even parasitic in nature; the *other* is rarely considered an equal and is often considered to be inferior. The instinct for xenophobia is universal in human cultures (and even in our primate relatives) and therefore an ancient inherited behavior. The violence it can provoke is a characteristic of every known human culture. Even among foragers, archeological evidence points to many instances of violent death at the hands of another human. Ötzi, for example, apparently died of an arrow wound (Holden, 2001). The point is that cooperative reciprocity—one of the hallmarks of our species—is, and has always been, selectively applied (E.O. Wilson, 2012: 57–71).

Agricultural societies

Textbooks sometimes indicate the emergence of agriculture as a point on the timeline of human population growth, as though it were a sudden occurrence. It was anything but. More likely it evolved gradually over tens of thousands of years, perhaps in the following scenario.

Foraging humans, as early as 45,000 years ago, followed big game among seasonal territories and used fire as a weapon in the hunt. Fire stimulated the growth of edible plants, which were selectively harvested and perhaps coincidentally found in human refuse piles in subsequent years. Over time it became easier to return to these reliable sites than to search far and wide for edible vegetation, and the groups that relied on these food sources gradually became more reliant on particular species in certain areas. It was at first a commensalism, but it grew into a remarkable mutualism between useful plants and their human symbionts. For the chosen plant species the arrival of humans was a boon, as their numbers increased dramatically with the new attention. Human numbers more or less did the same.

People changed plants by selecting (at first unconsciously, but with growing purpose) characteristics that were most desirable. Plants changed people as well. The new diet brought on physiological changes—and not all welcome, for the decrease in diet diversity ushered in some new human health concerns. Domestication also changed human behavior, particularly in the time devoted to certain activities, in the regularization of the landscape, and in social structure. In essence, humans too were becoming domesticated, and the new reliance on cultivation transformed human culture (Diamond, 1997: 117; 1987: 64–66; Johnson and Earle, 2000: 127; Abbo *et al.*, 2005; E.O. Wilson, 2012: 93).

The process as I have described it is one advocated by David Rindos in *The origins of agriculture* (1984). It is the view that agriculture developed through unintentional co-evolution. The human selection of plants and animals was entirely for short-term gain, with no long-term plan for societal change. Rindos points out that many nonhuman species (from ants to chimpanzees) have also co-evolved with other species, and that such mutualistic relationships increase the carrying capacity of both participants. One difference in the human case is that some initial domestication may have been for non-food items, such as plants for ritual or adornment. A second difference in human society is that cultivation moved beyond the incidental and haphazard to the intentional and specialized—in which humans preferentially protect some favored species at the expense of others—and finally to agricultural domestication, in which human behaviors like irrigation, tillage, weeding, storage, and settlement come to revolve around particular domesticates. With agricultural domestication both the domesticated species and the human society become dependent on one another, trending toward an obligate symbiosis (1984: 138, 144, 260).

Agriculture as a more formal way of life emerged in different regions of the world at different times, roughly 9000 to 4000 years ago. There were at least eight independent centers of origin, and agriculture did not develop until much later in other places. Part of the reason for the variability in agriculture was the availability of domesticatable plants and animals, a component of the geographic endowment with which various groups found themselves. Domestication is really just a fancy name for intense and repeated selection that results in desirable traits. For plants, selection—which was long done without the intention of making better food— could have been for fruit or seed size, less bitterness, oily seeds, or the length of stems or fibers. Certain plants are more easily domesticated than others, since they already have desirable characteristics in the wild, are genetically pliable, and offer humans the advantage of rapid growth, high yield, and easy storage. Grains, legumes, and squash were among the first domesticated plants, followed much later by berries and fruit and nut trees. Animal domestication—defined as animals selectively bred in captivity—happened in the same way at roughly the same time, but was limited to fewer candidate species. Smaller or larger, more or less hair, greater meat, milk, or egg production; all may be desirable characteristics for humans. Some animals have a diet, growth rate, aversion to captivity or aggression that makes them undomesticatable. Thus we rely on only a few dozen domesticated animals, highlighted by sheep, goats, cattle, pigs, and horses among the mammals, and chickens, ducks, geese, and turkeys among the birds. Notably, candidate species for domestication were not evenly distributed around the world during the emergence of agricultural society. Jared Diamond makes the case that the greater complement of domesticatables on the Eurasian continent provided those peoples with a sociocultural advantage over peoples of other continents (Diamond, 1997: 117–119, 157–175; E.O. Wilson, 2012: 92).

In areas where domestication was feasible, people could produce more food per unit of land by cultivation and animal husbandry than could be supported by foraging alone. In this way the advent of agriculture allowed for a population density increase. Clearly, though, it was not a case of agriculture beginning and foraging ending—the two lifestyles coexisted for thousands of years in many regions and currently coexist in some. Still, over time most human populations have trended toward cultivation and pastoralism. The sedentary lifestyle has the effect of increasing the number of children born per woman and reducing infanticide, which further increases population density and provides more hands to work the land. From the advent of agriculture until very recently, most of the human population has been directly involved with food production. There are advantages to the agricultural life, not the least of which are the ability to store food for times of need, a population-fueled military advantage over rivals, and a reliable source of protein. These are advantages of security, both in the defense against rival groups offered by the strength of numbers and in the defense against starvation offered by stockpiled food (Diamond, 1997: 88–89; Johnson and Earle, 2000: 146).

Diamond has pointed out, however, that the transition to agriculture brought a number of societal issues that, over time, would grow into problems, some of which have environmental implications. With the arrival of agriculture we see comparatively poor diets (versus forager diets in the best of times), more health problems, and increased gender discrimination. Production and storage of food encouraged social stratification of a type that was not commonly seen in egalitarian foraging groups; it is with the rise of agriculture that we see the emergence of a working class under the direction of a ruling class, militant territoriality, and (arguably) increased aggression. Clearly, the transition to agriculture was a trade-off of sociocultural evolution that solved short-term problems while inviting long-term problems. Diamond has called it the worst mistake in the history of the human race (Diamond, 1987; Apicella *et al.*, 2012).

The weakening of egalitarian social structure was in part due to raw population numbers: at some point it becomes impossible to know everyone in your society. It's not that social bonding is lost, of course, only that it becomes hierarchical. Just as in forager society, there is pressure on the individual to follow the norms of his or her social circle. But stratification means that bridging to other circles—in the context of commerce, for example—is possible, necessary, and even advantageous for the individual. Thus collective action is less tightly controlled by one's family or social stratum and more directed by elites of the greater society. The opportunity for out-of-group networking is simultaneously a critical factor for social function and an invitation for individual prospecting (Siegel, 2009).

Agriculture and environmental change

The evolution of agriculture signals a major change in environmental perception. Land cleared for agriculture became home, and wildlands, once thought of as home, slowly became less frequently traveled, then foreign and foreboding, and eventually a place to be feared and cleared (Dutton, 2009: 20; E.O. Wilson, 2012: 93). Plants and animals, once co-inhabitants of the wild, slowly became domesticated (or shunned), then stockpiled, and then items produced primarily for trade. There is a progression here from the instinctual notion of *possession* to the legal concept of *property* to the marketplace concept of *commodity*. Gradually, this progression drove a wedge between human and nonhuman (Hodgson, 2015: 102–128).

How did this conceptual change alter the natural environment? The effects are written in sediment layers around the world. Erosion increased with land clearing. Invasive species in the form of weeds, hitherto an unknown concept, followed human agriculture and displaced indigenous vegetation. Weeds too are domesticates, though unintended and undesired; perhaps they are better thought of as parasitic domesticates (Rindos, 1984: 123). Whatever we call them, they began to thrive with agriculture. Additionally, microbial pathogens flourished in the comparatively high-density human settlements, particularly when humans lived closely together with livestock. From our seat in the 21st century it is easy to see these behavioral changes as the beginnings of an environmentally destructive human existence—and perhaps they were. Considered from the perspective of the parochial group, however, these sociocultural changes make perfect sense. A more stable food supply helps ensure individual and kin survival. Social stratification, at least as it begins, is a form of reciprocation. A larger population raises the group ability to compete with other groups. These basic selection pressures were the forces behind the sociocultural transition, and environmental effects were incidental.

Agriculture and environmental values

Like foraging society, agricultural society is strongly reliant on the direct acquisition of natural resources—but the idea of ecological utility has changed. Over thousands of years of domestication and manipulation, people came to rely on a few species and processes that were eventually assigned economic value and traded as commodities. Stability seems to have been one of the benefits of the transition to sedentary society, as it offered defense against both human rivals and seasons of want. But if stability was a benefit, equity was a casualty. The comparatively egalitarian structure of the foraging group gave way, in most agricultural societies, to stratified and even exploitative relationships. Hierarchical social structure changed the nature of social reciprocity. Direct social reciprocity came to be replaced with a market economy, in which relationships among people are increasingly defined by impersonal exchange and money is increasingly equated with value. Market-based exchange is a system of reciprocity, but not necessarily one of common purpose (Johnson and Earle, 2000: 135; Graeber, 2011: 214–238).

The transition to sedentary life similarly altered concepts of beauty, sanctity, and morality. In a more hierarchical, stratified society, these concepts became important social cohesion mechanisms that unintentionally weakened ties with the natural world. With settlement came a growing sense of connection to a place of homes, hearths, and ceremonial structures; in this sense place-making and community building became a concerted action of social identity. Wilderness, by contrast, came to be seen by some as a foreboding place without the controlled safety of the garden (Cronon, 1996; Northcott, 2015: 19–20). It is also in this era that we see a general decline of pantheism and the emergence of monotheism—a hierarchical stratification of spirituality that mirrored the stratification of society. Through the course of this evolution, people came to see themselves on a different social plane than the elements of the natural world (Lerro, 2000: 144, 174, 291).

Like foragers, traditional cultivating societies are rich with rituals to honor and placate ancestral spirits and to promote fertility and food production. Much ritual is aimed at defining the local community and negotiating relationships among its members. Chanting, music, adornment, and dance convey a sense of common "origins, purpose and destiny"; they are "the ties that bind families into groups" and "encourage compliance" (Johnson and Earle, 2000: 126, 250). However, within stratified agricultural society there are new opportunities for individualism: ostentatious displays of skill, power, surplus (shown through both generosity and wastefulness), and costly possession. Cultural expression, in this sense, is both a pathway to individualism and an opportunity for social mobility (Lerro, 2000: 144, 174, 291; Dutton, 2009: 150; Graeber, 2011: 238, 387).

Extractive societies

Just as agriculture developed alongside and within foraging societies, extraction overlaps with both. By *extraction* I mean the large-scale ability to remove useful products from the land, water, or air. When exactly this began is difficult to say (and it depends on definitions of scale, for humans have always extracted raw materials from the Earth). Forests were being managed for harvest in Europe as early as the 5th century, and mining for flint, ochre, quartz, and shale was common among far earlier humans (Dart and Beaumont, 1967: 408; Mirov and Hasbrouck, 1976: 111; Bunker, 1984; Dickson, 1990: 42–43; Walker and Shipman, 1996: 176). Extraction from the rivers (water power, irrigation, and drinking water), sea (fish, marine mammals, and shellfish), land (wild animals and plants, nutrients, agricultural commodities, peat, metals, rocks and minerals, fossil fuels) and atmosphere (nitrogen converted to fertilizer) followed, and these raw materials paved the way for mechanized production, human population growth, and global commerce. The modern outcome is a social arrangement in which some people consume an astonishing amount of extracted material. The average modern American, for example, will use some 14,500 kilograms of iron ore, 630 kilograms of copper, and 350 kilograms of zinc in a lifetime, fueled by 310,000 liters of petroleum and washed down with millions of liters of freshwater.[2]

The era of extraction may have begun in the midst of small-scale agriculture, but it truly became a global environmental force with the emergence of a market economy based on voluntary exchange of private property (Johnson and Earle, 2000). The property of interest for this discussion consists of natural resources—an extension of domesticated agricultural commodities—that were harvested, processed, marketed, and consumed by an increasingly specialized population. This too is a trade-off, either unconsciously accepted or instituted by circumstances in the course of sociocultural evolution. The benefits of the market economy ostensibly include the freedom of ownership, entrepreneurship, and decision-making within a stable infrastructure (like a government) and a framework of agreed-upon rules and standards (such as systems of law, money, and credit). It allows for individuals (or groups) to acquire resources that may be rare in their region by exchanging items of surplus; it provides ordinary people with the opportunity to improve their social position; it includes elements of both freedom and responsibility. The negative aspects of the trade-off arguably include the encouragement of hedonic selfishness at the expense of collective good: the loss of equity as wealth is accumulated by a few at the expense of the many, the removal of human interconnection with the natural world and the facilitation of environmental destruction in the name of economic growth. In David Graeber's words, certain aspects of the market economy are "designed to eliminate all moral imperatives but profit" (Graeber, 2011: 320).

The market-based economic system emerged as smaller agricultural communities were coalescing into states—higher systems of organization with authority over larger populations in particular territories. As population density increased, states evolved as the best means of "managing internal resources and responding to external threats" (Cohen, 1978: 51). Social division, restriction, and inequality were intensified as states formed, with power in many cases concentrated in a single person or in a small group of elites. The intensification of extraction is closely tied with the rise of nationalism—social identity on a larger scale, with (at least nominally) common beliefs and values and (real or perceived) common competitors or enemies. According to one theory, some emerging states were driven by competition to pursue courses of emulation and innovation to "offset the perceived relative power advantage of another state" (Taliaferro, 2006: 471). Building and maintaining power demands resource extraction. Hence the possession of natural resources, or access to them, was the original basis for national wealth. Of course, not every emerging state has the capacity or impetus for major resource extraction. In those that have, according to this view, leaders acting in the interest of the nation commandeer natural resources to compete with other states. It seems to have made little difference whether the state is monarchical, socialist, or democratic; all have become extractors at one level or another (Taliaferro, 2006).

States are social entities that, like smaller groups, seek their own preservation. They rely on cooperation among their members, with some internal balance of power as an uneasy goal. As with agricultural communities, though, the population of extractive states is too large for intimate knowledge and direct reciprocity between all members; thus there is division into cultural and socioeconomic factions. Historically, states have also been highly xenophobic; nationalism is tribalism on a larger scale. Identification with a group that is too large to personally interact requires common ideology, ethnicity, history, or sociocultural behaviors (or at least the perception of such commonalities) and the "belief that the group requires its own state if it is to survive" (Taliaferro, 2006: 473). To the extent that individuals perceive these commonalities to be legitimate, the national group-think can co-exist with smaller subgroups based on politics, religion, family, and— as we encountered in the first chapter—those motivated by labor and demographic solidarity (Taliaferro, 2006: 491–492).

The emergence of the extractive nation-state triggered a rapid trend toward urbanization. In the United States, for example, the population working directly with agriculture fell from about 90% in 1800 to 40% in 1900 to less than 2% in 2000. Rural population in the US fell from 60% to 20% in the last century, mirrored by a drop from 87% to 50% worldwide over the same period (Dimitri et al., 2005).[3] The story of urbanization flows from intensified agriculture. As agriculture communities grew denser and the capacity for long-term food storage increased, there were more people available for non-agriculture work. Necessity bred innovation in the transportation of water and food to the cities, and this in turn fueled further population growth. Eventually resource extraction and technological advances began the transition of urban areas from centers of agriculture to centers of industry. As they grew, cities consumed former agriculture land and exceeded local limits of food and resource production; this necessitated greater transport from farther distances. The reverse is also true— the growing urban waste stream required transport to rural areas for disposal (Mumford, 1956).

Early industrial cities were notorious for their poor air and water quality, which far exceeded the local processing capacity. Waste accumulation in cities bred disease, both infectious and noninfectious. Friedrich Engels described the urban living and working environment of 19th-century Europe in explicit language:

> Heaps of refuse, offal and sickening filth are everywhere . . . the atmosphere is polluted by the stench and is darkened by the thick smoke of a dozen factory chimneys . . . the creatures who inhabit these dwellings . . . must surely have sunk to the lowest level of humanity.

> (Engels, 1958 [1845]: 71)

Why, given these horrid living conditions, have people flocked to cities throughout the age of extraction? The answer is that this is another sociocultural trade-off. Cities offer employment, engagement, opportunity, and at least the perception of security. A cost of urbanization is the sense of environmental self-sufficiency: it is the removal of human consumers from the source of the resources they consume, and it is the illusion that resource procurement and waste disposal can be consistently and harmlessly dealt with elsewhere (Mumford, 1956; Johnson and Earle, 2000: 380).

In comparison with forager and traditional agricultural societies, the age of extraction presents some important changes in social structure. These changes are well represented by the concept of social *distance*—the theoretical level of connections among people, in terms of their perception, sympathies, level of acceptance, and frequency of interaction with one another. Within close-knit, highly bonded foraging groups, as we have seen, there is incentive for close and regular interaction. We might think of this as a small social distance among group members. Through the course of sociocultural evolution, the increased population density drives stratification by class, status, wealth, and other characteristics, thereby increasing the social distance among people. This has implications for social decision-making and collective action (Akerlof, 1997; Ethington, 1997).

Extraction and environmental change

With the capacity for large-scale resource extraction came the human ability, for the first time, to change the environment on a global scale. From our modern perspective this is most obviously seen in the atmosphere, as deforestation and fossil fuel combustion have altered the concentration of greenhouse gases, particulates, and other atmospheric contaminants over the past two centuries. But our understanding of global atmospheric phenomena is recent, and extractive society has been blind to these long-term and long-distance effects for much of its history. More obvious to individuals in early nation-states were the local and regional effects of extraction: deforestation, erosion, mass wasting, depletion, and pollution. Some early industrial cities were nearly unlivable (literally, given the incidence of disease) and rural or wild areas were increasingly being encroached upon for resource extraction. Government oversight, laws, and economic structures that permit and regulate industrial growth lagged behind environmental problems, so degradation was initially without remedy. Additionally, as the scope of extraction grew, local individuals increasingly had less control over local resources; rather, resource extraction and processing were directed by a distant political or economic power. This powerlessness fomented a growing sense of frustration with declining environmental quality and associated feelings of inequality and exploitation. Thus we see in this period the first major and concerted protests over environmental destruction and contamination, including calls for a reduction in coal smoke in cities and for reforestation in rural areas (Johnson and Earle, 2000: 385; Radkau, 2014: 11–12).

Extraction and environmental values

The age of extraction has been one of wholesale appropriation of the harvestable commodities of nature. A difference from the other sociocultural branches considered here is that extractive societies increasingly harvest resources not for personal, kin, or group use, but for the highest bidder in the market. The market works in the other direction as well, since remote interests can own and exploit a resource far from their own home, and therefore far from the ramifications of extraction. In this way extracted resources have become a driver of the global economy. Such a system is dependent upon stability: the ability to control environmental conditions. In this era it has become clear that wealth can buy you a certain amount of stability, in the form of floodwalls, irrigation systems, drainage networks, firebreaks, reservoirs, and the like. In these ways, environmental engineering can manage environmental fluctuations to maintain local stability—often by transferring the instability to other people in other places.

In extractive societies the romantic movement has blossomed, both in celebration of the perceived perfection in nature and in response to the perceived ills of society. In contrast to the evil, foreboding nature of an earlier age, romantic authors and artists found peace, majesty, harmony, and tranquility in the wild, even as—and in part because—the wild was being commodified. Romantics reinvigorated the spiritual connection with nature in extractive societies, even as natural products and resources were readily bought and sold on the market. Indeed, it is with the rapid expansion of extraction and industry that we see the loss of the sanctity bemoaned by Locke, Thoreau, Rousseau, Marsh, and Muir. Some see in extractive and industrial societies a loss of the sacredness of place, as cities become merely interchangeable sites for habitation. The romantic response is to seek out, commune with, and defend places of natural purity (Northcott, 2015: 163–188).

Morality in extractive societies becomes at once more and less complicated. It is no longer only about sociocultural rules of interaction and reciprocity with fellow group members, though these are our moral instincts. People in extractive societies increasingly become members of many interlocking groups, and less interaction is face-to-face. More actions are undertaken by a state or corporate interest, and the rules of small-group morality are less applicable. As a consequence, equity has taken a major hit in the age of extraction—in this era the haves separated themselves from the have-nots. Urban areas, often multicultural but seldom socially harmonious, became a juxtaposition of the very wealthy and the very poor. In terms of environmental morality, since natural resources are commonly bought and sold it becomes more acceptable for some people to treat them as objects with only market value. For others, who reject such a view, the desire to change environmentally-destructive actions emerges as a social movement (Box 5.1).

Synthetic societies

Following the branching tree model of sociocultural evolution, we have seen that some forager societies—the stage at which all human societies began—remain on Earth, though most have evolved into, been subsumed into, or been eliminated by agriculture and industry. Much of the human population still exists in some form of agricultural society. A subset of these have industrialized through intensive extraction of natural resources. A still smaller subset, industrialized in both agriculture and manufacturing, have evolved to become societies utterly dependent upon technology and human infrastructure. I will refer to these as synthetic societies, after Bookchin's (1962) work

Box 5.1 Environmental social movements

Environmentalism as a social movement—or a set of social movements—emerged in the era of extraction and industrialization and has evolved dramatically over the past 150 years. As reviewed by Robert Gottlieb (2005), some of the earliest American environmental social actions were responding to resource exploitation of the 19th century, seeking to curb abuse with proper resource management and to preserve wilderness in its pristine state. In the early 20th century, urban issues of public health, sanitation, and planning developed as movements separate from, but parallel to, ecological preservation and conservation. The environmentalism that emerged from the world war era added new concerns of destructive technology, population growth, and resource limitation.

In the 1960s the environmental movement gained new popular support, even as it became intertwined with many other causes. Rachel Carson brought the world's attention to the dangers of synthetic chemicals in a period of antinuclear, antiwar, civil rights, labor rights, and feminist movements. Gottlieb finds similarity in these social causes as cultural critiques, in the way they challenge authority, and even in their tendency toward activism and radicalism. One of many consequences of the 1960s counterculture was the era of environmental regulation of the 1970s. For some people this linked environmentalism with policy-making and regulation—measures that have since fueled considerable backlash.

Environmentally minded groups have proliferated in recent decades, but much environmental action is undertaken by a few major organizations, such as the Sierra Club, the Nature Conservancy, Greenpeace, and the World Wildlife Fund. These are professionalized, politicized, big-budget institutions that consequently draw some criticism for being part of, rather than opposed to, the elite establishment. There are also many grass-roots organizations aimed at place- and issue-specific action, justice, and change that reach beyond the traditional scope of resource management to advocate for social reform. Gottlieb suggests that the diversity of modern environmental organizations—in terms of scope, issue, method, and audience—can obscure the overarching objective of environmentalism. Clarity may be gained through recognition that ecological objectives and social objectives are intimately related. In Gottlieb's view, the environmental movement could benefit from "a redefinition that leads toward an environmentalism that is democratic and inclusive, an environmentalism of equity and social justice, an environmentalism of linked natural and human environments, an environmentalism of transformation" (Gottlieb, 2005: 404).

Our synthetic environment. Synthetic society differs markedly from other branches of the sociocultural tree, particularly in its materials, biotechnology,
wealth, and conceptions of community.

Synthetic materials

The world war era ushered in the synthetic age, most clearly in the invention of
new materials. The ability to synthetically fix atmospheric nitrogen into fertilizer
through the Haber-Bosch process tripled the amount of available nitrogen fertilizer and made the human population surge of the 20th century possible.
Chemistry also brought us pesticides that revolutionized agriculture while pre-
senting new threats to both human and ecological health. These synthetic
chemicals provided a new means of reducing weedy competitors, fungal pathogens,
and invertebrate parasites or predators in the short term, even as they selected for
resistant pests to be dealt with by new chemicals in the future. Material synthesis
has brought us plastics, composites, and polymers for clothing, containers, building
materials, and packaging, providing convenience while dramatically increasing
the production of non-biodegradable waste. Even edible material is produced in
highly synthetic ways: products of confinement facilities and monocultures are
treated with artificial color and flavor, processed for long shelf life, packaged in
plastic and mass-marketed.

Synthetic biology

Synthetic biology is nothing less than the human modification of life forms and
processes, and it has transformed life in affluent societies. Through the process of
genetic modification (GM), biotechnology has produced dozens of new plant,
animal, and microbial varieties that provide rot resistance, cold tolerance,
increased nutrition, insect and herbicide resistance, and other useful characteristics. Individuals of many developed societies commonly eat GM food and wear
GM clothing every day, often without knowing it. The quest for new and marketable traits has precipitated the bioprospecting industry, in which bits of
interesting biodiversity are scavenged (often from cash poor but biologically rich
parts of the world) for the creation and marketing of novel organisms (Guha and
Martinez-Alier, 1997: 109–127). Advances in medicine and nutrition have
allowed us to manage many diseases and conditions that were formerly life
threatening, resulting in a dramatic increase in average life expectancy (in nations
with access to the technology). Gene therapy holds the promise of extending life
further for those with debilitating disease.

Perhaps the most astonishing effect of synthetic biology has been the
development and widespread use (in certain societies) of birth control. By
allowing for family planning—often in the form of later and fewer pregnancies—
readily available contraception has dramatically reduced the number of births per
female in the industrial and post-industrial world. Unprecedented in human
history, people are now choosing to invest more heavily in fewer children—or to

invest in their own advancement with no children—thereby snubbing the ancient evolutionary imperative of maximizing one's own offspring (Richerson and Boyd, 2005: 149). One of the many implications of this is a divide in world population growth, such that populations are stable or even shrinking in developed nations but still rapidly increasing in developing nations.

Synthetic nature

Many people in synthetic societies have very little connection with the natural world. As we have seen, much of the food production process is industrialized, removing people from any idea of where their food comes from. Indoor climate control is common in homes, workplaces, vehicles, stores, and entertainment venues. A small percentage of people seek regular immersion in a natural setting; when they do, much of the experience is by way of auto-tours, paved trails, and comfortable lodges. Hunting and fishing are in decline. Fewer children grow up with significant time outdoors. As a proxy for the ecological world, pet ownership is enormous. (In fact, Americans spent about $60 billion on their pets in 2015—more than the 30 smallest national gross domestic products (GDPs) combined.[4]) There are, of course, affluent sub-cultures that are pushing back against this loss of connection with nature. Gardening is popular, and farmers' markets featuring locally and organically grown foods are growing in number and scope. Bird watching and nature photography are common hobbies. Still, in the United States only 5% of food is grown organically, only 8% is grown at home or purchased from local vendors, and only about 50% of people are engaged at least minimally in outdoor recreation.[5] Considering that these were all near 100% only a century ago, these numbers are striking.

Synthetic wealth

For much of human history, wealth (if the word had any meaning at all) was associated with natural objects: food, skins, shells, tools. While natural objects still have value, much of the wealth in synthetic societies is only a representation of actual goods, in the form of money, credit, and corporate shares. About half of modern Americans, for example, hold stock in corporations. By 2000, corporate entities represented over half of the 100 largest economies in the world, and the top 200 corporations' combined sales surpassed the combined economies of 182 nations. The world's richest 1% reached a telling milestone in 2015: possession of as much wealth as half of the world's population. Oxfam International issued an even more extreme picture in 2017, estimating that half of the world's wealth is controlled by just eight men.[6] But disparity is only part of the issue here. The other part is that much of the wealth of the 1% is invested in corporate entities that are under intense pressure to grow, or else lose market share and renewed investment. Thus much of the world's wealth is only indirectly connected with resources. It is instead invested in people—or rather in ideas of people—that promise to accrue more wealth. The system is based on a model of continuous growth while reliant upon non-renewable and finite resources, an irony to which many an investor is blind (or willfully ignorant). The result is more wealth controlled by a smaller group of people who are more disconnected from their actual resource base than at any time in human history.

Synthetic community

All of these changes, incredibly rapid on the evolutionary timescale, have had profound effects on the structure of affluent communities. Family structure, long a basic unit of culture, is changing, with a greater percentage of one-parent households. In 1960, 22% of children in the United States lived in a single parent household; it is now over 50% (Ellwood and Jencks, 2004). A similar, though less extreme trend is seen in the European Union. The new individualism demands a large investment in prestige and position, and a smaller investment in children (or a larger investment in fewer children). The average age of first child bearing has increased in affluent nations, just as the overall fertility has declined. Marriage rates have declined and divorce rates have increased. The "traditional" model of a nuclear family surrounded by extended family, while far from extinct, is no longer the path taken by the overwhelming majority (E.O. Wilson, 2012: 244).

For many individuals in synthetic society, group life is more connected but also more anonymous than it was for previous generations. Groups beyond the family form complex networks with many disparate sub-groups, such as co-workers, friends, ethnic groups, religious affiliations, online communities, and political or special interest groups. These multifaceted group dynamics can result in diffuse social connections that tend to assort by relative income levels. In some situations a multitude of weak social connections, particularly within a social structure of many contradictory authority figures, can dramatically reduce social participation (Siegel, 2009). Furthermore, even in the midst of complex social circles, the loss of personal connection has strained social cohesion. For example, a number of scholars have observed that both social exclusion and social isolation are exacerbated in synthetic society, resulting in diminished workplace and community solidarity (Mason, 2015: 209).

Social exclusion has probably been a characteristic of all human communities; it is an artefact of our propensity to form social groups. This is not to say that it is a good thing, only that it is an evolved behavior of our species. Individuals have long been excluded from certain groups for all manner of reasons, including appearance, race, ethnicity, gender, age, ideology, religious affiliation, and many others. Exclusion based on socioeconomic status is by no means the least of social stigmas, and it has arguably reached a crescendo in synthetic society. Simply stated, people generally associate with their socioeconomic peers. This is exacerbated by social isolation—when "the wealthiest fraction of a society feel that they can insulate themselves from the common fate and buy their way out of the common institutions" (Barry, 1998: 7). In such situations, according to scholar Brian Barry, access to opportunity, justice, democratic principles, and even an individual's sense of belonging can be undermined for many by the elite few. Real or perceived, intentional or incidental, exclusion and isolation can weaken interpersonal trust, increase social distance, and deteriorate social cohesion (Barry, 1998; Wilkinson and Pickett, 2010: 38–54).

Synthetic community can thus present an odd social arrangement. The internet age has made new connections possible, greatly enhancing social networks (though a quick scan of the comments on any posting will remind you that xenophobia is alive and well). At the same time within-group social bonding in synthetic society appears to be on the decline. The result is the sort of society in which a person might close a major financial transaction with a complete stranger and not know the names of his neighbors. Of course, there are cooperative, reciprocal, and even altruistic acts to be found, both in concert with neighbors and directed at distant individuals whom the altruist will never meet. Furthermore, even though synthetic life can be highly removed from nature, it offers unprecedented opportunity to understand the character of natural resources, of other cultures, of nonhuman species, of unfamiliar places, and of one's personal environmental footprint. Still, the overwhelming forces of synthetic society facilitate individual behavior and inhibit collective action (Adger, 2003; Richerson and Boyd, 2005: 188, 224; Siegel, 2009).

Environmental change in synthetic societies

The environmental impacts of synthetic society are ubiquitous. The age of synthetic materials and chemicals has been implicated in many human health concerns, including cancer, developmental deformities, and hormone disruption. It would be unfair to condemn the age of synthetic materials altogether, however, for synthetic chemicals, materials, and biology have done much to improve human health for some. Even so, plastics and other disposables have surely increased the size of our waste stream, and with some exceptions synthetic societies are not great re-users or recyclers. At the heart of the consumption-based lifestyle is a great deal of energy; the average American uses nearly twice the energy of the average European and three to five times more than average inhabitants of agriculture societies.[7] Much of this energy is produced with fossil fuels, and so synthetic societies are altering the atmospheric content of greenhouse gases in a major way. This has global implications of climate change, ocean acidification, coral bleaching, and associated issues. The negative effects of material and energy consumption—air and water pollution, waste dumps, deleterious effects of climate change—tend to be concentrated in less developed areas of the world that often have little capacity to regulate, prevent, or remediate environmental problems. Extraction of environmental goods and disposal of wastes are increasingly done under corporate auspices, often with tacit state approval, to the benefit of the wealthy and to the detriment of the poor. Thus basic human necessities, like clean water and air, a reliable, sufficiently nutritious and uncontaminated food supply, and adequate shelter are taken for granted in certain social circles but sorely lacking in others, who are sometimes residents of the same city.

Environmental values in synthetic societies

Value systems in synthetic society are widely varied. In keeping with the branching tree metaphor, perhaps we could say that this branch is socially splintered. The wealthiest people in the world are responsible for most of the energy and resource consumption and most of the waste production. The consumption is often blind, meaning that the consumer has little or no knowledge of the origin or ultimate destination of that which is consumed. There is also a large amount of luxury consumption. The value here is not only in the goods and services themselves, but increasingly in the *act of acquiring* the goods and services. And yet, it is primarily from the members of this most affluent society that many voices of environmentalism arise. It was, after all, some of the wealthiest communities of the world that launched the environmental revolution of the 1960s, that lobbied and petitioned for the first effective environmental legislation, and that have supported the dramatic growth of third-sector environmental organizations in the past half-century (McCormick, 1991: 66).

A school of thought championed by Inglehart (1977, 2000) holds that the affluent of the world, particularly in the synthetic age, have little trouble meeting their own material needs and thus have time and energy to devote to higher values like quality of life, equity, freedom, and environmental concerns. Inglehart has argued that such post-industrial values among affluent postwar generations are "the primary factor that has stimulated the emergence of progressive social movements such as the peace, feminist, and environmental movements" (Dunlap and York, 2012: 92). In this perspective, it is not the actual scarcity or degradation of resources that triggered the environmental revolution, but a shift in values enabled by wealth. The insinuation that environmentalism is the purview of the wealthy and not a concern of the poor has met with some criticism. One study, for example, has shown that individuals from less developed regions were more apt to express environmental concerns than wealthy respondents, particularly on the condition of their own community and personal health. Wealthier respondents were more likely to rate the quality of the global environment as poor and to express a preference for environmental protection over economic growth. These data imply that environmentalism is not simply a concern of the wealthy, but that the perspective between wealthy and poor can differ (Dunlap and York, 2008). Other surveys, however, have found environmental values to be only weakly correlated with affluence. The level and type of education and the degree of spiritual influence have been proposed as alternative factors (Ignatow, 2006: 457). In sum, the post-material explanation of environmentalism has lost its luster somewhat. To the contrary, it seems that environmental attitudes are both socioculturally and conceptually diverse.

Environmental values in synthetic societies occur within a sociocultural structure in which cooperative reciprocity is no longer an obvious requirement. The individual, freed from certain social obligations, may act in his or her own best interest. True, post-industrial people still feel compassion, they still feel responsibility to their fellow humans, and many still act on those feelings. But the consequences for not acting are no longer severe, no longer in existence at all, really, for group memberships are amorphous and transient. In fact, in many social circles it is personal status—measured by wealth and possession—that is the important factor, not cooperative behavior. Given leave of compulsory responsibility to the group, people are free to satiate individual desires. Whether or not this is a problem depends upon one's perspective. To John Bellamy Foster it is a moral crisis in which the wealthy are trending toward the selfish rather than self-interest, let alone collective interest (Foster, 2002: 44–46). Alexandra Maryanski and Jonathan Turner, by contrast, argue that the dissolution of social pressures for reciprocity is a good thing, allowing for "more choice, freedom, autonomy, and individualism" (1992: 169). Either way, it seems that the social cage—at least in some synthetic societies—has been broken.

Still, much of the impetus and advocacy for an environmental ethic has emerged from this deeply splintered synthetic society. In *Varieties of environmentalism*, Guha and Martinez-Alier argue that the environmentalism of the affluent world is more about changing "attitudes towards the natural world than a change in systems of production or distribution," and in most cases "run[s] parallel to the consumer society without questioning its socio-ecological basis" (Guha and Martinez-Alier, 1997: 18). These authors observe that affluent environmental concerns are often actualized by lobbying or litigation through established organizations, such as nonprofit environmental advocacy groups. While such groups certainly address local concerns, much of the call for change is directed elsewhere, to the places where deforestation and biodiversity loss are currently occurring. The concerns are frequently accompanied by directives that are not always welcome in less developed parts of the world.

Subsistence societies

If synthetic society represents the lifestyle of perhaps the wealthiest 5% of the world, the poorest 50% are living at or below a level of basic survival. In both urban and rural settings, the subsistence lifestyle is one of constant want for fundamental necessities like adequate nutrition, clean water, and secure shelter. The statistical trends only begin to tell the tale of the divide: a life expectancy about 75% of that in wealthy nations, infant mortality rate 10–15 times higher, incidence of HIV/AIDS about 15 times higher, childhood and maternal malnutrition rates nearly 30 times higher (Siegel, 2012). The population growth rate is also about ten times higher in less developed regions. This spells trouble for nations that do not have the infrastructure to support current populations and are on trajectory for a population doubling in the next few decades. National debt, corruption, political strife, and war exacerbate demographic problems. Life in such conditions is day to day. Subsistence societies are particularly plagued with deficient water quality and sanitation, suffering in great numbers from water-borne pathogens that are virtually unheard of in societies with municipal sewage systems and water treatment facilities. Air pollution, too, is a concern, as reliance on biomass for fuel and proximity to industrial centers increases the level of particulates, dioxins, metals, and sulfur and nitrogen oxides far beyond that which would be tolerated in synthetic society (Beckerman, 1995: 26–28).

It is difficult to characterize the social structure of such a vast and diverse sector of humanity. Perhaps the only meaningful observation is that they are generally denied the social capacity to advocate for their own needs.

Environmental change in subsistence societies

The journalist Anil Agarwal observed in the 1980s that extraction of natural resources by and for the affluent is the primary reason for environmental destruction in the developing world, and that the negative effects of this demand are borne primarily by the poor (Guha and Martinez-Alier, 1997: 3). According to the World Bank, "non-renewable mineral resources play a dominant role in 81 countries, which collectively account for a quarter of world GDP, half of the world's population, and nearly 70% of those in extreme poverty."[8] Extraction of renewable resources, such as timber, fish, and the palm oil considered in Chapter 2, is similarly common in the developing world, often to meet the demands of affluent society. Ideally, development and extraction can provide jobs, reduce poverty, and promote the growth of much-needed infrastructure. And there are some success stories. Too often, though, weak regulation allows unsustainable, exploitative, and environmentally destructive development. Ineffective governance also invites industry that is far cheaper in the absence of environmental and human rights regulation than in the presence of such regulation. Furthermore, the sheer population density and lack of adequate infrastructure contribute to environmental problems in less developed regions. Human and livestock waste, for instance, contaminate drinking water sources and fisheries in the absence of wastewater treatment facilities. Land cleared for agriculture can lead to erosion and impoverished biodiversity, and overgrazing or intensive irrigation can lead to desertification. Garbage, including toxic and electronic waste—some shipped overseas by synthetic societies for disposal—tends to accumulate in and around the homes of the very poor. On top of all this is a general political inability to remediate environmental degradation and to respond to environmental instability, mostly because of cost, coordination, and corruption. The displacement of peoples due to loss or degradation of their traditional resource base has given cause for a new term, proposed by Lester Brown in 1976: environmental refugees (Brown, 1976).

Environmental values in subsistence societies

For those in utter poverty, the environmental values of utility, stability, and equity are of foremost importance. Many subsistence livelihoods depend upon natural resources, and when those resources are degraded or acquired and extracted by others, local lives are irreversibly changed. In their essay "The environmentalism of the poor," Guha and Martinez-Alier (1997) make the case that the environmentalism of those in poverty is the action they take to resist resource misappropriation by the wealthy, which is often facilitated by the state. It is, the authors demonstrate, an environmentalism of protest, a "refusal to exchange the world they know, and are in partial control over, for an uncertain and insecure future" (1997: 12). In this perspective, resource use can be a deeply spiritual and moral issue for the poor, even while it may be a simple matter of commodity exchange for the affluent. The environmentalism of the affluent is in some ways foreign to those in a state of subsistence, for efforts to set aside wilderness, achieve gender equity, or save charismatic species within the context of nationalism and economic prosperity are less imperative to those whose very lives are dependent on basic resource access (Guha, 1989). As such, the environmental values of beauty and sanctity, surely as important to the poor as to the wealthy and perhaps more so, fade in the face of hunger and thirst. Guha relates the words of Mahatma Gandhi: "Even God dare not appear to the poor man except in the form of bread" (Guha, 1989: 71).

Sociocultural evolution in summary

Human environments, social structures, and cultural norms have undergone dramatic changes over the past 70,000 years. From the small-group life of the forager, in which existence is tenuous but social responsibilities are clear, certain human groups evolved to the sedentary agricultural life. Nature's products, now manageable and marketable, changed societal arrangements and altered human relationships with the nonhuman world. Eventually the human capacity to extract materials on a large scale and to buy, sell, and trade them without actual ownership increased the social distance between a subset of people and insulated them from the natural environment. In a select few societies, material wealth, military power, and technological innovation have allowed for a synthetic existence that is both inaccessible and debilitating for much of the world's population.

Our species has engineered its environment at every point along this evolutionary continuum. For much of this history (and prehistory), human social groups have been able to adapt to anthropogenic environmental change on the regional scale. A dual consequence of our sociocultural evolution is that it has: 1) allowed for anthropogenic environmental change on a global scale; and 2) compromised social mechanisms of collective action. Cooperative reciprocity, one of the inherited instincts that we may bring to bear on environmental problems, appears to have been weakened in the synthetic societies where collective action is needed most.

Environmental perspective depends upon one's position on the branching tree of sociocultural evolution. Within this diverse experience, though, every member of our species encounters environmental dilemmas in the social and mental space between the self, the other, and the nonhuman. In this space we wrestle with the things that we value, for they are often in conflict. We have evolved to become the preeminent consumers of our world, but our consumption is at odds with the stability and function of the nonhuman world. This is our socioecological dilemma, and it is considered in Chapter 7. On another level the ramifications of resource appropriation clash with our own perception of nature—what it is, what it means, and what we believe it ought to be. Such issues are spiritual and aesthetic, addressed in Chapters 8 and 9. Another environmental dilemma arises as a consequence of resource use and disparity. These are problems of socioeconomic evolution, and to these we now turn.

Notes

1 The term noble savage is first attributed to the playwright John Dryden in 1672.
2 Mineral Information Institute, 2007. www.kennecott.com/library/media/human% 20consumption.pdf, accessed June 2016; US Energy Information Administration 2016, https://www.eia.gov/tools/faqs/faq.cfm?id=23&t=10, accessed June 2016. Maupin, M.A., Kenny, J.F., Hutson, S.S., Lovelace, J.K., Barber, N.L., and Linsey, K.S., 2014, Estimated use of water in the United States in 2010: US Geological Survey Circular 1405, http:// dx.doi.org/10.3133/cir1405, accessed June 2016.
3 United Nations data, www.un.org/esa/population/publications/WUP2005/2005wup. htm, accessed June 2016.
4 American Pet Products Association (APPA), 2015, www.americanpetproducts.org/ press_industrytrends.asp accessed October 2016; World Development Indicators database, World Bank, http://data.worldbank.org/data-catalog/world-development-indicators, accessed April 2017.
5 Outdoor Foundation, 2016. Outdoor recreation participation report, www. outdoorfoundation.org/research.participation.2016.topline.html, accessed October 2016; USDA Economic research Service Organic Market Overview 2016, www.ers. usda.gov/topics/natural-resources-environment/organic-agriculture/organic-market-overview.aspx, accessed October 2016.
6 Credit Suisse Research Institute, 2015. Global Wealth Report 2015. https://publications. credit-suisse.com/tasks/render/file/?fileID=F2425415-DCA7-80B8-EAD989AF9341D47E, accessed November 2016; Hardoon, D., 2017. An economy for the 99%. Published by Oxfam GB for Oxfam International under ISBN 978-0-85598-861-6 in January 2017. Available at https://www.oxfam.org/sites/www.oxfam.org/files/file_attachments/ bp-economy-for-99-percent-160117-en.pdf, accessed January 2017.
7 CIA World Factbook 2016, https://www.cia.gov/library/publications/the-world-factbook/rankorder/rankorderguide.html, accessed November 2016.
8 The World Bank, 2017, www.worldbank.org/en/topic/extractiveindustries/overview#1, accessed November 2016.

Bibliography

Abbo, S., Gopher, A., Rubin, B. and Lev-Yadun, S. (2005). On the origin of Near Eastern founder crops and the dump-heap hypothesis. *Genetic Resources and Crop Evolution*, 52(5), pp. 491–495.

Adger, W.N. (2003). Social capital, collective action, and adaptation to climate change. *Economic Geography*, 79(4), pp. 387–404.

Akerlof, G.A. (1997). Social distance and social decisions. *Econometrica: Journal of the Econometric Society*, 5(5), pp. 1005–1027.

Ambrose, S.H. (1998). Late Pleistocene human population bottlenecks, volcanic winter, and differentiation of modern humans. *Journal of Human Evolution*, 34(6), pp. 623–651.

Apicella, C.L., Marlowe, F.W., Fowler, J.H. and Christakis, N.A. (2012). Social networks and cooperation in hunter-gatherers. *Nature*, 481(7382), pp. 497–501.

Barnosky, A.D., Koch, P.L., Feranec, R.S., Wing, S.L. and Shabel, A.B. (2004). Assessing the causes of late Pleistocene extinctions on the continents. *Science*, 306(5693), pp. 70–75.

Barry, B. (1998). *Social exclusion, social isolation and the distribution of income*. London: Centre for Analysis of Social Exclusion, London School of Economics.

Beckerman, W. (1995). *Small is stupid: blowing the whistle on the greens*. London: Gerald Duckworth.

Bird, R.B., Bird, D.W., Codding, B.F., Parker, C.H. and Jones, J.H. (2008). The "fire stick farming" hypothesis: Australian Aboriginal foraging strategies, biodiversity, and anthropogenic fire mosaics. *Proceedings of the National Academy of Sciences of the United States of America*, 105(39), pp. 14796–14801.

Bookchin, M. (as Lewis Herber). (1962). *Our synthetic environment*. New York: Knopf.

Bowman, D.M., Balch, J., Artaxo, P., Bond, W.J., Cochrane, M.A., D'antonio, C.M., DeFries, R., Johnston, F.H., Keeley, J.E., Krawchuk, M.A. and Kull, C.A. (2011). The human dimension of fire regimes on Earth. *Journal of Biogeography*, 38(12), pp. 2223–2236.

Brown, L.R. (1976). *Twenty-two dimensions of the population problem*. Worldwatch Institute Paper 5, March 1976.

Bunker, S.G. (1984). Modes of extraction, unequal exchange and the progressive underdevelopment of an extreme periphery, 1600–1980. *American Journal of Sociology*, 89, pp. 1017–1064.

Cohen, R. (1978). State origins: a reappraisal. In: H. Claessen and P. Skalník, eds., *The early state*. The Hague: Mouton. pp. 31–76.

Cronon, W. (1996). The trouble with wilderness, or getting back to the wrong nature. *Environmental History*, 1(1), pp. 7–28.

Dart, R.A. and Beaumont, P. (1967). Amazing antiquity of mining in Southern Africa. *Nature*, 216, pp. 407–408.

Diamond, J. (1987). The worst mistake in the history of the human race. *Discover*, May 1987, pp. 64–66.

Diamond, J. (1997). *Guns, germs, and steel: the fates of human societies*. New York: W.W. Norton.

Diamond, J. (2012). *The world until yesterday: what can we learn from traditional societies?* New York: Viking Press.

Dickson, D.B. (1990). *The dawn of belief*. Tuscon: University of Arizona Press.

Dimitri, C., Effland, A. and Conklin, N. (2005). *The 20th century transformation of US agriculture and farm policy*. Washington, DC: USDA Economic Research Service Economic Information. Bulletin 3.

Dunlap, R.E. and York, R. (2008). The globalization of environmental concern and the limits of the postmaterialist values explanation: evidence from four multinational surveys. *Sociological Quarterly*, 49(3), pp. 529–563.

Dunlap, R.E. and York, R. (2012). The globalization of environmental concern. In: P. Steinberg and S. Vandeveer, eds., *Comparative environmental politics: theory, practice, and prospects*. Cambridge, MA: MIT Press. pp. 89–112.

Dutton, D. (2009). *The art instinct: beauty, pleasure and human evolution*. New York: Bloomsbury Press.

Ellwood, D. and Jencks, C. (2004). The spread of single-parent families in the United States since 1960 (February 26, 2004). KSG Working Paper No. RWP04-008. Available at https://ssrn.com/abstract=517662

Engels, F. (1958 [1845]). *The condition of the working class in England*. Translation by W. Henderson and W. Chaloner. Stanford: Stanford University Press.

Ethington, P.J. (1997). The intellectual construction of social distance: toward a recovery of Georg Simmel's social geometry. *Cybergeo: European Journal of Geography*, 30. Available at https://cybergeo.revues.org/227

Foster, J.B. (2002). *Ecology against capitalism*. New York: Monthly Review Press.

Gamble, C. (2007). *Origins and revolutions: human identity in earliest prehistory*. New York: Cambridge University Press.

Gottlieb, R. (2005). *Forcing the spring: the transformation of the American environmental movement*. Washington, DC: Island Press.

Graeber, D. (2011). *Debt: the first 5,000 years*. Brooklyn: Melville House.

Guha, R. (1989). Radical American environmentalism and wilderness preservation: a third world critique. *Environmental Ethics*, 11(1), pp. 71–83.

Guha, R. and Martinez-Alier, J. (1997). *Varieties of environmentalism: essays north and south*. London: Routledge.

Hodgson, G.M. (2015). *Conceptualizing capitalism: institutions, evolution, future*. Chicago: University of Chicago Press.

Hogg, M.A. (2016). Social identity theory. In: S. McKeown, R. Haji and N. Ferguson, eds., *Understanding peace and conflict through social identity theory*. Switzerland: Springer International Publishing. pp. 3–17.

Holden, C. (2001). Ötzi death riddle solved. *Science*, 293(795), pp. 4–26.

Ignatow, G. (2006). Cultural models of nature and society: reconsidering environmental attitudes and concerns. *Environment and Behavior*, 38(4), pp. 441–461.

Inglehart, R. (1977). Political dissatisfaction and mass support for social change in advanced industrial society. *Comparative Political Studies*, 10(3), pp. 455–472.

Inglehart, R. (2000). Globalization and postmodern values. *Washington Quarterly*, 23(1), pp. 215–228.

Johnson, A.W. and Earle, T. (2000). *The evolution of human societies: from foraging group to agrarian state*. Stanford, CA: Stanford University Press.

Lane, C.S., Chorn, B.T. and Johnson, T.C. (2013). Ash from the Toba supereruption in Lake Malawi shows no volcanic winter in East Africa at 75 ka. *Proceedings of the National Academy of Sciences of the United States of America*, 110(20), pp. 8025–8029.

Lerro, B. (2000). *From earth spirits to sky gods: the socioecological origins of monotheism, individualism, and hyperabstract reasoning from the Stone Age to the axial Iron Age*. Lanham, MD: Lexington Books.

Maryanski, A. and Turner, J.H. (1992). *The social cage: human nature and the evolution of society*. Stanford, CA: Stanford University Press.

Mason, P. (2015). *Postcapitalism: a guide to our future*. New York: Farrar, Straus and Giroux.

McCormick, J. (1991). *Reclaiming paradise: the global environmental movement*. Bloomington, IN: Indiana University Press.

Mirov, N.T. and Hasbrouck, J. (1976). *The story of pines*. Bloomington, IN: Indiana University Press.

Mumford, L. (1956). The natural history of urbanization. In: W. Thomas, ed., *Man's role in changing the face of the Earth*. Chicago: University of Chicago Press. pp. 382–398.

Northcott, M.S. (2015). *Place, ecology and the sacred: the moral geography of sustainable communities*. New York: Bloomsbury Press.

Pinker, S. (2003). *The blank slate: the modern denial of human nature*. New York: Penguin.

Pretty, J. (2003). Social capital and the collective management of resources. *Science*, 302 (5652), pp. 1912–1914.

Radkau, J. (2014). *The age of ecology*. New York: Wiley.

Rampino M.R. and Ambrose, S.H. (2000). Volcanic winter in the Garden of Eden: the Toba super-eruption and the late Pleistocene human population crash. In: F. McCoy and G. Heiken, eds., *Volcanic hazards and disasters in human antiquity*. Boulder, CO: Geological Society of America. 345, pp. 71–82.

Richerson, P.J. and Boyd, R. (2005). *Not by genes alone: how culture transformed human evolution*. Chicago: University of Chicago Press.

Rindos, D. (1984). *The origins of agriculture: an evolutionary perspective*. Cambridge, MA: Academic Press.

Roebroecks, W. and Villa, P. (2011). On the earliest evidence for the habitual use of fire in Europe. *Proceedings of the National Academy of Science of the United States of America*, 108(13), pp. 5209–5214.

Sieferle, R.P. (2011). Cultural evolution and social metabolism. *Geografiska Annaler: Series B, Human Geography*, 93(4), pp. 315–324.

Siegel, D.A. (2009). Social networks and collective action. *American Journal of Political Science*, 53(1), pp. 122–138.

Siegel, J.S. (2012). *The demography and epidemiology of human health and aging*. New York: Springer. pp. 579–640.

Suddendorf, T. (2013). *The gap: the science of what separates us from the other animals*. New York: Basic Books.

Taliaferro, J.W. (2006). State building for future wars: neoclassical realism and the resource-extractive state. *Security Studies*, 15(3), pp. 464–495.

Thompson, W.S. (1929). Population. *American Journal of Sociology*, 34, pp. 959–975.

Tudge, C. (1996). *The time before history: 5 million years of human impact*. New York: Scribner.

Walker, A. and Shipman, P. (1996). *The wisdom of the bones*. New York: Knopf.

Wilkinson, R.G. and Pickett, K. (2010). *The spirit level: why greater equality makes societies stronger*. New York: Bloomsbury Press.

Wilson, D.S. (2002). *Darwin's cathedral: evolution, religion, and the nature of society*. Chicago: University of Chicago Press.

Wilson, E.O. (2012). *The social conquest of Earth*. New York: Liveright.

6   Socioeconomic evolution

Key points

- Our ancient system of interpersonal commerce has evolved into impersonal capitalism.
- Impersonal economic systems have simultaneously been implicated in environmental problems and praised as environmental solutions.
- Various alternatives to capitalism have been proposed as mechanisms to curb selfishness and rejuvenate cooperative reciprocity.

Modern environmental problems are complicated, but fundamentally they are driven by biological instincts in sociocultural context. These instincts include selfishness, nepotism, ostentation, and xenophobia, but also cooperative reciprocity, empathy, generosity, creativity, morality, and an appreciation for beauty. Our problems are complex because we are complex. Instincts do not dictate actions completely, of course, and in our best moments we can overcome our evolutionary demons for common benefit. Still, our response to global environmental problems is confounded by the tension between that which is good for our kind and that which is good for ourselves.

In the second chapter I proposed six values that can be extruded from a wide variety of environmental worldviews, and in the previous chapter I traced the evolution of these values through different phases of sociocultural evolution. In this chapter I will focus on two of the values—utility and equity—as they apply to environmental problems. These are questions of consumption, sustainability, and fairness, and in modern society such issues are addressed (or ignored) by economic policy and governance. Thus, this chapter examines the sociocultural evolution of economic systems. As with previous chapters, I offer a caveat: I do not intend to present a treatise on international political economy. Rather, I consider the emergence of free market capitalism, its shortcomings and merits, and alternative economic systems, all with an eye toward environmentalism.

Origins of capitalism

Capitalism, generally speaking, is a socioeconomic system that places individual rights and freedoms at the forefront. In this system private interests pursue profit via ownership, trade, and development of resources within the regulatory context of nation-states (Hodgson, 2015: 259). Capitalism is the dominant form of political economy in the world today, even in former bastions of socialism (Collins and Barkdull, 1995). In some forms, as in East Asia, government has a high degree of interaction and oversight of industry, finance, and development; in the continental European model, banks are central players in private funding; while in the Anglo-American system it is the stock market model of corporate finance that is dominant (O'Brien and Williams, 2013: 96). In all of these, though, the idea is the same: individuals or their organizations accumulate capital and use resources (both human and natural) in order to produce goods or services for profit. This system is ground zero for the debates of human development and environmental sustainability, and arguments for and against are drawn directly from our collective evolutionary heritage.

Ten thousand years ago human economic systems were very different from the modern global marketplace. Even so, we can see the origins of capitalism in the distant past. I will greatly simplify the history of economic development by reducing the rise of capitalism to the human acceptance of three mental models: credit, money, and incorporation.

The anthropologist Graeber (2011) makes a convincing case that credit (and debt) came first. We have seen that foraging societies are economically self-contained or nearly so, with complex and socially significant relationships of cooperation and reciprocity within the group. Goods (like food) or services (like protection) can be exchanged in kind, but are commonly repaid by enhanced reputation, status, loyalty, mating privileges, or the promise of future reciprocity. This is the oldest human economic system, and in a sense it is a kind of marketplace. Graeber argues that ancient economic transactions were nothing more than exchanges of social credits and debts:

> they are used to create, maintain and otherwise reorganize relations between people: to arrange marriages, establish the paternity of children, head off feuds, console mourners at funerals, seek forgiveness in the case of crimes, negotiate treaties, acquire followers—almost anything but trade in yams, shovels, pigs or jewelry.
>
> (Graeber, 2011: 130)

Within-group transactions lend themselves to socially mediated exchange. Out-of-group relationships are not as amenable to future reciprocity, and are therefore more dependent on the exchange of tangible goods. Harari (2015) notes that basic barter systems were maintained throughout much of the transition to agriculture; it was only with the emergence of cities that barter systems broke down amid complexities of specialization, storage, and long-distance transport. To deal with these new complications, people developed a mental model—a readily exchangeable proxy for goods and services that we call money. As Harari points out, some forms of money actually have physical value, like metal or grain or pelts or cattle. But most forms of money are physically worthless; the value is imaginary. Gold, the impetus behind so much of human history, was not particularly useful as a metal until the recent boom in small electronics. The linen and cotton of a hundred dollar bill have even less value, and yet anyone would scurry to pick it up and stuff it into their pocket if they saw it blowing down the street. Whatever the form, money is simply a "debt token"; it is a means of comparing and denoting perceptions of value (Graeber, 2011: 75, 130–136). As these tokens of exchange took on an equivalence with the commodities they represented, our species entered a market economy.

An important point here is that money is an abstraction. As such it separates the concept of value from the resource itself and from the labor necessary to procure and create. In so doing it removes the consumer from the realities of natural resources and human effort. In Graeber's words, money has the "capacity to turn morality into a matter of impersonal arithmetic" (Graeber, 2011: 14). The separation is not complete, for consumers still value—and are willing to pay more for—items that are hand-crafted or locally grown or original works. Still, such items are a small part of the modern shopping cart. Humans the world over (or nearly so) have accepted the idea that money represents value, often with no idea of the human or natural capital embedded in the purchase (Witt, 1999).

Naturally, money has greatly facilitated commerce, since it is easier to store, carry, exchange, and make change for a portable currency with mutually imagined value. The system works as long as everyone trusts the mental model. Whatever trouble it has caused, money is one of the greatest and most universal instances of human trust and tolerance in the history of our race. But before we feel too good about this wonderful innovation, Harari reminds us that it is not necessarily the neighbor, or the retailer, or the business partner that we trust, it is the paper that he or she holds (Harari, 2015: 180, 187). And some people will hoard and steal and guard this paper with their lives.

From the idea of money it is a short leap to not needing the promise that the paper represents some item of real value, nor from there to not needing physical exchange of money at all. This is the concept of "virtual credit money," and it appears to have arisen as an extension of social interaction (Graeber, 2011: 214; Harari, 2015: 310). Indeed, some of the oldest remaining artifacts from the cradle of human civilization are essentially ledgers of credits and liabilities (Graeber, 2011: 214–215). As civilization evolved, the extension of credit became a business venture unto itself. The availability of large, long-term, low interest loans has facilitated new enterprise. Credit has allowed explorers, employers, and entrepreneurs to grow their venture with the promise that future success will pay back the loan. By and large, the credit system works; people are able to pay back their loans more often than not, and they can also re-invest in their enterprise (or pursue a new one) to boot. In the past 500 years our faith in credit has allowed global production to increase by a factor of 240, and the number of businesses in the world now easily exceeds 100 million. But while the credit game has been lucrative for some, it has relegated others to lives of hopeless debt (Hawken, 1999; Graeber, 2011: 374; Harari, 2015: 305).

The reinvestment of profits back into production is the heart of capitalism, at least as imagined by Adam Smith in *The wealth of nations* (1776). Those who invest capital into a venture provide jobs and stimulate demand for other goods and services and thus produce more capital (Smith, 1784 [1776]). This is known as growing the economy, and it is just as imaginary as the money that it drives around in a circle. It is all based, you see, on the idea that the raw materials for ever-increasing production, such as energy, metal, land, and water, are in unlimited supply, or are at least in such great supply that their availability is guaranteed for the foreseeable future. It is also premised on the stability of nature—that the natural products and processes we need will be there whenever we need them. These are not necessarily sound assumptions, but before we examine them let's consider the third mental model of our current capitalistic world: the corporation.

For a long time only royalty had the wealth to fund new enterprise. Then an innovation in the medieval Middle East changed the game—merchants began to pool resources to finance trading expeditions and share the profits (Banaji, 2007; O'Brien and Williams, 2013: 52). The innovation made its way to Europe, and soon large infrastructure projects like canals were being funded the same way. In the 17th and 18th centuries the British and Dutch East India Companies expanded on the model. These were corporations as we think of them today: privately owned, with indirect government oversight, many investors who did not know one another, and a long-term vision of business, even as investors might come and go. For the first time, an individual with the means to invest could buy shares in a company and realize a profit (or loss) without really knowing the details of the enterprise, the actors, or their actions. It was another step in the removal of the consumer (in this case, both the buyer of commodities and the investor) from the resources being consumed and their social and environmental context. Further, it advanced a business model in which the corporation must show a profit—indeed, must show reasonably continuous profits—or risk losing investors, who could easily divest at any time with no future commitment (Graeber, 2011: 320; O'Brien and Williams, 2013: 61).

Of course, the transition to corporate capitalism did not all happen at once. But gradually, especially with the onset of extractive society and the industrial revolution, the corporate model gained traction. Today there are over 43,000 transnational corporations, some 1300 of which control 60% of global revenues (Vitali *et al.*, 2011). About three-quarters of the nations in the world have stock markets, and around 7% of people in the world directly own corporate shares or are indirectly invested, for example as members of pension plans (Grout *et al.*, 2009). Share ownership (and hence management decision-making) is concentrated in the hands of a few major investors, with limited oversight by the state or by general shareholders (Porta *et al.*, 1999). In this way a very small percentage of people control much of the world's resource base, and in order to maintain this control their corporations must show continuous growth.

Credit, cash, and corporation: these three innovations have changed the ways in which humans interact with one another and with the resources of the planet. For good or for ill, all three are products of sociocultural evolution. All developed as mechanisms that solved problems or that facilitated commerce, and none were designed with malicious intent. In fact, many argue even today that these inno-vations and the free market capitalism they support have been great advances for the human race. They are, after all, mechanisms of generating wealth, and in the best case they are aimed at procuring and providing social well-being—in the form of meaningful employment, reasonable income, and economic security—for many people. The mechanisms of capitalism also provide economic stability, it is argued, for the free market is self-correcting. Given a natural disaster, for instance, the market will adapt as investors pursue viable and profitable alternatives, and the economy will ultimately return to a state of growth (Mason, 2015: 4). And stable economic growth, the argument continues, raises the human standard of living. This is where we encounter equity, as critics of capitalism ask how the standard of living is determined and for whom it is being raised.

Labor and growth

Through the course of the industrial revolution the relationship between people, raw materials, and production fundamentally changed. For the first time, workers without common familial or cultural roots made their labor available on the market, and, once employed, were subject to the rules of whoever owned the capital. They were not quite powerless, though, for labor was a necessary part of production—it held value that could be used to demand reciprocation. Eventually laborers organized to protest wages and working conditions. As Paul Mason recounts, this collective force was good for more than just wage negotiations—it was a venue for mutual support: "During 1819, all over northern England, workers set up night schools and clubs, debated politics, elected delegates to town wide committees and formed women's groups" (Mason, 2015: 182). Collectives allowed laborers to share in the financial benefits of industrialization, even while the real wealth was being concentrated in the hands of a few. In order for those with wealth to produce more wealth, they had to compete. To compete they had to grow, and to grow they needed labor—and thus had to acknowledge the collective. It was not quite a workers' utopia, of course. Suitable working conditions were still a long way off, and rights were far from being inclusive or universal. Sweatshops, servitude, peonage, and even slavery existed then as now. Still, it was the beginning of an organized working class and the birth of a new sort of social solidarity (Graeber, 2011: 351; Robbins *et al.*, 2014: 104).

In mainstream capitalism the benefits (productivity, competitive advantage, and profit) are only realized with growth. Labor, while necessary for production, is a cost. Thus mechanisms which reduce labor costs while maintaining or increasing productivity are attractive to those with capital investment. For example, an owner could reduce wages, replace skilled workers with unskilled, or reduce the workforce through automation. All were attempted and met with violent labor resistance in early capitalism. The success of organized resistance led to a dramatic increase in labor solidarity movements, and by the World War I era labor unions were forces to be reckoned with. A response, used with great success by Henry Ford and eventually many others, was to make the work process ultra-efficient, such that fewer workers doing simple, repetitive tasks could actually increase productivity via assembly line. The production benefits of this approach are undeniable, but the effect on the individual worker is more dubious. Relegation to a menial, unskilled role, as Karl Marx argued, removes the individual from meaningful contribution to the enterprise (Marx, 1976 [1844]). It also makes the worker more expendable—and with expendability comes a lesser capacity to protest injustice (Robbins *et al.*, 2014: 105; Mason, 2015: 187–189).

Of course, another way to reduce costs and grow profits is to exploit natural resources in the cheapest way possible. Mass production, in Marx's words, can thus be "a progress in the art, not only of robbing the worker, but of robbing the soil" (Marx, 1976 [1867]: 637–638). This sort of capitalism is a great source of ecological stress, a topic of the next chapter.

Labor unions retained strength after World War II, both in the Allied nations and in certain quarters of the defeated Axis, where the right to organize was affirmed by the victors. Wages, taxes, and social welfare programs increased in the cold war era of capitalistic nations, with a corresponding growth in the number of white-collar, salaried positions. But the influence of labor unions has since waned, accompanied by what Mason (2015) calls the "atomization" of the workforce. By this he means that the workforce (particularly in developed nations) has become more stratified and splintered, and labor solidarity more disintegrated. By the mid-1980s:

> western capitalism, which had coexisted with organized labor and been shaped by it for nearly two centuries, could no longer live with a working-class structure of solidarity and resistance. Through off-shoring, de-industrialization, anti-union laws and a relentless ideological warfare, it would be destroyed.
>
> (Mason, 2015: 199)

Mason argues that labor in developed nations has since taken on a core–periphery model, in which a "core" of trained and educated employees hold salaried, credentialed positions with benefits, while the "periphery" are relegated to temporary, hourly, and expendable positions. The skilled industrial workforce in developed nations has contracted, prompting more people to find employment in the service sector. Manufacturing has become highly automated and increasingly takes place in less developed nations, where environmental and labor regulations are lighter and wages are lower. What this all means is that working class positions are less dependent on indispensable skills, that labor solidarity has been weakened, and that the workforce is consequently more isolated, vulnerable, and unfulfilled (Mason, 2015: 207; Chen, 2016).

Another front in the ongoing battle to maintain economic growth is the effort to ward off stagnation. Low consumer confidence, constricted productivity, curtailed borrowing, reduced investment and unemployment can feed on one another to the detriment of a market-based economy, leading to recession and even depression. In response, capitalistic nations have acted according to the economics of John Maynard Keynes (1883–1946), tinkering with the system repeatedly to stimulate growth. One such measure is for the central government to manipulate interest rates to encourage (or discourage) borrowing and spending. A second idea is the detachment of currency from a standard backing, like gold, thus enabling the creation of more money. In 1931 England abandoned the gold standard, and the US started down the same path in 1933—culminating in the complete separation of the dollar from the gold standard in 1971. Ever since, the global market has run on fiat money—paper with the illusion of value. The fictional wealth of printed money allows for increased spending and can therefore be used to ward off stagnation. Third, financialization, or the extension of credit far and wide, is a tool used to allow people (and businesses, and nations) to continue to consume despite the immediate ability to pay. Thus "credit cards, overdrafts, mortgages, student loans and motor car loans became a part of everyday life" (Mason, 2015: 16). This has spurred a new wave of consumerism in the affluent world, for nearly anything one desires is a mere card swipe or mouse click away, with no payment necessary until next month or next year—even in times of flat wages (Mason, 2015: 16–20).

The effects of financialization reach far beyond the personal credit card. In some respects the entire western economic system runs on credit and debt. Banks, for instance, have the ability to create and lend money that they do not physically possess. Such loans must be paid back with interest, which requires the borrowing entity to expand its economic capacity. In many cases this can only be achieved with further use of credit, and the debt-spiral continues to grow. Much has been written about this peculiar system, but I will highlight just two problems: an ecological and a social side effect. First, the ecological effect. The modern economic house of cards is built upon ever-increasing credit, and ultimately access to more credit is based on ever-increasing demand for natural resources. The system is perpetuated in part because it is profitable. Indeed, in modern capitalism much monetary exchange is not for goods or services, but in service of debt. When debt itself is a commodity, there is incentive to create more of it. The dilemma is twofold: we can't create more natural resources, and the ecological stress we generate can diminish ecosystem services (Dietz and O'Neill, 2013: 103–106).

The social side effect is that the system encourages economic disparity (Robbins *et al.*, 2014: 110). People, cultures, and environments in the developing world are exploited to feed the insatiable consumerism and demand for economic growth in synthetic society. In the affluent world there is a growing wealth gap, as the educated elite achieve a level of comfortable prosperity while peripheral workers become stuck on the debt treadmill in low wage, low benefit positions with little chance of advancement. The power is in the hands of those with the capital: the directors of corporate finance and the majority shareholders. The thriving affluent, far removed from menial labor and from the sites of resource extraction and waste disposal, have little reason to protest the system. To the contrary, they are deeply invested in a system of perennially greater production and higher profits. It is those who endure the hardships of resource extraction, those who must live with the associated pollution, those who work at the source of production, and those on the economic periphery who have legitimate cause for protest—but in many cases they lack the agency to change their situation. Certain people, it seems, always hold the advantage, while many others are always at a disadvantage (Wilkinson and Pickett, 2010).

The detrimental effects of capitalism on cooperative reciprocity were foretold in the mid-18th century by Adam Smith. Smith promoted the societal advantages of individual economic liberty, arguing that individuals acting in their self-interest could support the public good, for he saw "self-interest" as a component of reciprocity and the free market as a means to best meet the needs of all participants. And yet, Smith anticipated the problems of selfishness and greed. He saw that the privileged few could undermine the social contract and corrode the public good. In Smith's vision, the individual economic freedom of the market should not be an unlimited freedom. The freedom ought to end where injury to others begins (Smith, 1976 [1759]; Collins and Barkdull, 1995: 232).

According to Smith it is the "impartial spectator" of our social conscience that keeps us from straying from self-interest into selfishness. This ancient rule of social control is part of our evolutionary inheritance. Failing this, Smith argued, it should be government's role to simultaneously provide individuals the freedom to pursue self-interest while ensuring that economic actions do not result in individual or collective harm. Smith was not writing about environmental concerns, but the implications are clear. The "public good" includes the conservation of natural resources and ecosystem services, the provision for human health and dignity, and equitable access to biological and social necessities. In Smith's writing we can see the tensions between the capacities of free market capitalism to achieve "public good" and the human tendencies toward selfishness. Does capitalism promote the common good, including environmental concerns, or is it a machine of social and environmental destruction? Two and a half centuries after Smith posed the question it is still fiercely debated (Smith, 1976 [1759]; Collins and Barkdull, 1995).

Capitalism and environmental concerns

In *Ecology against capitalism*, John Bellamy Foster provides a multifaceted case against the economic system that has come to dominate the world. The overarching issue, he writes, is that "capitalist economies are geared first and foremost to the growth of profits, and hence to economic growth at virtually any cost—including the exploitation and misery of the vast majority of the world's population" (Foster, 2002: 10). Within this general and fundamental failing, there are several specific criticisms of capitalism.

I have touched on one argument already—the idea that impersonal capitalism removes the investor and the consumer from the material and context of production.

Here is a simple example. If I grow my own tomatoes, I know everything about their origin. I'm careful to build, not deplete, the soil in my garden, and I think long and hard to choose options of pest control that will not harm my own health or that of my family. If I own a tomato farm large enough to employ workers, their well-being is important to me, because I know them personally and a happy worker is a good worker. Now, imagine that I don't raise tomatoes at all but instead I buy them from a farmer one county away. It is her responsibility to take care of soil, plants, and workers, but I know her personally and I trust her judgement and reputation (and if I didn't, I would buy my tomatoes elsewhere). Her tomato operation, by the way, is capitalism at work—but it is the personal capitalism of face-to-face exchange. Adam Smith's "impartial spectator" is party to each transaction, providing a measure of assurance that people and resources are treated with respect.

The *impersonal* capitalism model goes like this: I buy my tomatoes from a supermarket. I don't know where they come from, how the land is cared for, what pesticides are used, or how the workers are treated. I don't know if the location of origin regulates environmental or human rights at all. The producers may in fact be fine, upstanding, and environmentally conscientious citizens, or they may be human-trafficking, drug-smuggling polluters. I have no way of knowing, and this essentially absolves me from a certain amount of social responsibility. The producer is also absolved from the responsibility of facing me, the consumer; thus the producer's "impartial spectator" has likewise been removed from the transaction. The story works the same way if I am an investor in the corporation that produces the tomatoes. Unless I am very diligent in my investment choices, I have no direct knowledge of how the operation is run and no obligation to find out. In the impersonal model, then, there is reciprocal exchange, but it seems that the cooperative aspect has been lost.

Simply stated, this argument is that impersonal capitalism circumvents our social assurances of forthright behavior. It removes our connection with the place, people, and resources by which the product is created (Foster, 2002: 88). This is not an argument against capitalism as such, only the socially and environmentally blind transactions toward which capitalism trends. Close connections between producer and consumer, while they still might be based on the free market, maintain the social checks and balances with which humans have evolved. Hawken *et al.* (1999) have called this natural capitalism—it is the inclusion of human social capital in the exchange of natural capital.

You might observe in the tomato example that I am simply a lazy consumer. I should eat only what I grow if I am so concerned about environmental quality and human rights, or I should do my homework on the companies in which I invest and from which I purchase tomatoes. Fair enough. But what if I need a new furnace or cell phone or car? These are complex items with many parts, manu-factured in many locations with raw materials from all over the world. There is not just one corporation involved here, there are many, and some are probably subsidiaries of others. The on-the-ground and in-the-factory actions of all of the players are often unknown and virtually unknowable. As a consumer, perhaps even a diligent consumer, I am woefully ignorant of the environmental and social costs of many of my purchases. The "invisible hand" of the free market is in this case based only on the cost of the tomatoes, for I know nothing else about them. Adam Smith, were he here, might sigh and shrug and invoke his fallback plan: if consumer choice can't guide the actions of the producer, then government regulation must. This brings me to a second criticism of free market capitalism (Smith, 1976 [1759]).

In the last half-century we have indeed experienced a dramatic increase in environmental protection efforts by way of government intervention. The late 1960s and 1970s saw a surge in environmental legislation in the United States, such as the National Environmental Policy Act, the Clean Water Act and Clean Air Act, as well as the creation of agencies like the Environmental Protection Agency and Natural Resource Conservation Service. Canada created its Department of the Environment at about the same time, as did Australia. Europe in this period initiated a series of Environmental Action Programmes aimed at waste avoidance and the reduction of emissions, effluents, and associated environmental damage through incentives, taxes, subsidies, and permits. Similar, though later, regulation has been instituted in South Korea, Japan, and elsewhere. Such regulation, while not perfect in its implementation or compliance, has certainly improved the air, water, and land quality of the nations that have enacted it. However, the lack of any substantial international regulation has meant that resource- and labor-hungry corporations, driven by consumer demand for low prices and investor demand for continuous growth, can seek to extract raw materials, employ inexpensive labor, and operate pollution-intensive manufacturing centers in regions of the world that are not as tightly regulated (Rothman, 1998). The resultant outsourcing of production facilities and jobs to less developed regions of the world—and the competition difficulties this has created for local business—has precipitated a push for deregulation in wealthier sectors. In theory, Adam Smith was correct that government regulation can protect the public good. Globally uneven regulation, however, simply moves the pollution, the exploitation, and the environmental damage to areas of the world that have a much smaller capacity to remediate such problems.

This raises the question of the global commons, a third environmental criticism of free market capitalism. As Garrett Hardin (1915–2003) famously described in *The tragedy of the commons* (1968), humans rely on the common *goods* of natural resources, such as fossil fuels, clean water, land, plants, and animals. We also collectively create common *bads* like pollution, contamination, garbage, and eroded soil. Capitalism gives entrepreneurs the right to purchase a portion of the commons at fair market value and to use these resources to create a marketable product. It also has assumed, until quite recently, that ecosystem services need not be considered in economic exchange (Gómez-Baggethun et al., 2010). It does not, however, often hold the entrepreneur accountable for the common bad. Thus any water pollution, greenhouse gas emissions, soil loss, or ecological stress—assuming these happen at levels allowed by regulation—are the responsibility of the public, not the private venture (Hardin, 1968).

Economists call these *externalities*, and those to which I refer here are specifically called negative externalities. If a paper mill in the United States, for example, is operating within the bounds of government regulation, it may be permitted to release a certain amount of effluent into the local river. If a dozen regional paper mills do the same, the river may have a pollution problem; often in this situation it is effluent of cellulose fibers that decompose in the river and thereby reduce the oxygen availability, sometimes resulting in the death of aquatic organisms. This is a loss of ecosystem function for the public. Since the cost is not borne by the business, the prices of its products are artificially low. Of course, some production owners may seek to reduce their environmental impact on their own. But voluntary implementation of pollution control measures may raise the price of the product, potentially placing the producer at a competitive disadvantage. So the effluent goes untreated, and the stream is degraded.

An important point here is that the common resource can be damaged *even if all participants are abiding by the rules*. So how can we prevent the degradation of the common resource? An obvious solution is simply to quantify the damage done (or ecosystem services used) by each participant and to make them pay for it. In some respects this is already happening, in the form of emissions trading, carbon credits, pollution taxes, and payments for ecosystem services (Gómez-Baggethun *et al.*, 2010: 1214). But Foster has argued that truly internalizing all of the environmental social costs of production is not an acceptable solution, for even if these costs could be calculated and incorporated the action would still result in degradation of the resource, and any loss of ecological function would lower the value of the commons and facilitate further degradation (Foster, 2002: 33–34).

Hardin theorized that self-interested individuals will seek to augment their production and profit by increasing their use of common resources at the expense of other users of the commons—and in fact, to the ultimate devastation of the common resource itself. In the same way, self-interested individuals (or states, businesses, or corporations) can generate negative externalities like pollution and cumulatively destroy the commons. "Freedom in the commons," according to Hardin, "brings ruin to all." Hardin's primary solution, like Smith's, was regulation: "mutual coercion, mutually agreed upon" (1968: 1243–1248). And indeed, many localities and nations have implemented regulations to prevent overexploitation of open access resources and to limit harvest, emission, effluent, and other environmental harms. Still, the individual economic freedoms of capitalism clash with the concept of common natural resources. Climate change caused by greenhouse gas emission is a good example. Burning fossil fuels is my right, and if I want to start a business that burns fossil fuel on a large scale that is my right as well. Regulation of carbon emissions is only just beginning to be proposed—and is hotly contested—but even if I am limited by regulation, my carbon emissions contribute to a major environmental problem. Climate change is already causing ecological and economic harm around the world, the pace and extent of which are almost sure to increase. In free market capitalism, though, I am not liable for these costs (at least not at present). In fact, I am to a certain extent locked into the system. If I am concerned about climate change and conscientiously alter my operation to use a non-carbon fuel, the market could work against me. My costs might be higher than those of the competition, and I'll have to rely on the consumer's willingness to pay for a climate-friendly but more expensive product.

The tragedy of the commons leads to the problem of equity. Who is profiting in this system, and who is suffering? Capitalism by definition is a system for those with capital, whether it is borrowed, earned, inherited, or shared. The individual, organization, or corporation with the wealth to invest bears the risk, and also stands to benefit the most. Others may benefit as well, like suppliers, employees, partners, subsidiaries, and affiliated individuals who have a job because of the endeavor. Local, regional, and national tax bases may also benefit, and to the extent that these taxes are used for the public good, each tax jurisdiction benefits too. Of course, resources used today may be non-renewable or otherwise spoiled in the process, and thus the action may be intergenerationally unfair. Additionally, the business enterprise may require materials or resources from other parts of the world, where environmental and labor laws are weak or non-existent; people in these areas may be exploited because of the enterprise, and no tax dollars come to support them in return. The negative externalities like pollution produced by the business may affect certain locations in particular, or large regions, or the entire planet. Wealthy populations will have the means to regulate and remediate these effects, while poor populations will not. This encourages the exploitation of people with the least capacity for resilience and resistance (Daly and Farley, 2004: 329). The point is that the free market system does not extend its freedom equally to everyone. It is a pay-to-play system.

Perhaps the greatest environmental argument against capitalism is that a system of constant growth is untenable, given that production relies ultimately on finite raw materials. Fossil fuels are nonrenewable. Arable land and photosynthetic capacity are limited. Minerals, freshwater, and ecosystem services are recyclable and renewable but not infinite. The specter of ever-increasing demand conjures a Malthusian image of humans surpassing the planet's capacity to meet their demand. Corporate capitalism, meanwhile, is short-sighted. It is designed to convert commodities into profits quickly. Long-term thinking, like conservation and restraint with regard to resource use, is discouraged, for it will only raise the price of goods and services. Besides, someone else will surely be willing to exploit the resource and out-compete the conservation-minded business. The whole system encourages unrestrained consumption fueled by the demands of an ever-growing human appetite (Foster, 2002: 48–49).

Arguments to this effect are not new. They reached a crescendo in the 1960s and 1970s, when Donella Meadows, Paul Ehrlich, E.F. Schumacher, Rachel Carson, Barry Commoner, and others drew Malthusian conclusions from projections of population growth, capitalism, and resource demand. Schumacher, in his book *Small is beautiful*, noted the two basic problems with a system of unlimited economic growth: finite natural capital (i.e. natural resources), and a limited capacity of ecosystems to function amid anthropogenic stress (Schumacher, 1999 [1973]: 17). Further, he recognized that the global market does not impose demands on resources evenly. Natural and human capital are being depleted, stressed, and exploited far more extensively and rapidly in areas lacking wealth and power. Short-term profitability, Schumacher argued, should not be the only motive for economic activity. It should also consider the effects on humans and on the environment (McRobie, 1999; Schumacher, 1999 [1973]: 28). Failing this, impersonal capitalism renders its participants blind to environmental and social consequences.

From the Miscellaneous Gripes file, let's consider a few other problems with mainstream capitalism. First, the market is hardly a level playing field. Businesses and the individuals who stand to profit from them have enormous influence over government policy. Thus government subsidies prop up some industries over others and favor some with weak regulation, loans, subsidies, and bailouts. The worst players among major corporations also find ways to evade taxes, with many profitable corporations paying no net income tax to any nation (Kristoff, 2016). In this way the system caters to those with the means to provide for themselves at the expense of those who do not. Second, the end consumer often has little idea about the social or environmental impacts of products because the purveyors are not required to disclose those impacts. The developed world has come a long way in terms of nutrition labeling for food—imagine if the consumer also knew about genetic modification, pesticide use, region of origin, and any sustainable practices or human rights or environmental violations of the parent company and its sub-sidiaries in the same way they knew about calories and sodium content. Too much for a label, I agree, but the internet would be a fine place for such information, available with a quick scan. Comprehensive labeling would allow for highly educated consumers and would promote freedom of choice—and it is therefore fiercely opposed by corporate interests (Smythe, 2009).

Third, since constant growth relies on continuous demand, it behooves the manufacturer to produce products that will need to be replaced or upgraded. This planned obsolescence can take the form of a substandard part in an otherwise high quality piece of equipment, or a version of the product that is due to be phased out and incompatible with future versions. The goal, of course, is to create the need for the next purchase. Fourth, many companies make it very easy to finance purchases and banks are eager to lend, even to consumers without appropriate means. This encourages the act of buying on credit and continues the cycle of debt, for those purchases come with interest and finance charges. Fifth, capitalism is accompanied by incessant marketing that understands well and preys upon the evolutionary penchant for acquisition, ostentation, and waste, especially as directed by peer pressure and celebrity endorsement. All things considered, the system is designed to encourage people to buy stuff they don't need from manu-facturers they don't know with money they don't have, and to buy more as soon as possible.

In summary, the environmental case against impersonal capitalism is rather strong. It removes the consumer from a knowledge of the resource base and the labor of production, thus weakening our collective social conscience. It creates social relationships of exploitation, not cooperative reciprocity. Uneven regu-lation shunts problems of extraction, pollution, and labor to developing regions of the world. It rewards entrepreneurs and investors with the profits of production but does not hold them accountable for accompanying problems, like pollution and ecological stress; instead, these are complications that the public must bear. It demands constant economic growth from a finite resource base. Given all these criticisms, well and loudly articulated over the last 50 years, one might think that capitalism has been checked, restricted, or slowed in response. This has not been the case. To the contrary, capitalism has expanded, regulation has been called into question, and impersonal business has come to dominate the global economy. Advocates for capitalism, far from acquiescing to environmental and social criticism, have instead argued that capitalism is a mechanism for the greatest good.

Capitalist counterarguments

In his book *Small is stupid* (1995), Wilfred Beckerman argues that capitalism is a great societal—and even environmental—force for the public good. Several of his points will be reviewed below, but in general the thought is this: poverty is the worst enemy of the environment, and economic growth spurs the innovation and infrastructure development that lifts people out of poverty. Far from seeking to slow growth, then, we should seek to grow the economy faster, for economic growth in developed nations provides expanding markets in developing nations. As people grow richer, Beckerman argues, they are more secure and are more likely to prioritize environmental problems. Their communities, also wealthier because of capitalism, will have more resources to allocate toward environmental solutions (Beckerman, 1995).

To the first criticism of capitalism that I have posed—the disconnection of the consumer from the natural resources and human labor of production—there is an obvious counterargument. For certain commodities, like tomatoes, it makes perfect sense for the consumer to have close connection with a small local producer. Of course, this means that tomatoes are only regionally and seasonally available; but if the price, quality, and experience are acceptable, local production is appropriate within the free market. However, we can't produce everything locally. It makes little sense for each region to have its own copper mine, seafood processor, and window factory. The necessary resources aren't available everywhere, for one, and it would be clumsy and redundant to have everything produced everywhere. Even if we could, consumers would probably still seek out the best deal, and it is quite likely that certain production centers would outcompete others. The system would thus revert to a global market. Additionally, there are efficiencies of scale with larger operations, even when taking transportation costs into consideration. Decentralized production can certainly work in some situations, but in general it is wasteful. We've already been through this, and we call it socioeconomic evolution. Small, Beckerman says, is stupid (Beckerman, 1995).

The criticism that capitalism allows for production of environmentally destructive "public bads" for which businesses are not held responsible also has a ready rebuttal. The market, the counterargument goes, also allows for the production of environmentally *friendly* products, services, and technologies that contribute to the "public good"—which are not reflected in market valuations and "that are usually ignored by those who are determined to conclude that economic growth is harmful" (Beckerman, 1995: 111). These include dramatic improvements in health care, nutrition, energy, transportation, and most other sectors, which are largely improved due to market-driven innovation. Beckerman also cites "public capital," such as hospitals, libraries, schools, parks, and the like, which are funded by taxes made possible by economic growth. This is not to imply that the market cares for the public good. It does not. But it will serve sustainable products to individuals who care just as well as it serves environmentally destructive products to those who don't care. The same argument can be made for recycled materials, organic foods, responsibly sourced goods, and ultra-efficient appliances—all are market driven. Beckerman acknowledges that there are negative externalities of production and that these are generally not accounted for in the market. He believes that environmental and social impacts need to be quantified, but stops short of the idea that the costs, once quantified, should be added to the costs of the good or services. This would slow economic growth, which in Beckerman's view is the opposite of what we should do (Beckerman, 1995: 111–113).

As to the tragedy of the commons, the capitalist might reply that problems of the commons are problems of open access (Daly and Farley, 2004: 161). Where there are clear and defensible property rights, there is no tragedy (Anderson and Leal, 2001: 22–26). Thus privatization of resources, the argument goes, makes sense if the goal is to maximize the efficiency of resource use and to prevent the scenario in which resources are over-subscribed and depleted to the satisfaction of none. The problem is that we can't easily extend private property rights to the ocean, to the atmosphere, or to ecosystem services like pollination, for example. These are subject to Hardin's tragedy, and unfortunately we are witnessing the results: the collapse of oceanic fisheries, the rapid increase of greenhouse gases in the atmosphere, and the demise of bees, respectively. The capitalist rebuttal is that *any* system in which natural resources are used by seven and a half billion people is going to have negative impacts on common property. At least capitalism takes place in the conduct of the market, and market principles have successfully solved some problems of the global commons. For instance, the worldwide phase-out of chlorofluorocarbons has slowed the loss of stratospheric ozone while allowing for a market-driven and environmentally friendly alternative. The same can be said for improvements in automobile fuel efficiency. These changes have come—are coming—about because of market pressures, but also because of regulation, which even Beckerman agrees is necessary to correct "market imperfections." Left unregulated, he observes, "the environment will not be managed in a socially optimal manner" (Beckerman, 1995: 140).

That globally uneven regulation disproportionally allows for dubious enterprise in developing regions of the world is not the fault of the market, the capitalist might claim. The market simply responds to regulation where it exists. (Of course, a keen observer might point out that corporations and wealthy individuals spend an enormous amount of money every year opposing and circumventing regulation.) As to the broader question of regulating quality of life and exploitation, the mantra is this: the free market provides the greatest economic good for the greatest number of people. The problem, of course, is that some values are not easily converted to dollars or bought and sold on the market, and in some ways this makes them less amenable to regulation. Indigenous tradition, for example, as well as spiritual fulfillment, access to beautiful and sacred places, freedom, security, psychological well-being—none of these have an easily quantifiable market value or easily defined criteria for regulation. Further, attempts to commodify and regulate these intangibles by assigning them market values reduces the irreducible, and will effectively destroy each (Foster, 2002: 32). Thus the purchase and clear-cut of old growth tropical forest makes perfect sense economically but no sense environmentally or for the human inhabitants of the forest. Until the intangibles are recognized as immeasurable values and offered globally uniform protection, there will continue to be market-driven inequity.

The criticism that I billed as potentially the greatest—that constant growth is not possible with finite resources—is dismissed as a non-issue by Beckerman (1995: 55–57). Despite dramatically increased rates of use of minerals and fossil fuels since the "limits to growth" arguments of the 1970s, he points out, reserves have increased and prices have fallen. New reserves of resources are found as demand grows, and there is no reason to expect this to end in the near future. The capitalist argues that the free market discourages waste and therefore results in the most efficient use of those resources. This view is extremely short-sighted, of course, meaning that nonrenewable resources will ultimately be depleted, no matter the efficiency of use. A wonderfully efficient running form does not matter much if the runner is sprinting toward a cliff. But Beckerman does not expect us to go over the cliff anytime soon. Furthermore, in his view, when it does happen it will be gradual, not immediate, and in situations of gradually growing scarcity, capitalism spurs innovation. As nonrenewable resources become scarce, inefficient or prohibitively expensive, there will be great financial incentives to develop and market new alternatives. Thus, for example, fiber optics will replace copper, aquaculture will replace wild fish harvest, and hydrogen-based fuel will replace carbon-based fuel, just as LED lights are currently replacing incandescent lights. And yet, environmentalists contend, even the alternatives rely on raw material, and we have only so much raw material. The alternatives also require energy, and the amount of work achieved cannot exceed the energy used to achieve it. The free market ultimately cannot save us from the problem of resource limits, it can only tell us *not yet.*

Foster points out a fallacy in this view of free market innovation as the answer to resource depletion. The market, he reminds us, is designed for profit. Scarce resources are highly valuable, particularly if there is resistance to an alternative. As long as there are people willing to pay big money to maintain a lifestyle of consumption, there will be purveyors at the ready. So the market may not facilitate a shift to cleaner fuels, or protected fisheries, or more efficient vehicles, or less wasteful lifestyles. It just means that the dirty fuels, threatened fish, gas-guzzlers, and waste disposal will be available only to those who can afford them (Foster, 2002: 99).

Alternatives to capitalism

Economic systems are fundamentally about what is produced or procured in a society, how and where the production is done, how (and by whom) the produced goods or services are consumed, and who profits. Regardless of where you stand on the matter of capitalism as curse or savior, it is undeniable that much of the world—largely driven by the demands of synthetic society—has accepted it as a way of life. It is also undeniable that, however theoretically appropriate, and however much good for the greatest number, the free market has been environmentally and socially destructive for many, particularly those in a state of subsistence. Corporate capitalism in particular has promoted individualistic behavior over mechanisms of social control. In response, a number of alternatives to mainstream capitalism have been proposed or employed, all aimed in various ways at checking the human tendency for selfishness.

The mixed economy

This first category is really not an alternative to capitalism, it is more of a tempered capitalism. A number of ideas have been proposed to allow the best aspects of the market—like innovation and job creation—to continue while regulating the more dubious practices. One such system proposes that private business should exist but under a much stronger regulatory structure, such that actions of financial institutions are subject to government oversight, thus curtailing socially and environmentally destructive lending. In this "mixed economy" model the social essentials—food, water, energy, health care, waste treatment—are state-owned, supported by relatively high taxes. This is essentially a hybrid between capitalist and socialist structures. It exists in various forms, from the democratic socialism of Scandinavian nations to the community capitalism model of Jiangsu Province, China (Nee and Cao, 1999; Brejning, 2013: 55–56). The idea is still at heart reliant on the system of production and optimistic about the innovation of new technologies to solve future problems. Is such a model environmentally better? It depends, of course, on the level and intention of regulation. It is plausible that environmental degradation and contamination could be effectively managed within a given nation in a system of regulated technocentrism. In fact most developed nations of the world essentially have some version of this system already (though the internal regulation is variable). The real question is whether regulation can encourage environmentally and socially sensitive business on a global scale. This seems unlikely in our nearly anarchical system of transnational corporate economics.

Participatory economics

Participatory economics is another form of capitalism, just one that aims to mitigate the profit-only motive (Helbing, 2013). One idea is that businesses should be run by worker cooperatives, rather than a few individuals with concentrated power. When workers have a voice, the thought goes, concerns about workplace conditions, equity, and ancillary effects are necessarily considered along with the quarterly profit report. In another vision, oversight by panels of stakeholders who are not employed by the business would be required prior to and during development, extraction, and production. In both models, people who have a vested interest in profit and also those with an interest in social and environmental concerns would have a seat at the decision-making table. Critics point out that such a wide variety of interests would make it difficult and far less efficient for any innovation or new development to move forward. It would be easy to see, for example, how bauxite extraction for aluminum manufacture could be nixed by local concerns anywhere in the world, thus requiring alternative materials that would make production prohibitively expensive. It is also conceivable that a worker-run cooperative seeking enhanced benefits would be nonviable in the face of competition from more draconian producers (Collins and Barkdull, 1995).

Another version of participatory economics approaches business from the direction of finance (Helbing, 2013: 17–18). Rather than practicing business on the model of impersonal loans from banks or unknown shareholders, could business enterprise be funded by interested individuals who understand and support the mission of the proposed work? This is being done already, albeit on a small scale. Community-supported agriculture is a subscriber-driven business, in which consumers invest prior to production and then share in the production, less overhead costs and profit for the producers. The slow money movement is similar: business is funded by individual investors independent of banks. The advantage of these models is that the investors have intimate (or at least virtual) connection with the mission, values, and practices of the enterprise. Business owners then have the obligation to remain true to their mission and values, or risk losing investors. It seems to work well for small operations, particularly in the local agriculture sector. It is harder to imagine a billion-dollar ball bearing factory being financed in this way.

Socialism

Socialism in various forms has been proposed or attempted as an alternative to capitalism. A common theme to socialist ideas is the notion of collective ownership. In this model some group of mutually interested citizens—in some variations the workers, but in other cases the general public or the state—holds all of the capital and completely controls the means of production. The idea of collective ownership, at least on paper, seems to hold some promise for the consideration of ideals other than profit and economic growth. A collective economy, for example, might be able to conserve common resources, or perhaps recognize the interdependence of human and ecological processes. The German philosopher Friedrich Engels (1820–1895) envisioned this, noting that humans can escape the evolutionary "struggle for existence" with a "social production . . . of conscious organization on a planned basis" (Engels, 1947 [1878]; Parsons, 1977: 49).

His collaborator Karl Marx (1818–1883), for his part, recognized the evolutionary origins of humans as a long process of communal ownership, in which the resources of nature were the "property of the community," with each individual as "proprietor or possessor" (Marx, 1993 [1939]; Merchant, 2008: 51). Further, Engels saw capitalism as a system of exploitation, waste, and pollution; a "huckstering of the Earth" by a few profit-seekers (Engels, 1932 [1844]; Parsons, 1977; Merchant, 2008: 53–54). From these and other early philosophical views, many forms of socialism have arisen. However, an economic system driven by a socialist environmentalism is as yet elusive. What might such a system look like?

We already know what it does not look like. The dominant socialist regimes of the 20th century—notably the Soviet Union and China—have been lessons in the capacity for socialist environmental degradation. Industrialization, militarization, and despotism in these socialist experiments have rivaled or exceeded the social and environmental problems of capitalism. Though systems of state control, they still sing the same refrain as capitalism—production, growth, and large-scale centralization—while largely ignoring the social and environmental costs of development. In Schumacher's view, a system that emphasizes equitable quality of life—one that combines group planning and individual freedom—would be an improvement, regardless of ownership (Schumacher, 1999 [1973]: 214–220). But some major attempts at socialism have demonstrated its failings: poor allocation of resources, inefficiency, inability to plan, consumer discontent, abuse of human rights, and a lack of incentive for innovation (Mason, 2015: 226).

Others have called for collective governance of technology and human rights by the working class in an ecologically oriented socialism, driven by the twin "issues of social justice and ecological justice" (O'Connor, 1998; Merchant, 2008: 192). In the vision of economist James O'Connor, an ecological socialism would have a local emphasis, but would also need regional, national, and international buy-in to adequately address interrelated and global environmental concerns. It would be based on reciprocity between both human interests and their ecological imperatives; it would be democratic and planned at multiple levels. O'Connor states that existing and past socialist regimes have largely failed to acknowledge the environmental conditions and human relations of production. Incorporating social movements that represent these views would lead to a more democratic, transparent, and sustainable system. In evolutionary terms, this is a call for a resurgence and extension of the cooperative reciprocity that impersonal capitalism tends to ignore or include only narrowly. In fact it is an attempt to *institutionalize* cooperative reciprocity, and that is where the difficulty lies (O'Connor, 1998; Merchant, 2008: 154, 194).

The political economist Elinor Ostrom has argued that specific resources can be successfully managed by a plurality of local interests in productive and sustainable ways. In fact, she has demonstrated that such management can be stable through collective ownership and self-organization, without coercive government regulation. Criteria that allow for such a model include clear boundaries of the resource and the users, clear rules of appropriation that are compatible with local ecologies, active participation of stakeholders in collective agreements, effective monitoring of both the resource and the users, clear sanctions for violations of the agreed-upon rules of use, and conflict resolution mechanisms that recognize the rights of individuals and the principles of self-governance (Ostrom, 2010: 653). These conditions are remarkably similar to the interpersonal, relational, and communal ways in which small bands of humans have managed resources for thousands of generations.

Ecocentric economics

A more radical approach to political economy calls for a restructuring of the ways in which humans interact with one another and with the world. Schumacher refers to this as a Buddhist economics; it is an ecocentric, rather than egocentric, approach to human livelihood. In this system, labor is useful if it is meaningful and fulfilling to the individual and community; it is not simply a necessity for individual or business profit. Work that builds the human character builds the society, and work that dehumanizes and demeans does the opposite. Given its emphasis on social interaction and ecological sensitivity, this sort of economic system is often associated with localism—a rejection of centralized corporate and national power (Soborski, 2013). Ecocentric economics does not deny that humans need material possessions for well-being, but it questions the value of consumption beyond necessity. In the same way, it acknowledges that humans rely on the resources of the natural world, and it therefore promotes a lifestyle that facilitates utility for the next generation. It is a system of voluntary simplicity, in which the acquisition of goods is not the measure of success or wealth. It also recognizes the difference between renewable and nonrenewable resources. Capitalism does not make such a distinction; energy and resources are simply regarded by their current unit price and used accordingly. Nonrenewable resources, in ecocentric economics, should be conserved; they should be used only for necessity in the absence of alternatives. Renewable resources, when used, should be renewed—meaning that trees should be planted, aquifers should be recharged, and fisheries should allow for reproduction of the next generation of fish. Ecocentric economics takes the long-term view (Schumacher, 1999 [1973]).

Schumacher's vision, slightly repackaged, is sometimes known as steady-state or zero-growth economy. A steady-state economy would still allow for private ownership, innovation, and market transaction, but the amount of material flowing through the system—and hence the level of consumption—is carefully managed. Resource use, in this system, would be limited by the rate of resource renewal, and waste production limited by the processing rate. Education, basic income, and employment would be guaranteed. Wage gaps would be regulated, as would lending. And a different model of progress and success would be used, measuring happiness, fulfillment, and quality of life as the bottom line instead of profit. This is all achievable with a major change in mindset and enough government oversight to make a free market capitalist shudder: bans, rationing, tradable permits, taxes, subsidized education, government-created jobs, subsidized income, mandated wage ranges, restricted lending, and restructured international finance rules. As encroachments on individual freedoms in the marketplace, these might be a difficult sell in the current political climate. In response, champions of the steady-state economy argue that business as usual is simply untenable (Daly, 1991; Dietz and O'Neill, 2013).

Bookchin (1982, 1986, 1989) extends ecocentric economics to the elimination of all hierarchies, such that decision-making would be collaborative and inclusive. He bases this on the egalitarianism of foraging societies, which (as characterized by Carolyn Merchant) are "neither superior nor inferior to nonhuman nature," but within it (Merchant, 2005: 148). His is a dialectic approach, in which all interested parties would have a seat at the table—a direct, face-to-face democracy—and therefore a role in seeking the best path forward for the collective. In this way the socioeconomic system would mimic a food web, in which (according to Bookchin) species are equal and their interaction achieves a natural balance. Bookchin's concept is regionalist; it is based on the idea that human societies must exist within the context of their biomes by choosing regionally appropriate agriculture, technology, and infrastructure. This, too, recalls the foraging society, in which people are limited by the capacity of their biogeographical setting. Needless to say, this model of political economy is a far cry from our current existence (and to Bookchin, this is exactly the point). It is unclear how such a transformation might be achieved.

The ecocentric economic systems proposed here might be variously seen as plausible, eccentric, radical, or outlandish. To the mainstream capitalist they make little sense, and are even counter-productive. The standard of living, in the prevailing capitalist view, is measured by production and consumption. For the individual or household, this translates into gross income and personal wealth, measured in terms of possessions and investments. For business and corporations, it is the quarterly profit report and stock value. For nations, it is the gross domestic product. All of this is premised on the idea that consumption and production are the goals themselves, and constant growth is the norm. The idea of minimizing production and consumption, the notion of zero-growth, the concept of planning beyond the next fiscal year, the question of personal and social fulfillment, none of these are compatible with the capitalism that is dominating the world today.

Sustainable development

The social environmentalist Foster argues that since the Earth's capacity to supply resources and absorb waste cannot be increased, the only way to achieve global economic stability is to reduce demand. He sees only three ways to do this: by stabilizing or reducing the human population, by improving technology, and by socioeconomic reform that reduces human material consumption (Foster, 2002: 97). The capitalist Beckerman rejects the notion of resource scarcity (Beckerman, 1995: 78). Instead he asserts that our greatest environmental problems are poverty and local pollution. He suggests that population stabilization, improved technology, and robust economic growth will yield the greatest good for the greatest number. These two views of the future represent the extremes of a polemic debate: to grow and develop faster or to constrain development and limit growth (Box 6.1).

Box 6.1 I=PAT and EKC

Ecologists and economists have long been interested in the relationship between demographic transition and ecological stress. In the early 1970s, Ehrlich and Holdren (1971), Commoner (1972), and others advanced the I=PAT hypothesis, suggesting that environmental impact (I) is directly related to population (P), affluence (A), and technology (T). This equation implies that economic growth and technological development are inevitably bad for the environment. Needless to say, this maxim has not held up well to scrutiny. Indeed, technological advances and even affluence can, in some cases, reduce the ecological footprint and improve environmental quality.

Some two decades later, economists proposed an alternate hypothesis: the environmental Kuznets curve (EKC; Grossman and Krueger, 1991, following Kuznets, 1955). The EKC is an inverted U-shaped curve, predicting that environmental impacts will increase with per capita income to an inflection point, after which increasing wealth will decrease environmental impacts. The implication is that economic growth is the best path to environmental quality. This model, too, is an imperfect descriptor of a complex relationship (Carson, 2009). It is unclear, for instance, exactly how we should measure environmental impacts; per capita emissions, deforestation, waste generation, and ecological footprint might all yield different results. Further, such metrics are not necessarily reliably acquired or readily comparable among nations. Finally, there are many other variables at play, including geography, population density, social policies, trade relationships, and inequality. Carson (2009) summarizes by observing that there is no clear case for a universal causal relationship between income and environmental impact. At best, EKC research has been able to establish that economic growth, while not an environmental panacea, will not necessarily result in greater environmental impact. Part of the uncertainty— and environmental opportunity—lies in the choices that societies make regarding the wealth they generate.

Both ends of the spectrum, at least as represented by these scholars, are in agreement on one important point: they both detest the idea of sustainable development. This is curious, since sustainable development is seen by many others as a middle ground. It is purportedly a system that allows for economic growth while limiting deleterious effects on future growth. It seems sensible enough. Why would it be rejected by both Beckerman and Foster? Beckerman claims that sustainable development inappropriately mixes the technological (i.e. the appropriation and transformation of resources) with the moral (i.e. the consideration of what ought to be done regarding society and environment). He prefers to focus only on utility, with a goal of optimization—the most effective use of a resource. But this begs the question: optimization for whom? For instance, would this optimize the existence of nonhuman species? Certainly not, for Beckerman. He describes the "absurd" scenario of abandoning human development that negatively impacts any other species. This would halt all human activity. The circle of optimization cannot logically be so large. How about the optimization of human welfare? Beckerman allows that this might be a reasonable goal, but argues that the valuation of social and environmental welfare and the projection of values for future generations are poorly defined. If these are accounted for, and if the appropriate period of time for intergenerational optimization is defined, Beckerman sees the market as the best mechanism for achieving it. In the absence of quantified values, Beckerman argues that sustainable development is based only on subjective morality (Beckerman, 1995: 125–140). Foster, for his part, sees sustainable development as "primarily an economic concept serving narrow economic ends." It is, in Foster's view, equivalent to sustained economic growth, and no model of constant growth can be maintained indefinitely. Instead, he advocates for a departure from capitalism: "a global society that elevates the status of nature and community above that of the accumulation of capital; equality and justice above individual greed; and democracy above the market" (Foster, 2002: 79–82).

Despite criticism from many sides, sustainable development has gathered some momentum as an economic course of action. In 2015 the United Nations (UN) adopted an Agenda for Sustainable Development, including 17 goals to be achieved by 2030. The goals are lofty. They include the desire to end poverty, to end hunger, and to promote equality, education, and welfare. They call for sustainable agriculture, sanitation, and energy for all. The goals do not call for a halt to economic growth; rather, they promote sustained growth, with meaningful employment and suitable infrastructure for the entire human population. Regarding natural resources, the goals call for efficient and sustainable use and the reduction of waste while halting land degradation and biodiversity loss and significantly reducing pollution. Goal 16 is to "promote peaceful and inclusive societies for sustainable development, provide access to justice for all, and build effective, accountable and inclusive institutions at all levels."[1]

Some might say that these are beyond lofty—they are utopian. If truly achieved (by 2030 or any other year), I suspect it would be a first for the human race. Perhaps bands of human foragers have approached some of these ideals, driven by their reliance on one another and on the interpersonal social pressures for cooperative reciprocity. But even our ancestral foragers changed the condition of the land and drove other species to extinction, and their cooperation probably did not extend much beyond their own group. They can be forgiven, certainly, for theirs was a world of seemingly endless resources and constant threats, and theirs was a kill-or-be-killed existence. Our world is different. Our resources, while not immediately approaching exhaustion, are subject to fierce competition on the playing field of international political economy. Our social groups are circles of disparity, with some facing a scarcity of basic necessities while others enjoy obscene wealth. The UN Sustainable Development Goals call for people to set selfishness and xenophobia aside in favor of compassion and cooperation. Clearly, our species has a great capacity for beneficence. But in a world dominated by individual interests it seems that the social mechanisms of cooperative reciprocity have been undermined. Can we overcome our parochial selfishness to achieve global equity? This is the great question of our time.

Note

1 United Nations Sustainable Development Goals, 2016, www.un.org/sustainabledevelopment/development-agenda/, accessed February 2017.

Bibliography

Anderson, T. and Leal, D. (2001). *Free market environmentalism*, 2nd edition. New York: Palgrave Macmillan.

Banaji, J. (2007). Islam, the Mediterranean and the rise of capitalism. *Historical Materialism*, 15(1), pp. 47–74.

Beckerman, W. (1995). *Small is stupid: blowing the whistle on the greens*. London: Gerald Duckworth.

Bookchin, M. (1982). *The ecology of freedom: the emergence and dissolution of hierarchy*. Palo Alto, CA: Cheshire Books.

Bookchin, M. (1986). *The modern crisis*. Philadelphia: New Society.

Bookchin, M. (1989). *Remaking society*. Montreal: Black Rose Books.

Brejning, M.J. (2013). *Corporate social responsibility and the welfare state: the historical and contemporary role of CSR in the mixed economy of welfare*. Farnham: Ashgate.

Carson, R.T. (2009). The environmental Kuznets curve: seeking empirical regularity and theoretical structure. *Review of Environmental Economics and Policy*, 4(1), pp. 3–23.

Chen, V.T. (2016). The spiritual crisis of the modern economy. *The Atlantic*, December 21, 2016.

Collins, D. and Barkdull, J. (1995). Capitalism, environmentalism and mediating structures. *Environmental Ethics*, 17(3), pp. 227–244.

Commoner, B. (1972). The environmental cost of economic growth. *Chemistry in Britain*, 8(2), pp. 52–56.

Daly, H.E. (1991). *Steady-state economics: with new essays*. Washington, DC: Island Press.

Daly, H.E. and Farley, J. (2004). *Ecological economics: principles and applications*. Washington, DC: Island Press.

Dietz, R. and O'Neill, D.W. (2013). *Enough is enough: building a sustainable economy in a world of finite resources*. London: Routledge.

Ehrlich, P.R. and Holdren, J.P. (1971). Impact of population growth. *Science*, 171(3977), pp. 1212–1217.

Engels, F., (1932 [1844]). Outlines of a critique of a political economy. In: K. Marx, ed., *The Economic and Philosophic Manuscripts of 1844*. Translation by M. Mulligan. Moscow: Progress.

Engels, F. (1947 [1878]). *Herr Eugen Dühring's revolution in science*. Translation by E. Burns. Moscow: Progress.

Foster, J.B. (2002). *Ecology against capitalism*. New York: Monthly Review Press.

Gómez-Baggethun, E., De Groot, R., Lomas, P.L. and Montes, C. (2010). The history of ecosystem services in economic theory and practice: from early notions to markets and payment schemes. *Ecological Economics*, 69(6), pp. 1209–1218.

Graeber, D. (2011). *Debt: the first 5,000 years*. Brooklyn: Melville House.

Grossman, G.M. and Krueger, A.B. (1991). *Environmental impacts of a North American free trade agreement*. Cambridge, MA: National Bureau of Economic Research, working paper 3914.

Grout, P.A., Megginson, W.L. and Zalewska, A. (2009). One half-billion shareholders and counting: determinants of individual share ownership around the world. Presented at the 22nd Australasian Finance and Banking Conference August 18, 2009, Sydney, Australia.

Harari, Y.N. (2015). *Sapiens: a brief history of humankind*. New York: Random House.

Hardin, G. (1968). The tragedy of the commons. *Science*, 162(3859), pp. 1243–1248.

Hawken, P. (1999). Commentary. In: Schumacher, E.F. (1999 [1973]). *Small is beautiful: economics as if people mattered*. 2nd edition. Vancouver, BC: Hartley & Marks. p. xv.

Hawken, P., Lovins, A. and Lovins, L.H. (1999). *Natural capitalism*. Boston: Little, Brown and Company.

Helbing, D. (2013). Economics 2.0: the natural step towards a self-regulating, participatory market society. *Evolutionary and Institutional Economics Review*, 10(1), pp. 3–41.

Hodgson, G.M. (2015). *Conceptualizing capitalism: institutions, evolution, future*. Chicago: University of Chicago Press.

Kristoff, N. (2016). Corporations game the tax system at our expense. *New York Times*, April 14, 2016, A23.

Kuznets, S. (1955). Economic growth and income inequality. *American Economic Review*, 45(1), pp. 1–28.

Marx, K. (1976 [1844]). Comment on James Mill. *Economic and Philosophical Manuscripts of 1844*. Translation by C. Dutt. New York: International Publishers.

Marx, K. (1976 [1867]). Capital: a critique of political economy. In: F. Engels ed., *Book one: the process of production of capital*, Vol 1. Translation by S. Moore and E. Aveling. New York: Vintage.

Marx, K. (1993 [1939]). *Grundrisse*. London: Penguin Press.

Mason, P. (2015). *Postcapitalism: a guide to our future*. New York: Farrar, Straus and Giroux.

McRobie, G. (1999). Commentary. In: Schumacher, E.F. 1999 [1973]. *Small is beautiful: economics as if people mattered*. 2nd edition. Vancouver, BC: Hartley & Marks. p. 28.

Merchant, C. (2005). *Radical ecology: the search for a livable world*. New York: Routledge.

Merchant, C., ed. (2008). *Ecology*. 2nd edition. Amherst, NY: Humanity Books.

Nee, V. and Cao, Y. (1999). Path dependent societal transformation: stratification in hybrid mixed economies. *Theory and Society*, 28(6), pp. 799–834.

O'Brien, R. and Williams, M. (2013). *Global political economy: evolution and dynamics*. 4th edition. New York: Palgrave Macmillan.

O'Connor, J.R., ed. (1998). *Natural causes: essays in ecological Marxism*. New York: Guilford Press.

Ostrom, E. (2010). Beyond markets and states: polycentric governance of complex economic systems. *Transnational Corporations Review*, 2(2), pp. 641–672.

Parsons, H.L., ed. (1977). *Marx and Engels on ecology*. Westport, CT: Greenwood.

Porta, R., Lopez-de-Silanes, F. and Shleifer, A. (1999). Corporate ownership around the world. *Journal of Finance*, 54(2), pp. 471–517.

Robbins, P., Hintz, J. and Moore, S.A. (2014). *Environment and society: a critical introduction*, 2nd edition. Chichester, UK: Wiley-Blackwell.

Rothman, D.S. (1998). Environmental Kuznets curves: real progress or passing the buck? A case for consumption-based approaches. *Ecological Economics*, 25(2), pp. 177–194.

Schumacher, E.F. (1999 [1973]). *Small is beautiful: economics as if people mattered*, 2nd edition. Vancouver, BC: Hartley & Marks.

Smith, A. (1976 [1759]). *The theory of moral sentiments, or an essay towards an analysis of the principles by which men naturally judge concerning the conduct and character, first of their neighbours and afterwards of themselves*. Indianapolis, IN: Liberty Press.

Smith, A. (1784 [1776]). *An inquiry into the nature and causes of the wealth of nations*, 3rd edition. London: Strahan & Cadell.

Smythe, E. (2009). In whose interests? Transparency and accountability in the global governance of food: agribusiness, the Codex Alimentarius, and the World Trade Organization. In: J. Clapp and D. Fuchs, eds., *Corporate power in global agrifood governance*. Cambridge, MA: MIT Press. pp. 93–123.

Soborski, R. (2013). *Ideology in a global age: continuity and change*. London: Palgrave Macmillan. pp. 140–168.

Vitali, S., Glattfelder, J.B. and Battiston, S. (2011). The network of global corporate control. *PLoS One*, 6(10), p. e25995.

Wilkinson, R.G. and Pickett, K. (2010). *The spirit level: why greater equality makes societies stronger*. New York: Bloomsbury Press.

Witt, S. (1999). Commentary. In: Schumacher, E.F. (1999 [1973]). *Small is beautiful: economics as if people mattered*, 2nd edition. Vancouver, BC: Hartley & Marks. p. 31.

7 Socioecological evolution

Key points

- Romantic ecologists have portrayed ecosystems as holistic, balanced, self-regulating entities, but scientific ecology has provided evidence to the contrary.
- Ecosystems are temporary associations of organisms, and their function is subject to anthropogenic stress.
- Certain human social structures alleviate ecological stress and promote ecosystem services.

We have evolved as social organisms within an ecological context. It follows that social structure and cultural character are largely attributable to ecological endowment: domesticatable animals and plants, geomorphology, weather and climate, soil quality, and the availability of harvestable natural resources. The inverse is also true—human social structure and cultural character shape ecological systems. People and their institutions alter their abiotic surroundings and exert strong selection pressures on the evolution of other living things. Thus the advent of agriculture, the age of extraction and industry, and the emergence of post-industrial synthetic society have sculpted the environment, at first locally and now globally. Clearly, human and nonhuman have co-evolved. In fact, the mutual influence is so ubiquitous that it hardly makes sense to think of either in isolation. Together, they function as a socioecological system.

Socioecological systems are partially defined by the ways in which people conceptualize nature. As we have seen, mental models of nature are wide and varied. The nonhuman world is both our mother—the giver of life and sustenance—and a source of unknown dangers. Where some see a pristine paradise, others envision a marketable commodity. Some imagine a world in which they are insulated from natural systems altogether. Still others consider all of nature to be a self-regulating, sentient organism. Mental models like these are in cultural competition, and the models that prevail inform our relationship with and behavior toward the nonhuman world.

In this chapter I review some western concepts of nature under the changing cultural influences since Darwin. In particular, I explore the paradox that Darwinian ecology presents: that all life is co-originated and interrelated while also brutally competitive. This paradox has played out over the past few centuries as romanticized conceptions of nature have been challenged by rational science. Over the same period of time, human sociocultural evolution has altered ecological conditions. As concepts and conditions have changed, so too have our environmental challenges. Through the course of this chapter I will suggest that environmentalism is in the throes of a re-conceptualization of ecological systems. What this means in practice is that we should no longer be concerned with the preservation of some proper version of unspoiled nature. Rather, our greatest challenge is to sustain the ecological processes that support human life.

(Near) death of a superorganism

Ecology is a young science as compared with disciplines like astronomy, physics, and chemistry. But in some ways it is the oldest of sciences, for the earliest experimental subjects of our ancient ancestors were plants, animals, and ecosystems. Of course, no one studied ecology for its own sake and left record of such until Aristotle, and another two millennia would pass until ecology was recognized as a science in its own right. This birth—or reincarnation—took place in the midst of a western world budding with industrialization and capitalism, under the influence of materialism tempered with romanticism. It was in this context that Ernst Haeckel defined the field after the work of a colleague: "Ecology is the study of all those complex interactions referred to by Darwin as the conditions of the struggle for existence" (Egerton, 2013: 229).

The sociocultural setting in which ecological science emerged would influence it for the next century. It was on one hand the product of a materialist, reductionist movement. In this sense ecology was driven by the desire to isolate, identify, categorize, and catalogue living things in the Linnaean approach to life. Categorization opened the door to appropriation and even to exploitation. But there was also a holism to this new science of ecology: in the spirit of Alexander von Humboldt, it was an effort to understand the perfection in nature—to perceive the ways in which living things interact as a single entity. To those of this holistic persuasion, human encroachment sullied nature's vitality. Extraction and manipulation were therefore an affront to the spirit (Worster, 1994).

Darwin was an impetus for both perspectives. His ecology banished the supernatural from worldly interactions, positing instead a system of desperate individual struggle for life in forms that are far from perfect and immutable but instead subject to selection and change. At the same time, Darwinian evolution also demonstrated the interrelation of all organisms, showing that humans are part of nature, not above it, that living things depend upon one another, and that all life comes from a common ancestor (Worster, 1994: 31–39). There is conflict in Darwin's view of life, for it holds that individual self-interest and benevolent cooperation occur simultaneously. This is an important tenet of the science of ecology.

In the decades after Darwin's publication this ideological struggle was played out nowhere more dramatically than the American frontier, where the wonders of nature (having been wrested from indigenous peoples) lay exposed either for the taking or for the cherishing. American diplomat George Perkins Marsh (1801–1882) was an early advocate for the latter, warning in *Man and nature* (1864) of the negative effects of deforestation and linking the conservation of natural resources to human welfare, even as Thoreau at about the same time connected wilderness to the human soul. Both Marsh and Thoreau saw grandeur in nature, though their conclusions differed. Marsh wrote of the need to protect the balance and harmony of the nonhuman world, but saw human dominion as the means to achieve this. Thoreau might have agreed about the balance and harmony, but was an advocate of the oneness of humans and nature, of humans *in* nature. He wrote of the "oversoul," the moral spirit that pervaded the cosmos and bound all things together. Thoreau's world was a being unto itself: "the Earth is not dead, inert mass; it is a body, has a spirit, is organic and fluid" (Thoreau, 1971 [1854]: 340; Nash, 1989: 36). This holistic animism is in sharp contrast with Marsh's man-as-manager, but the discrepancy was nothing new. In the perspectives of Marsh and Thoreau we see both the nature/human dualism of Descartes and the paradox of Darwin.

Whether motivated by the image of spirit or steward, the American conservation movement was off and running. The innovation of land set apart for the public good was soon to follow, with the first major dedications of Yosemite in 1864 and Yellowstone in 1872. Thus began a nature preservation movement that has since spread around the world, resulting in millions of hectares of protected terrestrial and aquatic habitat. Of course, one thing that spurred the protection of natural wonders was the perception that they were being rapidly lost to the plow and the saw. The last decades of the 19th century were a time of wholesale deforestation, drainage, and slaughter in the American west. These two attitudes—appropriation and preservation—represent the peculiar dichotomy that is the root cause of so much environmental concern.

The classic romantic-versus-utilitarian approach to nature is depicted in the friendship and rivalry between John Muir and Gifford Pinchot. Muir, the Scottish-born force behind the establishment of Yosemite National Park, sought God through nature. He was a holistic preservationist who, like Thoreau, found perfection in the natural world and corruption in the designs of human society. His relationship with nature was visceral, emotional, and ecstatic. Muir's ecology reflected his biocentrism: the organisms and ecological communities in unspoiled nature were as God intended them to be. Any deviation or destruction instituted by humans was disrespectful to both the creatures and to God's plan. Nature, in short, was a sacred cathedral. Muir appreciated Darwinism for its humbling implications. It placed all living things on the same level, all interconnected, all reliant upon one another (Nash, 1989: 42). Pinchot, meanwhile, was no less a nature enthusiast but held the philosophy of a utilitarian. His conception of nature drew upon the competitive aspects of Darwin's ecology. Nature's products, to Pinchot, were to be put to use for human benefit. Forests were to be harvested and re-planted. Landscapes could be sculpted. In a word, nature should be *managed*. Pinchot was not averse to the concept of preservation—in fact he was responsible for establishing many ecological sanctuaries in the United States. Nor was he advocating ecological degradation. His was a strategy of wise use, of renewal, of sustainable harvest. Wilderness for the sake of wilderness made little sense to a man of efficient utility (Miller, 2001).

The same socioecological conflict is evident in the work of biologists Charles Elton and William Wheeler in the early 20th century. Elton (1900–1991), author of *Animal ecology* (1927), was perhaps the first community ecologist and is credited with developing the concepts of the food chain, food web, energy pyramid, and the ecological niche (Worster, 1994: 295–300). The niche is a particularly critical concept in modern ecology. It is the way of life of a particular species; it defines the role of the organism in its environment. The functional niches of different species are an important aspect of the ecosystem concept. Here we encounter the ideological divide. In one line of thinking, the ecosystem and its constituent niches allow for a reduction of the system to its base parts. It provides a means of expression and evaluation of the ecosystem in the terms of physics and economics (Worster, 1994: 306). Seen in this individualistic light, much of the Darwinian struggle for existence comes down to the battle for niche space.

Considered in another way, the ecosystem and its interconnected niches seemed to confirm holism. William Wheeler (1865–1937) was a Harvard entomologist who studied the various functional behaviors within ant and termite colonies. Such colonies, to Wheeler, act with a common purpose and constitute a *superorganism*. By extension, the cooperative communities in the natural world, each comprised of species with particular functions, could similarly be seen as superorganisms. In Wheeler's view the collective has emergent properties—it is more than a collection of solitary individuals (Worster, 1994: 323). The British mathematician-cum-philosopher Alfred North Whitehead (1861–1947) carried the thought further: in nature, each species, indeed each organism has a part to play, and as each is a critical member of the whole, each must have intrinsic value. As part of a greater unit, every living thing has worth (Nash, 1989: 58–60). An avowed opponent of reductionist materialism, Whitehead's philosophy held that the properties of an entity can only be understood in its relationship to other entities. Humans, in this light, should act accordingly by respecting interdependence (Worster, 1994: 319). The notion is better remembered from Muir's earlier and more lyrical prose: "When we try to pick out anything by itself, we find it hitched to everything else in the Universe" (Muir, 1911: 110).

Interestingly, many early American ecologists—while at odds over the proper human relationship with nature—shared the ecological perspective that ecological systems occur as a unit. The view was best expressed by the great American botanist Frederick Clements (1874–1945). Clements was influenced by Darwin but was particularly a disciple of Herbert Spencer, who subscribed to a notion of universal holism (Worster, 1994: 212–214). Ecological systems, as Clements followed Spencer's logic, behave like organisms. They are born as colonized habitat, they mature through the ordered succession of each species by another, and they reach maturity—the endpoint of change—as a climax community. A mature ecosystem that is disturbed by natural disaster or human encroachment will, left to its own, revert back to the climax community dictated by the regional climate (Clements, 1916). Clementsian ecology is therefore the ecology of the super-organism. It is directed toward an endpoint by the living things themselves; it is autocatalytic. One can see in the Clementsian perspective the romantic influence: there is expectation of purpose, direction, and order in nature that progresses toward the proper state, the highest order of existence. Clements' holistic vision of the ecological superorganism dominated ecological thought for the next half-century and, while it is no longer the predominant perspective, it is alive and well today (Spieles, 2010: 17–21).

The ecology of Thoreau, Muir, Wheeler, and Clements is drawn at least in part from a benevolent interpretation of Darwinian evolution. This is the notion that organisms, as kin, cooperate toward certain purpose. It recalls the chivalry of an earlier age. Nature romanticized behaves like a human in its growth and in its intention, prone to corruption but called to return to purity. As observed by the modern philosopher Kate Rigby, there is a promise of purpose and self-actualization here (both in nonhuman nature and in people) that is "jeopardized [by] human society" (Rigby, 2014: 64). Human and nonhuman alike, in this perspective, are intended to reach their full potential.

But Darwin's theory says nothing of the sort. To the contrary, Darwinian evolution recognizes the individualistic brutality and purposelessness of the natural world. An ecology premised on such an understanding of the world would have to be based on individual organisms living or dying according to the happenstance of competition and their abiotic conditions. Just such an ecology was proposed by the American ecologist Henry Gleason (1882–1975) as a rebuttal to the Clementsian system. Gleasonian ecology is not an orderly and cooperative march toward a climax community; rather, it is a chance collection of species that happen to coexist as long as conditions allow in an environment that is always changing. The niches that species occupy are not crafted out of regard for harmony or cooperation; they are the product of opportunity, natural selection, and the requisite suffering and death. To Gleason, the species associations we see and regard as proper are purely coincidental. In this ecology there is no goal, no endpoint, and no superorganism (Gleason, 1939; Nicolson, 1990).

Gleasonian ecology throws some treasured ecological beliefs into jeopardy. If individual organisms migrate continuously and independently, finding the opportunity for growth only where chance conditions allow, then there are no idealized communities, only temporary associations. If organisms are all coming and going in a world of random fluctuation, then a nature of harmonious balance is unlikely. If associations of plants and animals are temporary, then that which we think of as an "ecosystem" is merely a transitional accident.

The concept of native species is a good example. In some modern societies there is a professed preference for native species and a contempt for those deemed non-native. Actually, though, the native/nonnative distinction is arbitrary. The range of every species changes over time as environmental conditions change, and so there is no correct or proper distribution of organisms. In the United States, for instance, a species is deemed native if it was present when European men first began to catalog the species of the new world. This definition is meaningless in most other parts of the world. Even if it were meaningful, the equation of *native* with *desirable* is inconsistently applied. Honeybees and earthworms, for example, are both nonnative to North America (by the prevailing definition), but both lauded for their contributions to humankind. Prairie dogs and coyotes, both native by definition, are scorned. Native species and desirability are both social constructs. Of course, it is true that invasive species are a socioecological problem— they do millions of dollars of agricultural, silvicultural, and aquacultural damage every year—but this is precisely the point. Species value, practically speaking, is mostly about human preference (Spieles, 2010: 71–83).

Gleasonian ecology challenged the notion of an orderly, progressive natural world. But romanticism dies hard, and Gleason faced a tough crowd. Gradually, field evidence has supported his individualistic ecology, but this has not prevented the conception and management of ecosystems as holistic units (Spieles, 2010: 22). The idea that certain species are *supposed* to be in certain arrangements in certain places is powerful. In some sense this notion has become the vision of what is ecologically *right* with the world, and that which humans do to prevent or alter the right sort of nature is wrong. Aldo Leopold captured this attitude most memorably: "A thing is right when it tends to preserve the integrity, stability and beauty of the biotic community. It is wrong when it tends otherwise" (Leopold, 1949: 224–225).

Leopold's life and work illustrate the conceptual tension of his time. Initially a forester in the utilitarian model of Pinchot, Leopold advocated for the extermination of predators and the human use of nature's commodities. But he was also influenced by Muir to question pure anthropocentrism, asking "whether the principle of highest use does not itself demand that representative portions of some forests be preserved as wilderness" (Leopold, 1921: 718). His ecology was clearly Clementsian, calling the climax community "a base-datum of normality, a picture of how healthy land maintains itself as an organism" (Leopold, 1941: 3). Later in life he experienced a sort of conversion, leaving the church of utilitarianism to become a biocentrist, urging his readers to "think like a mountain" and adopt a "land ethic" (Leopold, 1949: 224–225). "Harmony with the land," he wrote, "is like harmony with a friend. You cannot cherish his right hand and chop off his left... The land is one organism" (Leopold, 1966 [1938]: 145–146). With such holistic and romantic words he inspired generations of ecologists and environmentalists. And yet he was at some level still a mechanist, speaking of the "cogs and wheels" of nature with the fervor of a Gleasonian individualist (Leopold, 1991 [1932]: 165–166). The historian Donald Worster wonders if Leopold was attempting to reconcile the different conceptions of the ecological world and thereby heal a rift so long a part of the human experience (Worster, 1994: 290). Whether he consciously intended such a reconciliation or not, Leopold's legacy is an expression of the human–nature dilemma.

The 20th-century environmental movement was partially, and initially, about this dilemma. It was driven by Thoreau, Muir, and Leopold's vision of nature unsullied by humans—a nature of pure inspiration—and the effort to protect it from destruction at the hands of humans. There is irony here, in that: 1) the pristine nature to be protected from society was in fact a highly manipulated construct of society; and 2) the western society that advanced the notion of pristine nature had, not so long ago, held a very different opinion of the natural world. To the first point the journalist Charles Mann recounts the many ways in which the American landscape had been sculpted by Native American harvest, fire, and ecological engineering, long before the descendants of European settlers yearned for the primeval (Mann, 2005). To the second point, environmental historian William Cronon notes that wilderness was equated with a barren and fear-filled wasteland only a few centuries prior to the wilderness protection movement. The shift in mindset, Cronon argues, was a function of the romantic frontier. There was by the American mid-20th century an association of sacredness with wilderness—it was where one could commune with God—and a sense (among some) that protecting it was morally right. The wild frontier also represented "the last bastion of rugged individualism," where a person could find his own destiny (Cronon, 1996: 8–10, 13). These memes quickly became part of American culture. Our modern understanding of natural history and the violence with which the "wild" was claimed from its prior inhabitants should throw a dubious light on the sanctity of unspoiled nature, but the image persists nonetheless. Clearly, wilderness—or at least the concept of wilderness—has deep connotations for the human psyche. Nature as superorganism, one that matures to fill its proper place in the balanced, harmonious world—this image fits nicely into the myth of pristine wilderness.

The science of ecology, however, has shown this ideal to be false (Wu and Loucks, 1995; Rohde, 2005; Kricher, 2009). Most scientific ecologists now accept a Gleasonian view of the natural world. Certainly, there are mutualisms and associations in ecological communities. But species that commonly appear together tend to have independent ranges according to environmental gradients and their own physiological tolerances. Further, pollen core analyses have shown that species distribution has shifted dramatically and independently over geologic time. Other ecologists have questioned the normalcy of equilibrium in ecological systems, observing instead that ecological communities appear to be in a constant state of change. All of this points to an ecology of organisms, not superorganisms.

In this perspective, ecosystems are temporary associations in which species individually assemble and sort through competition, inhibition, and facilitation, and are eventually replaced by better competitors until the system is upset by disturbance, after which re-assembly begins a new trajectory (Walker and Salt, 2012). Cyclic ecological processes place great emphasis on physical factors which limit growth—called ecological stressors—and the periodic upheaval of disturbance. Since ecological stress and disturbance change over time, the ranges of species are constantly in flux. This is nothing new. In fact, it is how associations of organisms have changed since the appearance of life on Earth. What is new, at least on a geologic timescale, is the ability of one species to stress and disturb the others. It seems that humans excel in this area.

Anthropogenic stress and disturbance

Humans were changing their ecosystems before they were human; that is, even our ape-like ancestors altered the world around them. As members of our species honed their hunting skill, began to use fire, and learned to domesticate plants and animals, they exerted great evolutionary force on the nonhuman world. From an ecological perspective, the whole of human history can be seen as a great set of selection pressures.

Even as the human understanding of nature has changed in recent centuries, nature itself has changed in response to human activity. As we have seen, pollution, overharvest, disruption, and degradation have been (and still are) major by-products of extraction and industry. Such negative externalities are ecological stressors; they tend to increase or decrease physical, chemical, and biological factors that can determine which organisms are able to survive in an area. For example, human development tends to break ecological habitat into small, disconnected, and isolated fragments. Anthropogenic harvest simplifies food webs by removing predators and other dominant species, which are often replaced by invasive species introduced by human agency. Human-derived waste can deplete oxygen availability in aquatic ecosystems. In such ways we are purveyors of ecological stress. We also alter disturbance regimes. As we have come to own land and possess natural resources, we have become less accepting of the disruptive events of nature. Many are beyond our control, but not all. We suppress fire, prevent floods, and minimize storm surge. We lessen drought with irrigation, we manage inundation with drainage, and we attempt to control pest outbreaks with chemical treatment. The modern human quest to maintain ecological stability is part of the greater conceptual conflict of environmentalism. In order to promote vital ecological services, treasured ecosystems, and cherished species, preservation-minded individuals and organizations are manipulating flood cycles, managing fire, mechanically and chemically removing undesirable species, and introducing desirables in order to re-create, restore, stabilize, and protect valued landscapes. The very stability that is sought, however, is often undermined by global anthropogenic change and by the impermanent nature of ecological systems (Spieles, 2010: 55–68).

Altering disturbance regimes is in itself a stress to some organisms, for many species depend upon a certain frequency, intensity, or duration of disturbance as part of their life cycle. Conversely, ecological stress can lead to disturbance, as when tree mortality triggers a forest fire. The upshot is that all human societies have transformed the conditions of the nonhuman world. By changing stress and disturbance regimes, we (often unwittingly) select for certain organisms and ecological functions and select against others. Ecologist Eugene Odum (1913–2002) clarified the matter, showing that stress drives ecosystems toward more transitional characteristics (Odum, 1985). Stressed ecosystems are commonly populated by species with short life spans, great dispersal ability, wide tolerance, rapid growth, and prodigious reproductive capacity. These are called r-strategists, and generally we recognize them as nuisance invaders. They are the dandelions and cockroaches of the world. Odum noted that the inverse is also true: stressed ecosystems support fewer K-strategists, those of slow growth, slow reproduction, poor dispersal, and narrow tolerance. These are typically species which humans value, such as koala bears and giant sequoias. In sum, Odum proposed that eco-logical stress selects for species that are less desirable for humans at the expense of species we find to be more desirable.

Actually, he showed much more than this. Stressed ecosystems also leach more nutrients, support less diversity, and store less carbon than unstressed systems. They are less productive, and more of the photosynthetic product goes unused within the ecosystem. They more easily become dominated by a few species, resulting in simpler food chains. Parasitism increases with stress, and mutualism decreases. Further, the detrimental effects of stress are not easily reversible. Later ecological scholars showed that cumulative stress can degrade ecosystem structure and function to a threshold of change, beyond which the environment favors new dominant species and different processes. Post-threshold, a reduction in stress will not necessarily allow the ecosystem to revert to its previous state, meaning that certain ecological services can be lost and not easily retrieved. As Odum was publishing early work on ecological stress the scenario was being played out in ecosystems around the industrialized world. Lake Erie became the infamous example, as industrial and agricultural effluent transformed it from a clear-water state to a turbid, oxygen-deprived algal bowl that was pronounced dead in the late 1960s (Odum, 1985; Sweeney, 1993).

The point is that anthropogenic stress can drive ecological systems toward characteristics that are less useful and less attractive for humans. We value certain qualities—certain ecological services—of the nonhuman world. The concept of ecological service is a useful way of highlighting desirable, and even marketable, aspects of the nonhuman world. But at the most fundamental level, ecosystem services exist because of specific ecological structures and functions that are not easily commodified. These structures and functions depend upon adequate bio-logical diversity, habitat heterogeneity, landscape connectivity, and suitable disturbance regimes. The stresses of extraction, industry, and the synthetic age compromise these ecological attributes and jeopardize ecosystem services (Peterson *et al.*, 2010).

Odum's insight came at a time of colliding mental models: romanticism and rationalism, objective thought and idealistic vision. The romantic notions of wilderness, balance, and harmony did not disappear, but were joined by scientific concerns of the post-world-war era. Precisely because of the economic productivity of (relative) peacetime, it quickly became apparent that the new synthetic society was threatening ecological services. In the US the use of war-era synthetic chemicals as pesticides prompted Rachel Carson to write *Silent spring* (1962), igniting a revolution of concern for ecological and human health. A new pros-perity and mobility led to a surge in outdoor recreation as many explored parks and wilderness areas, prompting an increase in natural area preservation initiatives. The renewed interaction with the land precipitated outcry over perceived degradation from extraction, industry, emission, and effluent. Air that was not deemed breathable and waters not deemed fishable or swimmable resulted in major regulatory actions of the 1960s and 1970s. There was a corresponding increase in the membership and fundraising for environmental nonprofit organizations which protected land, lobbied for political support, advocated for environmental quality, and rallied millions of people to the cause. All of this, expressly stated or not, was done in the name of ecological stress reduction for the protection of ecosystem services (Worster, 1994; Radkau, 2014).

At the same time another thread of the environmental movement was taking shape in recollection of the dire prognostications of an earlier age. Malthus (1888 [1798]) had predicted that population, as it grows exponentially, will eventually outgrow the linear increase in food supply. The unfortunate result would be starvation and death for many and survival for few (a notion that had a profound influence on Darwin). In the post-world-war era, even in the midst of incredible innovation in agriculture that Malthus could not have foreseen, modern-day Malthusians took up the ominous message with renewed vigor. A number of postwar apocalyptic publications—no doubt influenced by the atrocities of war—pitted the growth of a destructive human population against the Earth's capacity to support life: *Population roads to peace or war* (Burch and Pendell, 1945); *Our plundered planet* (Osborn, 1948); *Road to survival* (Vogt, 1948). Along with these works, explosive world population growth inspired the neo-Malthusians of the environmental revolution. For example Garrett Hardin, in *Tragedy of the commons* (Hardin, 1968), criticized policies that promoted overbreeding; he later decried efforts to provide food to famine-stricken Africa, likening the Earth to a metaphorical lifeboat with space for only a limited number of people (Hardin, 1974). Paul Ehrlich published *The population bomb* in 1968, warning of imminent mass starvation:

> In the 1970s and 1980s hundreds of millions of people will starve to death in spite of any crash programs embarked upon now. At this late date nothing can prevent a substantial increase in the world death rate, although many lives could be saved through dramatic programs to "stretch" the carrying capacity of the Earth by increasing food production and providing for more equitable distribution of whatever food is available.
>
> (Ehrlich, 1968: xi)

The message was amplified by *The limits to growth*, published by Donella and Dennis Meadows, Jorgen Randers, and William Behrens in 1972.

While the environmental apocalypse predicted in the cold war era has not come to pass, these and many other environmental advocates may be credited with bringing the world's attention to the consequences of ecological stress. The crisis was not perceived as a deficiency of the natural world; that is, there was nothing wrong with the ecological systems themselves that was causing this threat. It was instead seen as a problem of human society as applied to ecological constraints. Populations, we know, have carrying capacities in their environment. The carrying capacity represents an upper boundary to population growth, beyond which individual organisms will not have the means to survive. Applied to humans, the message is clear: Earth has a limited capacity to support life. Ecological stress reduces that capacity, and the human population may be well on its way to surpassing that limit, if it has not already.

Social stress and ecological stress

The criticism of the social ills that would allow such a tragedy has come to be known as social ecology. As noted in Chapter 3, social ecology—though hardly a single school of thought—is generally more confrontational than scientific ecology. It is more an assessment of how things ought to be than how they are. Here, I will explore just one of the many realms of social ecology in order to illustrate an important link with the discussion above. The social-ecological systems (SES) approach studies the ways in which human social systems can promote or suppress the sustainable utility of natural resources. The basic premise of SES is that social organization and governance can influence the function of the ecological systems on which they depend (Fischer-Kowalski and Weisz, 2016).

Drawn from the work of Ostrom (2010), SES suggests that social organization which mandates collective decision-making, accountability, reciprocity, and proportional costs and benefits among participants can manage ecological resources in a stable way. By contrast, social arrangements that allow power differentials, unequal regulation, unfair access, or undue burden are prone to ecological stress and diminished ecological function. Here, then, is the connection between ecological service and our legacy of sociocultural and socioeconomic evolution. Social cohesion offers behavioral control mechanisms that minimize anthropogenic stress and promote critical ecological processes. Accordingly, the SES approach holds that social dysfunction must be addressed prior to—and as a necessary precursor for—the solution of ecological problems (Box 7.1; Robbins et al., 2014: 115; Fischer-Kowalski and Weisz, 2016).

This social theory is a version of systems ecology, in that it conceptualizes ecological systems as nested, mutually dependent networks with dynamic structure and function. Even as individual participants (e.g. organisms, species, institutions) come and go, a system with relatively stable architecture can maintain certain functional states. In ecological literature, such a system is said to be *resilient* to disturbance—that is, it can maintain function amid upheaval. Stressed ecosystems are those that have lost internal diversity, connection, or functional redundancy and are thus more apt to lose function in the face of change. Connecting this theory to human social systems is still a relatively new endeavor. The idea is that certain sociocultural attributes (like the Ostrom-esque qualities listed above) can confer robust functional capacity to human communities. There are many potential complications here, to be sure. Market pressures, demographic factors, resource dependency, and similar factors can make the theory difficult to

---

Box 7.1 Coupled human and natural systems

Human social systems have co-evolved with ecological systems, but until quite recently these systems have been treated as separate entities in both academic and political circles. Considered together, coupled human and natural systems (CHANS) can provide new insight on environmental problems and solutions (Liu *et al.* 2007). One observation from this school of thought is that CHANS have changed over time. Historically (and pre-historically), human influence on natural systems was comparatively local and low-intensity. Modern extraction, industry, and affluent lifestyles have exerted an increasingly global, rapid, and intense pressure on natural eco-logical systems.

A central point to CHANS research is that human activities have direct and indirect effects on ecosystems services, and that ecosystems services have corresponding effects on human societies. These effects do not follow political or ecological boundaries. Nor are they symmetrical; that is, human and ecological communities do not generate or bear stress equally. Thus, human behavior in one locality can influence ecosystem services in many places around the world, just as global ecological processes can affect local actions.

One difficulty with modern CHANS is that human regulatory structures have traditionally operated at the level of interpersonal and hierarchical groups, while maintenance of global ecosystem services requires inter-nationally-coordinated action. Liu *et al.* (2007) therefore suggest that CHANS should be a focus of future environmental work, not only in terms of understanding linkages but also in the reconsideration of govern-ance, policy, and decision-making. Critical ecological processes may be protected with governance that fosters globally interconnected socioeco-logical systems, and they will likely fail in the absence of such governance. This challenge is effectively a call to stop thinking about human and non-human systems as merely co-existent and to start thinking about them as co-evolving and co-dependent.

---

test. Still, a body of scholarly work is providing evidence that links social behavior with functionally sustainable ecological systems. Key attributes to resilient social organizations appear to be inclusivity, communication, cooperation, reciprocity, and trust (Adger, 2000; Walker *et al.*, 2004; Barnes-Mauthe *et al.*, 2015; Fischer-Kowalski and Weisz, 2016).

Whether or not these principles are applicable to all human social systems is debatable—indeed, this question is representative of social ecology in general. As enticing as the intersection between scientific and social ecology is, it still needs more study. Even so, it is an intriguing line of thought, and one that I find to be consistent with our evolutionary origins: *Human social systems and ecological systems influence one another. Human activity can stress ecological systems. Low-stress ecosystems more effectively provide ecological services. Societies based on equity and cooperative reciprocity exert less stress on ecological systems and stabilize ecosystem services.*

Global ecology

Certain branches of social ecology have called for nothing short of an upheaval and re-invention of human society (Merchant, 2005: 139–161). Deep ecology, ecofeminism, animal liberation, and Gaianism all represent a revival of the softer side of Darwinian ecology—that of interrelatedness and harmonious balance. The intrinsic value of nonhuman nature, an egalitarian biocentrism, holism, and universal animism all experienced a renewed popularity in the environmental revolution of the 1960s and 1970s. In various ways, and not always in agreement, these ideologies advocate the protection of wilderness, alternatives to capitalism, mystic communion with the nonhuman world, and nature-as-religion. Such philosophies are by design quite distant from modern scientific ecology. This makes their tenets difficult to rectify with our current understanding of the natural world. Intrinsic value, for instance, only makes sense if value is judged by something or someone other than humans. Biocentric egalitarianism denies the well-established mechanism of natural selection. And animism implies a vital force that pervades and connects the entities of the universe—a force which has not yet been shown to exist beyond the human imagination.

Some versions of these worldviews equate *beneficial* states of nature with *correct* states of nature—what their adherents find to be *good* with what is *right* (Robbins *et al.*, 2014: 77). Critics have observed that this is more about promoting a particular political creed than achieving a better understanding of the ways in which the natural world actually functions. Bookchin (1989), for example, has argued that biocentrism and deep ecology deny humanity's central role in finding solutions to its own environmental problems; they fail to recognize that environmental problems have their roots in social inequity. Cronon (1996), Guha (1989), and others criticize biocentric ecologies as the perspectives of post-industrial privilege, seeking to impose their views on less privileged people who must work the land, sea, or forest in which they live in order to survive.

Revisiting the phenomenon of Gaianism illustrates the difference between understanding the ecological environment and moralizing it. As proposed by James Lovelock in 1972, the hypothesis stated that Earth is a complex, co-evolving system with self-regulating mechanisms (Lovelock, 1972). This basic observation is plausible. The biosphere is indeed a complex system, and many such systems have internal feedbacks which maintain the system within a range of function. The Earth's producers, for example, sequester carbon in a way that would ultimately cool the planet, but for consumers and volcanoes, which spew carbon back into the atmosphere and counteract cooling. These cycles demonstrably contribute to our understanding of global systems. Even to say that such systems have evolved is not problematic, for they were not always so. To say they evolved simply means that the participants and processes have changed over time. But the notion of Gaia has grown far beyond that which Lovelock initially proposed. The idea that global processes are directed by a superorganism to maintain suitable conditions for human existence makes a certain ecological condition the *correct* condition, and it makes the defense of that condition the *right* thing to do. Donald Worster—to cite just one critic—questions why the global harmony was not active several billion years ago, but only became active for the edification of modern humans (Worster, 1994: 382). In my estimation, much social ecology that trends toward spiritual ecology falls into the same trap. It is thought that conceives an ideal world for the thinker, and it elevates that thought to a moral imperative.

Scientific ecology, too, has come to consider global processes in recent decades, mostly—again—out of concern for anthropogenic stress and fragile ecosystem services. Global atmospheric change, first quantified in terms of carbon dioxide by Charles Keeling in 1958, has become a stress of great concern. Agriculture, extraction, industry, and urbanization: all have contributed to increased greenhouse gases in the atmosphere, and it is now well established (but widely denied politically) that anthropogenic emissions are correlated with global temperatures. The rising temperature itself is a concern, but some ancillary effects are perhaps more urgent. Atmospheric carbon dissolves in surface waters, making the oceans measurably more acidic. Warmer and more acidic water has resulted in the loss of coral reefs; all of these conditions plus deoxygenated dead zones threaten our already overharvested fisheries. Meanwhile, anthropogenic stress has been implicated in a global biodiversity decline, that which environmental author Elizabeth Kolbert and others have called the sixth great extinction in the history of our planet. Such global stressors are pushing ecological services to the brink (Keeling *et al.*, 1976; Karl and Trenberth, 2003; Kolbert, 2014).

But acidified oceans, deoxygenated lakes, and diversity-impoverished forests are not right or wrong. They are simply conditions of stress for certain organisms, conditions that are by-products of human activity. Some species are thriving in the midst of human-induced stress; it's just that they happen to be species that humans find undesirable or useless. Correspondingly, some desirable ecological functions are at risk of being lost and replaced by functions that do not serve humans as well. Healthy coral reefs, for example, are breeding grounds and nursery areas for many commercial fish species. Bleached reefs are dominated by algae and do not provide the same nursery function. Grasslands provide fodder for millions of grazing animals that feed millions of people. Grassland soils made saline by over-irrigation or saltwater intrusion become barren and no longer support grazing mammals. Forests provide long-term carbon sequestration, reducing the climate-changing effects of greenhouse gases in the atmosphere. Clear-cut and eroded land may not support the growth of trees, and so the functions of a forest are lost. There are many examples of such stress-induced shifts in ecosystem function (Scheffer *et al.*, 2001). All of them evoke value judgements not according to what sort of nature is inherently right or wrong, but instead by what is critical for human survival.

To modern scientific ecology, then, the emphasis is less about protecting particular species in their historic habitat or species associations as a unit (though there are still Clementsian efforts to do just this). Global change has made it clear that the distribution of species will change and that ecosystems do not seek and maintain a proper state. Rather, conservation in the midst of constant change is (or should be) more concerned with stabilizing the ecological functions on which our species depends.

This is not to say that the prioritization of particular species is folly. The Endangered Species Act, the International Union for the Conservation of Nature (IUCN) Red List, and many environmental organizations focus on the protection of iconic species. In part this is residual romanticism; in part it is just good marketing. Certain species simply capture the human imagination. Many people want to protect charismatic species, and will vote with ballots and dollars to do so even if they will likely never see those species in the wild. Conservation ecologists can work with this interest to protect the habitats and processes that popular species (and ultimately humans) need. It is much easier to interest people in protecting the orangutan, for example, than it is to interest them in facilitating carbon sequestration.

What this means is that scientific ecology has moved away from the expectation that ecosystems will self-assemble in the correct association. Rather, it has trended toward the active manipulation and management of ecological systems to protect vital functions. Prevailing theory is that ecological processes are resilient to an extent; they have the capacity to absorb disturbance and maintain function, even as species come and go. Cumulative stress, however, reduces resilience and increases the likelihood that a major disturbance will shift function into an undesirable state (Walker and Salt, 2012). In response, many conservation biologists have become ecological engineers. Through active intervention to minimize stress, maximize diversity, and manage disturbance regimes, vital ecological processes may be restored and maintained. Some ecologists, like Michael Rosenzweig, suggest that active management can allow functional, low-stress ecosystems to occur alongside areas of more intensive human activity. The catch is that people must recognize and prioritize the ecological attributes that make services possible (Rosenzweig, 2003).

The ecological engineering approach has shown some success on a local scale (Mitsch, 2012). Small patches of habitat, stressed by fragmentation, nutrient load, invasion, and erosion have been rehabilitated through land acquisition, regulation, prescribed disturbance, and selective planting. Such applied ecology is now a major focus of many nonprofit organizations and governmental agencies. When the stressors are global, however, they are not so easily managed with local action. Salt marsh restoration in the face of sea level rise, forest rehabilitation amid acid rain, fishery recovery in deoxygenated oceans—these are all beyond the capacity of the ecological engineer. These problems will not be solved without social action on an international scale.

Ecological change, changing ecology

What began as the discipline of ecology is now many disciplines; in this sense the field has changed a great deal since the time of Darwin and Haeckel. In another sense, it is much the same, for ecologists still struggle with the Darwinian paradox. Are ecological systems fundamentally driven by competition, appropriation, and the individual struggle for survival? Are they systems of kinship, cooperation, and mutual benefit? The answers appear to be yes, and yes. Yes, natural selection is a messy process, and the price of life is suffering and death. But also yes, there are many opportunities for and instances of cooperation and coexistence. Pending evidence to the contrary, these do not appear to be cooperation in the super-organism sense, nor does coexistence occur according to some supernatural directive. Furthermore—given our understanding of ecological stress, disturbance and the shifting pressures of evolution—it is now clear that the romantic ideals of natural balance, harmony, native species, and climax communities are figments of our collective imagination. Part of the hard work of environmentalism is aligning our mental models with ecological realities. But the lessons of reality are not all bad. Living organisms, given the chance, can and do interact with one another for common benefit. Now, as we recognize that human social problems are compromising ecological systems, it seems that the species that most needs to cooperate is our own.

Bibliography

Adger, W.N. (2000). Social and ecological resilience: are they related? *Progress in Human Geography*, 24(3), pp. 347–364.

Barnes-Mauthe, M., Gray, S.A., Arita, S., Lynham, J. and Leung, P. (2015). What determines social capital in a social–ecological system? Insights from a network perspective. *Environmental Management*, 55(2), pp. 392–410.

Bookchin, M. (1989). *Remaking society*. Montreal: Black Rose Books.

Burch, G.I. and Pendell, E. (1945). *Population roads to peace or war*. Washington, DC: Population Reference Bureau.

Carson, R. (1962). *Silent spring*. Boston: Houghton Mifflin.

Clements, F.E. (1916). *Plant succession: an analysis of the development of vegetation*. Washington, DC: Carnegie Institution of Washington.

Cronon, W. (1996). The trouble with wilderness, or getting back to the wrong nature. *Environmental History*, 1(1), pp. 7–28.

Egerton, F.N. (2013). History of the ecological sciences, part 47: Ernst Haeckel's ecology. *Bulletin of the Ecological Society of America*, 94(3), pp. 222–244.

Ehrlich, P.R. (1968). *The population bomb*. New York: Ballantine.

Elton, C. (1927). *Animal ecology*. New York: Macmillan.

Fischer-Kowalski, M. and Weisz, H. (2016). The archipelago of social ecology and the island of the Vienna school. In: H. Haberl, M. Fischer-Kowalski, F. Krausmann, and V. Winiwarter, eds., *Social ecology: society–nature relations across time and space*. New York: Springer. pp. 3–28.

Gleason, H.A. (1939). The individualistic concept of the plant association. *American Midland Naturalist*, pp. 92–110.

Guha, R. (1989). Radical American environmentalism and wilderness preservation: a third world critique. *Environmental Ethics*, 11(1), pp. 71–83.

Hardin, G. (1968). The tragedy of the commons. *Science*, 162(3859), pp. 1243–1248.

Hardin, G. (1974). Commentary: living on a lifeboat. *BioScience*, 24(10), pp. 561–568.

Karl, T.R. and Trenberth, K.E. (2003). Modern global climate change. *Science*, 302(5651), pp. 1719–1723.

Keeling, C.D., Bacastow, R.B., Bainbridge, A.E., Ekdahl, C.A., Guenther, P.R., Waterman, L.S. and Chin, J.F. (1976). Atmospheric carbon dioxide variations at Mauna Loa observatory, Hawaii. *Tellus*, 28(6), pp. 538–551.

Kolbert, E. (2014). *The sixth extinction: An unnatural history.* New York: A&C Black.

Kricher, J. (2009). *The balance of nature: ecology's enduring myth.* Princeton, NJ: Princeton University Press.

Leopold, A. (1921). The wilderness and its place in forest recreational policy. *Journal of Forestry*, 19(7), pp. 718–721.

Leopold, A. (1991 [1932]). Game and wild life conservation. In: S. Flader and J. Callicott, eds., 1991. *The river of the mother of God and other essays by Aldo Leopold.* Madison, WI: University of Wisconsin Press. pp. 165–166.

Leopold, A. (1941). Wilderness as a land laboratory. *Living Wilderness*, 6, p. 3.

Leopold, A. (1949). *A Sand County almanac.* New York: Oxford University Press.

Leopold, A. (1966 [1938]). Conservation. In: L. Leopold, ed. *Round river.* New York: Oxford University Press. pp. 145–146.

Liu, J., Dietz, T., Carpenter, S.R., Folke, C., Alberti, M., Redman, C.L., Schneider, S.H., Ostrom, E., Pell, A.N., Lubchenco, J. and Taylor, W.W. (2007). Coupled human and natural systems. *AMBIO: A Journal of the Human Environment*, 36(8), pp. 639–649.

Lovelock, J.E. (1972). Gaia as seen through the atmosphere. *Atmospheric Environment*, 6(8), pp. 579–580.

Malthus, T.R. (1888 [1798]). *An essay on the principle of population: or, a view of its past and present effects on human happiness.* 99th edition. London: Reeves & Turner.

Mann, C. (2005). *1491: New revelations of the Americas before Columbus.* Alfred Knopf.

Marsh, G.P. (1864). *Man and nature, or physical geography as modified by human action.* New York: Scribner.

Meadows, D., Meadows, D., Randers, J. and Behrens III, W.W. (1972). *The limits to growth.* New York: Universe Books.

Merchant, C. (2005). *Radical ecology: the search for a livable world.* New York: Routledge.

Miller, C. (2001). *Gifford Pinchot and the making of modern environmentalism.* Washington, DC: Island Press.

Mitsch, W.J. (2012). What is ecological engineering? *Ecological Engineering*, 45, pp. 5–12.

Muir, J. (1911). *My first summer in the Sierra.* San Francisco: Sierra Club Books.

Nash, R.F. (1989). *The rights of nature: a history of environmental ethics.* Madison, WI: University of Wisconsin Press.

Nicolson, M. (1990). Henry Allan Gleason and the individualistic hypothesis: the structure of a botanist's career. *Botanical Review*, 56(2), pp. 91–161.

Odum, E.P. (1985). Trends expected in stressed ecosystems. *Bioscience*, 35(7), pp. 419–422.

Ostrom, E. (2010). Beyond markets and states: polycentric governance of complex economic systems. *Transnational Corporations Review*, 2(2), pp. 641–672.

Osborn, F. (1948). *Our plundered planet.* New York: Little, Brown & Co.

Peterson, M.J., Hall, D.M., Feldpausch-Parker, A.M. and Peterson, T.R. (2010). Obscuring ecosystem function with application of the ecosystem services concept. *Conservation Biology*, 24(1), pp. 113–119.

Radkau, J. (2014). *The age of ecology.* New York: Wiley.

Rigby, K. (2014). Romanticism and ecocriticism. In: G. Garrard, ed. *The Oxford handbook of ecocriticism.* Oxford: Oxford University Press. pp. 60–79.

Robbins, P., Hintz, J. and Moore, S.A. (2014). *Environment and society: a critical introduction.* 2nd edition. Chichester, UK: Wiley-Blackwell.

Rohde, K. (2005). *Nonequilibrium ecology.* Cambridge, UK: Cambridge University Press.

Rosenzweig, M.L. (2003). Reconciliation ecology and the future of species diversity. *Oryx,* 37(2), pp. 194–205.

Scheffer, M., Carpenter, S., Foley, J.A., Folke, C. and Walker, B. (2001). Catastrophic shifts in ecosystems. *Nature,* 413(6856), pp. 591–596.

Spieles, D.J. (2010). *Protected land: disturbance, stress, and American ecosystem management.* New York: Springer.

Sweeney, R.A. (1993). "Dead" Sea of North America? Lake Erie in the 1960s and '70s. *Journal of Great Lakes Research,* 19(2), pp. 198–199.

Thoreau, H.D. (1971 [1854]). *Walden.* Shanley, J.L., ed. Princeton, NJ: Princeton University Press.

Vogt, W. (1948). *Road to survival.* New York: W. Sloane Associates.

Walker, B., Holling, C.S., Carpenter, S. and Kinzig, A. (2004). Resilience, adaptability and transformability in social–ecological systems. *Ecology and Society,* 9(2), p. 5.

Walker, B. and Salt, D. (2012). *Resilience thinking: sustaining ecosystems and people in a changing world.* Washington, DC: Island Press.

Worster, D. (1994). *Nature's economy: a history of ecological ideas.* Cambridge, UK: Cambridge University Press.

Wu, J. and Loucks, O.L. (1995). From balance of nature to hierarchical patch dynamics: a paradigm shift in ecology. *Quarterly Review of Biology,* 70(4), pp. 439–466.

8 Sociospiritual evolution

Key points

- Spirituality and religion are ancient products of sociobiological and sociocultural evolution.
- Spirituality can play an important role in personal well-being, and religion can confer social well-being.
- Religious spirituality offers a model of interpersonal accountability, though it can be hampered by parochial xenophobia.

Through the course of evolution, our species has developed certain characteristics that lend themselves to environmentalism. We are cooperative and reciprocal social organisms. We have the ability to form and evaluate mental scenarios. We have norms of sociocultural expectation. Just as these qualities can shape our social and ecological surroundings, they can be shaped by those surroundings. We have seen how sociocultural evolution has challenged systems of cooperative reciprocity, even as it has threatened the stability of ecological services. We have also seen that mental models of the natural world can differ from the realities of ecological structure and function. This chapter is devoted to another sort of mental model that can simultaneously define and confound environmentalism: our sociospiritual nature.

Conceptual scenarios do not only occur in the individual mind. We share our mental models, and they in turn are subject to the forces of sociocultural selection. Interpretation of the universe is a cooperative and competitive enterprise. Thus, as other elements of culture have evolved, so too have our spiritual perceptions. From the first efforts to make sense of the inexplicable, to rituals of honor, passage, and group bonding, to romantic visions of the supernatural, to scientific theories of human cognition—all are part of our spiritual legacy. Today, it leaves us pondering what—if anything—about our world is *sacred*, and what this might mean for our collective behavior.

Spiritual origins

On the ceiling of the Sistine Chapel Michelangelo painted *The Creation of Adam*, that famous fresco of the finger of God reaching out to touch the finger of man. It depicts the moment of creation, or perhaps the moment of intellectual endow- ment, from the Most High to that which He made in His own image. It captures in breathtaking imagery the questions that humans have contemplated as long as we have had the ability to contemplate anything: Who are we? Where do we come from? What is our place in the universe?

The biblical interpretation of *The Creation of Adam* has ready answers to these questions, of course. We are God's highest creation. We come from His hand. We are here to do His will. Such is the certainty of monotheism. But spiritual explanations of the human condition are as widespread and diverse as culture itself. Thousands of spiritual traditions (and an unknowable number of others that are now extinct) revere stories of humans, nature, and the supernatural to explain their origins just as Michelangelo's brushstrokes explain it for the Judeo-Christian. Actually, though, Michelangelo seems to have incorporated a hidden message into *The Creation of Adam* that might suggest a different tale. In 1990 a physician named Frank Lynn Meshberger observed something that had apparently eluded everyone else for over 470 years. The cloth surrounding God and his angels in the fresco is an anatomically accurate silhouette of the human brain. This can hardly be a coincidence, for Michelangelo was both a perfectionist and a master of human anatomy. What, then, was his reason for this portrayal? Meshberger proposed that Michelangelo was illustrating God's gift of intellect to the human race. But another interpretation is that the great master was implying that God, angels, and the story of creation exist only within the human mind (Meshberger, 1990).

I don't know Michelangelo's true purpose, and maybe no one ever will. In any case, the juxtaposition of the miraculous spark of life with the physical lobes and sulci of the brain presents a perfect framework for an exploration of environmental spirituality. For millions of people, the natural world is sacred because it holds the spirit or expresses the creation of the divine. Nature is thus sanctified, and cultural rituals for the reverence of nature are the essence of environmentalism. For millions of others, spirituality is an evolutionary adaptation of the structure and neurochemistry of the brain. It plays a vital role in behavior, mental health, and social cohesion, but it comes from within our own neural function and is entirely natural, not supernatural. Hence, human perception of the universe is divided by a conflict between the spiritual and the material. Perhaps Michelangelo was depicting just this controversy.

I have been using the term *spiritual* and will continue to do so, but it may be useful to compare it with the term *religious*. There are nearly as many definitions of these terms as there are authors who write about them. I will loosely follow con- cepts offered by Jared Diamond in *The world until yesterday* (2012: 329). Spirituality is a broad perspective that generally includes one or more of the following: 1) A belief in the supernatural; that is, a belief that there is a force (or are forces) that we cannot sense but that explains certain actions or circumstances that we experience. For example, a spiritual person might believe that a drought is happening for a providential reason that we are not meant to know or understand. 2) A belief in mysticism, that is, a belief in the human ability to commune with the supernatural by prayer, meditation, or other means to seek guidance, to offer thanks, or to petition. 3) A belief that one is part of something bigger than one's self, and that this connection gives life meaning. Part of this is the sense that the self extends beyond the physical, and that the soul can interact with a greater spiritual energy for a common purpose. Religion by some definitions includes these things as well, but note that the three items listed above may all be accomplished individually. Religion, in contrast, includes things that are more socially oriented, such as: 1) Social membership, with visible signs of commitment, like attendance, financial contribution, recitation, or participation in rituals. These serve to show and re-affirm that one is part of the religious community. 2) Common rules of morality, which are well-known to group members and required for group membership. Religion, then, is about monitoring the behavior of others as much as it is about one's own behavior. The Christian environmentalist Cal DeWitt has defined religion as "the passion to live rightly on Earth and to spread right living" (Tippett, 2016: 40). Clearly, there is a social component to religion (as DeWitt defines it) compared with spirituality (as I have defined it). Of course, many religious and spiritual traditions include some but not all of these items, and many individuals subscribe to some but not others. But this gives us a place to start.

If we compare spirituality and religion to environmentalism we see some clear connections. Supernatural belief is central to animism, pantheism, and Gaianism. Mystical beliefs are part of the worldview of many cultures. Holism—the understanding of the natural world as one interconnected entity with emergent properties—is a characteristic of many conceptions of nature. Moreover, demonstrated adherence to a system of morality is an aspect of group interaction and social membership. Religions can function as social control mechanisms, encouraging cooperative reciprocity and discouraging hedonic selfishness (D.S. Wilson, 2002: 162). Just as social control is central to religion, it is central to the social contracts that are the basis for environmental equity. I do not therefore equate environmentalism with spirituality or religion; I only note that they share some characteristics.

As far as we know, nonhuman animals exhibit nothing like spirituality or religion. There is some speculation that our hominid cousins (like Neanderthals) may have had some sort of ritual behavior, but even if they did, with their extinction spirituality became distinctly human. How did these mindsets and behaviors arise in our species?

One model, of course, is that a supreme being bestowed the capacity for spirituality on humans alone, as depicted by the finger of God in Michelangelo's work. Alongside the general lack of evidence for this (and perhaps it is an event for which there could never be evidence), there are some logical problems. For one, the thousands of different spiritual traditions and creation stories are in many ways contradictory with one another and with physical laws, such that they cannot all be factual. It is odd that a supreme being would provide contradictory information. Second, many traditional accounts of spirituality rely upon Cartesian mind–body dualism, meaning that the "gift" of spirituality to humans and other living (and even nonliving) things is in the form of an extrabiotic vital energy. Such an energy has not yet been identified (and perhaps is not identifiable); this makes the vital force of organisms and the mystical connection between them difficult to ascertain. Third, the purpose and direction of nature espoused by some spiritual environmentalists is at odds with that which appears to be its primary mechanism: evolution by natural selection. Natural selection, being directionless, is not a process that implies a purpose or goal for living things. Still, to a true believer, no amount of logic or reason will dislodge strength of conviction. In the words of early Christian philosopher Tertullian (c.155–c.240 CE), "if we believe, we desire nothing further than to be Believers" (1722 [c.220]: 25; Stamos, 2008: 46–49, 180–181).

But a great many people *do* desire to believe further, and many have proposed that there are better explanations for the emergence of human spirituality, namely evolutionary explanations. David Stamos, in *Evolution and the big questions* (2008: 178–185), examines spirituality and religion in terms of sociocultural evolution, sociobiological evolution, and theistic evolution. Having already explored sociocultural evolution, we can quickly get to the theory: spiritual explanations, stories, and beliefs about the natural world, as well as associated rituals, are memes. They originate as mental models in the brains of individual people, and they spread by communication, imitation, and education (likely with mutations, additions, and deletions along the way) to the collective intelligence of one or more social groups. Most importantly, the environmental sociospiritual memes that survive to this day (e.g. that there is an extrabiotic spirit in all living things, that life on Earth is directed by a supreme being, or that Earth itself is a self-regulating organism) have out-competed other memes, not necessarily because they are true, but because they resonate with human psychological biases. For instance, they are presented as easy-to-remember stories, they are proclaimed by highly respected people in positions of power, they are subscribed to by the majority of one's group, they include co-selected memes of reward for the believer and punishment or exclusion for the non-believer, they discourage criticism, or they are tied to ritual. As noted above, such ideas are important mechanisms of group bonding, which explains why thousands of different cultures all have unique stories of spiritual connection with nature.

As we have seen, sociocultural evolution happens on a foundation of—and in conjunction with—sociobiological evolution. As such, the components of spirituality exist at various places along that spectrum of instinctive to entirely learned behaviors. Humans have an innate capacity for imitation, for example. Our genetic inheritance also seems to include an instinctual obedience to authority, a propensity to seek agency and purpose in events and occurrences, a tendency toward binary classification (e.g. good and evil), a penchant for reducing variation to prototypes, and a "predisposition toward indoctrination" (E.O. Wilson, 1975: 186; Stamos, 2008: 187). Clearly, such traits would confer real survival advantage on the prehistoric savanna, as our ancestors needed to sense and categorize their surroundings, quickly identify friend or foe, and follow the direction of a leader at a critical moment to flee, strike, or defend. Such instincts are not as absolute as the blushing response; they are statistically variable in a population. Thus some people aren't particularly obedient to authority, while others are. An illustration of this point is provided by an often-cited study which found that two-thirds of participants readily administered an apparently painful electric shock to another person simply because they were instructed to do so by an authority figure—they were obedient even to the point of hurting another. One-third of the participants refused to go so far in following orders (Milgram, 1974). So the expression of these instincts can vary, but taken together they present a plausible mechanism by which memes could easily be taken up and churned into spiritual beliefs through the process of cultural evolution. In other words, our genes predispose us to spirituality and religion (Dissanayake, 1992: 159).

Why should this be so? Why would our genetic inheritance prime us for spiritual thoughts and religious behaviors? One perspective is that biological and socio-cultural evolution are God's mechanisms for enacting His plan. This is known as theistic evolution. Some theistic evolutionists suppose that a supreme being set up the processes of evolution, but then, once life on Earth began, allowed evolution to proceed undirected. Others see every step of evolution guided by a vigilant God. In both scenarios, the results of evolution are an expression of the Supreme Being, with humans as the ultimate achievement. This means that God's chosen mechanism is evolution by natural selection, complete with all of the suffering, starvation, disease, deformity, and death it entails. It also means that every chance contingency and every random mutation over billions of years that resulted in the evolution of our species was either pre-ordained or guided; that essentially, there is no such thing as chance—that God has "loaded the dice in our favor" (Stamos, 2008: 203). To some, this implies a universal determinism that is not only cal-loused but also terribly arrogant—to believe that a system of suffering would be set into motion just so that our species could walk the Earth. Additionally, there is the question of the immortal soul. If we humans indeed have a soul but are also the product of evolution, at what point in evolutionary history did the soul become a characteristic of living things? Or was it always there, meaning that vile parasites and pathogenic bacteria also have a soul? These contentious thoughts are the unsteady ground on which the theistic evolutionist must stand (Stamos, 2008: 196–213).

Another explanation of our genetic propensity for religious spirituality—absent the direct influence of God—is that these characteristics were not directly selected for, but that they emerged incidentally from a collection of skills. We have seen this before: this theory is that religious spirituality is a spandrel. In this perspective, the various instincts described above each confer a survival advantage of their own. It is easy to imagine, for example, that obedience to authority would offer a survival advantage quite apart from any spiritual or religious connotation. If all of these instincts were thus inherited for other reasons, it could be that spiritual beliefs and religious behavior emerged as a by-product. By analogy, this is like riding a bicycle. Bike riding could hardly have evolved in and of itself, for there were no bikes until 1817. But evolution did hone our skeletomuscular structure, our spatial balance, and our ability to coordinate vision with motor skills. These and a pair of ridiculous-looking shorts work nicely together on a two-wheeler. Just so, according to the spandrel theory, the characteristics of obedience, conformity, binary classification, and agency attribution provide the foundation for the incidental emergence of spirituality and religion (Seybold, 2010: 96).

Other scholars, however, see clear survival advantages to religious spirituality itself. Individuals of early human societies who were true believers—or even those who were simply good at learning spiritual ways and conforming to rituals—may have had a better chance of winning a mate and producing offspring. They may have also been more mentally, physically, and emotionally healthy, thereby improving their odds of survival. It is plausible, too, that religious spirituality offers real survival advantages for the social group. Most obviously, a group that follows an authority figure with unquestioned devotion might have a survival advantage in times of crisis. In more mundane, day-to-day life, rituals have a spiritual connotation but are generally connected to real-world survival. The treatment of illness, the timing of planting and harvest, the preparation of food, and personal hygiene are all ritualistic in many cultures, as are the processes of choosing a mate and raising children (Stamos, 2008: 187).

Then there are taboos, those culturally (and perhaps genetically) transmitted customs that prohibit certain behaviors within a social group. Bohm *et al.* (2009: 4–6) speculate that taboo, along with animism and mysticism, was a dominant formative agent in early human cultures. In some cultures, taboo behavior is thought to provoke the gods and invite supernatural retaliation; violators are subject to severe punishment or banishment. The incest taboo is well known and virtually universal, but many others were common among tribal peoples (and some still are). Taboos against touching tribal leaders, on the treatment of the dead, on the avoidance of particular places, on the killing or eating of certain animals, on the creation of images or use of names (e.g. in reference to a god)—all restrict individual behaviors for spiritual reasons. In some cases, we can see the primal morality of social control in the observance of taboo-based restrictions on personal excess and self-gratification. Others are clearly linked with personal and community health, like incest avoidance, burial of the dead, and prohibition on the consumption of toxic or disease-causing food items.

Interestingly, another common category of taboo involves interaction with the nonhuman world. In the Shona people of Zimbabwe, for example, the avoidance of sacred sites and species is similar to modern nature reserves and protected species in developed societies. The fruit-bearing muhacha tree may not be cut down. Mountains are not to be encroached upon. Certain animals, like the praying mantis, are not to be killed. The Shona also have taboos against urinating in water and soiling water with soot, both protections against community resource degradation. These are, in effect, all rules of environmental sustainability. But they are not part of the culture because of a collective agreement to conserve and protect resources. Taboo plants, animal, and spaces are avoided because they are thought to harbor spirits that will make violators disappear or go insane. Cutting down a muhacha tree is believed to be an action that will stop the rain. Mountains are considered sacred because the vapor rising from them is thought to predict the weather. Killing a praying mantis will adversely affect the cows' milk production. Soiling water with soot is said to dry up the well, and urinating in a river is said to bring on painful disease. None of these have any scientific basis, but as social/ spiritual/ecological rules they constitute an environmental ethic (Chemhura and Masaka, 2010).

Taboos, then, are a sort of sociospiritual cage, distinguishing behaviors that are acceptable from those that are not. In many cases they appear to be ancient wisdom of social and environmental co-existence—instances of traditional ecological knowledge—and perhaps they are. An important point to remember, however, is that taboos (and many religious doctrines, for that matter) are culturally and geographically specific. A serious taboo for one culture might be utter nonsense to another. Likewise, shifting populations, altered conditions, and changing climates can reduce a bit of ancient wisdom to a cultural liability. Orlove (2005) recounts an example in the fate of the Norse settlement in Greenland (c.984–1400). The reasons for the demise of this civilization are complex, but they clearly center upon a few food sources which were critical for survival. It seems that these European settlers relied almost entirely on the seal and caribou hunt to supplement their cattle, making them vulnerable to climatic shifts that altered migration patterns or prohibited grazing. They ultimately struggled with starvation, apparently in the midst of abundant oceanic fish that they would not eat. Diamond (2005: 228–230) speculates that for one reason or another (like a refusal to adopt Inuit practices, or a belief that local fish were unclean) the Greenland Norse developed a fish-eating taboo. This might have indeed been cultural wisdom as long as other food sources were plentiful. But then the seal hunt failed, and the weather did not provide for hay production, and their cultural instincts became a hindrance. In a changing world, a sociospiritual cage that is too rigid can become a trap.

In summary, then, spiritual beliefs and religious practices are products of our sociobiological nature and sociocultural evolution. Universal human characteristics like obedience, agency assignment, and binary classification make the human intellect fertile ground for spirituality. The character of our collective intelligence and interpersonal dynamics makes our social groups fertile ground for religion.

Material foundations

If the traits that provide for religious spirituality are genetically heritable they would need to have a physical basis that could be acted upon by natural selection. There is a growing body of evidence to this effect (Hamer, 2004; Alper, 2006: 155–158; Stamos, 2008: 192–195). While the instinct for spiritual thought and religious behavior is far too complex to relate to a single gene or a particular neurotransmitter, these characteristics do appear to have a physiological foundation. First, there is neurological evidence. Seizures of the temporal and parietal brain lobes have been shown to give patients mystical feelings, visions, and out-of-body experiences. The same sensations can be generated by electrical stimulation of these brain regions. Second, meditation and prayer have been shown to alter brain wave activity, particularly by reducing blood flow to the section of the brain that distinguishes self from non-self and is thus associated with spatial orientation. The implication is that reduced activity in this region can result in a feeling of spatial disorientation, or a sense of being everywhere at once. Third, surveys of identical and fraternal twins, raised together or apart, on measures of religious interest, values, and fundamentalism indicate that about half of the variation in response is genetically influenced. This means that a spiritual disposition is partially heritable (and so is an absence of spiritual disposition). Fourth, spiritual states of mind are chemically inducible with psychedelic drugs. This is true not only of modern pharmaceuticals, but also of ethnobotanical agents used for thousands of years to evoke extra-somatic experiences in human minds. Finally, research by geneticist Dean Hamer has identified a gene implicated with spiritual sensation. This gene codes for a protein involved in the "packaging" of neurotransmitters like dopamine, adrenaline, noradrenaline, and serotonin. Alteration in the amounts of these neurochemicals is associated with "every facet of self-transcendence, from loving nature to loving God, from feeling at one with the universe to being willing to sacrifice for its improvement" (Hamer, 2004: 73). The particular allele associated with increased feelings of self-transcendence has a single difference in its nucleic acid sequence: cytosine in place of adenine. As hypothesized, subjects with the cytosine allele scored significantly higher on personality traits of self-transcendence, spirituality, and holism. Hamer does not claim that this is the only spirituality gene, just that it is one of many. But as these neurotransmitters moderate our emotions, values, and mental models of the universe, their genetic foundation is a significant discovery indeed.

Such evidence is trending toward Michelangelo's hidden riddle—that spiritual enlightenment comes from our own brains—and away from the "finger of God" model of spirituality. This is a large and jagged pill to swallow for many people. While we are considering it, let's add two important corollaries. First, if "altered" brain states—caused by seizures, stimulation, pharmaceuticals, or meditation— can temporarily blur the boundaries between self and the rest of the universe, then our "normal" brain structure and function must work to *clarify* the division between self and other. What this means is that our brains have evolved to make us think that we are separate from nature. Descartes, were he here, might take a measure of vindication from this thought. Second, if Hamer's gene is one of many that affect neurotransmitter activity, and if a small difference in that one gene can affect spiritual personality, then the number of possible spiritual mindsets must be very high (Stamos, 2008: 194–195). Hamer estimates that there might be 50 such genes (Hamer, 2004: 77). Imagine that individual A happens to have 95% "spiritual" alleles while individual B has only 5% spiritual alleles. Individual A achieves a neurobiological state of transcendence easily and often, while individual B does not understand what transcendence feels like. It makes sense that individual A is a true believer and individual B is not. But then consider that every other percentage is also possible, and you no longer have a dichotomy of believe-it-or-not, you've got a continuum of spiritual and religious experience. Further, if natural selection resulted in this continuum of possibilities, then each possibility (or many of them) must be acceptable in terms of individual fitness and of value to group survival. What all of this means is that spirituality varies greatly among humans, and it makes no more sense to vilify people for their degree of—or lack of—spirituality than it does to vilify them for the color of their skin.

But we do seem to hold people accountable for their degree of spirituality, and this is just as prevalent in environmentalism as it is in every other aspect of modern society. Those who feel nature in their soul, who find spirit in the nonhuman, who see the Earth as God or Goddess are often frustrated by those who do not. And those who seek to sustain ecological processes for purely practical reasons are bewildered by and often dismissive of spirituality. This conflict is not just a social construct; it is built into our physiology. Our sociocultural evolution—indeed, our view of self, other, and nature—can thus be viewed as an ongoing struggle to reconcile the spiritual and the material.

Sociospiritual evolution

If we accept the premise that a spiritual mindset has a genetic basis, and if we acknowledge that spirituality is ubiquitous among human cultures (or nearly so) but variable among human individuals, we can begin to construct an idea of how spirituality came to be such an important part of environmentalism. Here, then, is a speculative scenario of sociospiritual evolution (Diamond, 2012: 367).

With the evolution of the mental capacity for time-shifting scenario building, the human brain was able to compare perceptions of reality with its own simulations of *possible* realities. As we have seen, this ability seems to be a mental skill that separates humans from other animals, and it likely played (and still plays) an important role in sociocultural evolution. It is also plausible that this mental ability allowed for the attribution of unexplainable events to supernatural agents. Death of close relatives, for example, and environmental disturbances, and the behavior of animals, and the origin of one's group—all would have defied explanation among our ancient ancestors. And so mental models filled in the gaps and became stories told around the campfire. Through the course of meme selection and mutation these became culturally specific and group-defining spiritual explanations. Based on anthropological studies of modern foraging societies, it seems likely that these early scenarios revolved around "ancestor worship and nature spirit worship" (Stamos, 2008: 180). They are thus the beginnings of what we think of as spirituality (Diamond, 2012: 345–346).

As spiritual explanations became embedded into cultures, they became associated with rituals and taboos—rites of passage, ideas of sanctity, prohibitions against certain actions—to honor the spirits of ancestors, to appease the gods, or even in an attempt to control natural phenomena. According to Bruce Lerro (2000), rites and spells in indigenous spirituality are often aimed at harnessing the power of nature, for the spirits of nature are believed to be accessible to the human spirit. Rituals also took on the role of social identity. One who knows the spirits, follows the example of the chief and faithfully keeps the rituals and taboos is one of us, and those who do not are not. Actually, rituals and taboos are more than this. They are a proxy for morality; they are an authentication of one's intentions (or what Diamond calls badges of commitment). Here we should remember that the spiritual mindset even among our early ancestors was likely a continuum from true believer to skeptic. The observance of rituals and taboos identified one as a true believer. Those of a contrary mindset could perhaps fake the commitment— though this might not be easy—or find assistance in ethnobotanicals or in meditation or trance-based ritual to accept the commitment, and hence be accepted by the community. Persistent skeptics were probably not great candidates for survival and reproduction. Social pressure to conform to particular rites and moral codes, on pain of banishment, is the beginning of what we think of as religion (Lerro, 2000: 20; Diamond, 2012: 361).

Belief in supernatural agents and participation in rituals goes beyond the confirmation of group membership. It confers real benefits to both group and individual. Alper (2006) has postulated that spirituality is an evolved survival mechanism that relieves us from the anxieties of the future—particularly the reality of our own death, but generally of things we cannot control. Spiritual mental states alter brain function and induce feelings of unity, peace, tranquility, and timelessness. These responses are commonly seen in intense religious experiences and transcendental meditation (and incidentally, similar feelings are expressed by some who experience deep immersion in nature). In the midst of fear, grief, terror, uncertainty, or strife, spirituality provides comfort and assurance. Jared Diamond offers a second benefit: that spiritual beliefs and religious practices confer survival advantage through social support. Shared thoughts (e.g. prayer or chant) and activities (rituals) facilitate group cohesion. Shared spirituality provides organization, unquestioned obedience, and socially mandated reciprocity which could provide survival advantages during a crisis. Given these advantages (and the social pressures wielded against the non-compliant), it is easy to see how spirituality and religion became a characteristic of many, if not all, human cultures (Diamond, 2012).

Animism thus became entrenched as polytheism (or paganism), of which perhaps a few thousand cultures remain of the many that have existed throughout human sociocultural evolution. It is worth pausing here for a moment to recall the relationship of the animist with the natural world and with fellow humans. To the animist, one's psyche is not independent of the spirits of nature; rather human spirits and natural spirits are collective. It follows that one's spiritual life can only make sense in geographical and ecological context. Ceremony and ritual, then, are about *becoming* nature, not merely representing it. Taboos, as we have seen, often have an element of environmental sustainability, as does the sanctity affixed to particular animals, plants, or places. The group cohesion enforced by adherence to ritual adds an element of social conscience. This fosters egalitarianism on the small scale, perhaps even extending beyond blood relatives. These all sound like idyllic social and environmental behaviors, and in many tribes throughout the existence of our species they may well have been (though the rose-tinted vision must be tempered by the practice of banishing nonconformists). The good will of the tribe, however, rarely extends to people or environments that are external to the tribe. Ritual-based moral codes apply to those who know and obey the rituals, and sanctity applies to known places. Unknown people and places are disregarded at best, and beneath contempt at worst (Lerro, 2000: 66; Diamond, 2012: 45–53; Northcott, 2015: 157–158).

The spiritual mindset is prominent in foraging cultures, for many foraging customs and behaviors originated in the absence of a scientific understanding of the world. Thus, the rituals and taboos we see today are those that survived the process of sociocultural selection over millennia. Further, there is a strong element of sociobiological selection at play here. Small, intimate, spiritually oriented cultures select for true believers. For most of its history (and prehistory), then, the evolution of our species has favored an animistic spirituality.

The emergence of monotheism presented a challenge to pagan animism that has since swept through and beyond the western world. Monotheism grew out of and existed alongside polytheism, but eventually came to dominate it. Exactly how monotheism has out-competed polytheism is a matter of some debate. In his book *From Earth spirits to sky gods* (2000), Bruce Lerro presents a convincing case that the stages of spiritual and religious evolution are a direct response to the stages of social change as they occurred from roughly 6000 to 500 BCE. Animistic spirituality is an egalitarian relationship between human and natural spirits, just as foraging society is egalitarian in structure. Everyone in such a culture has direct access to the spirits, for all spirits are part of one collective. With the stratification of society (which happens for a host of reasons, like population growth, domestication, resource stress, and others) comes the stratification of spiritual life. This means that social hierarchy parallels the development of religious and spiritual hierarchy. Gradually, some in the society (the chief, the priest, the shaman) come to have access to the spiritual world that the average citizen does not. The spirits are no longer reachable except through the intercession of the holy man. In Lerro's words, with the commodification of natural objects, the spirits gradually get "moved" from their seats within the objects and organisms of nature to a "transcendental space" in the sky. With the accumulation of wealth, particularly among upper classes, comes a social separation that "minimizes collectivist obligations" and gradually undermines cooperative reciprocity. With the specialization of labor, political hierarchy, and centralization comes a gradual acceptance that the spirit God and the self are both individuals, and that neither are located in the objects of nature (Lerro, 2000: 144, 174, 291).

At the most basic level, it seems that monotheists were better at teaching their faith to children and proselytizing to potential converts, and thus grew in number as many polytheistic traditions waned. This precipitated a fundamental shift in thinking, such that the sacred—once understood as places and entities of the Earth—now had their true home in God's realm, which is not of the Earth. To the monotheist there is but one Spirit, not a spirit for every creature and object of the Earth. Even human souls are not of this world and are destined for a better place (pending successful adherence to the religious code during one's lifetime). Earthly objects and creatures are placed here for man's utility, management, and dominion. Indeed, Roderick Nash points out that much language in the Bible refers to wilderness as cursed land that God's people must protect themselves against and work to subdue. Accordingly, we have seen how Judeo-Christianity enabled the age of extraction and industry, effectively (if unintentionally) encouraging individualism and social hierarchy. This is what prompted Lynn White to call it the most anthropocentric religion ever conceived (White, 1967; Nash, 1989: 88).

The romantic movement of the 18th and 19th centuries imagined a nuanced monotheism, one that recalled and employed animism in guise. To the romantic, God's spirit is in the natural world, and immersion in nature is a means to place one's true self before the creator. In many ways, the romantic movement is a spiritual tussle not only with the bleak and oppressive realities of extractive, industrial, material society, but also with the oppression of the dominant hierarchical monotheism. The notion of a benevolent, harmonious, balanced nature in mystical connection with the human spirit is an attractive meme that is still an influential aspect of environmentalism (Thacker, 1983).

Inexorably, modern science has eaten away at the premise of romanticism, showing time and again that the material, not the spiritual, explains the workings of our bodies, our world, and the universe. But even as romantic spiritualism was challenged it experienced a rebirth, as exemplified by Lynn White's 1967 criticism of the dominant western worldview. According to Nash (1989: 95), White's purpose was not to tear down Christianity, but rather to reform it. White (1967) called for a new Christian environmental ethic that melds elements of eastern and American Indian spirituality with Christianity, rejecting man's dominion over nature and recasting the Christian as a steward of God's creation. With an appeal to St Francis of Assisi, White imagined an ecological theology in which humans are stewards, acting with a love of nature that is not self-interested but done for the love of God's creation. The Christian Stewardship (or Creation Care) model has since become a popular green interpretation of traditional doctrine. Nash points out that this is still very anthropocentric, for the steward is the select of God, taking care of the Earth in order to achieve the great reward (and to avoid eternal punishment). Furthermore, since the Bible does not include specific instructions on how the good Christian is to manage the Earth, many uses can be rationalized. White's spin is creative, but it does not quite equate Christianity with the biocentric spiritual traditions of the world.

Some material environmentalists have trouble accepting even this re-imagined view of spirituality. The evolutionist Stephen Jay Gould, for example, saw the notion of humans-as-stewards as the ultimate hubris. If there are, as some ecologists estimate, some ten million species on the planet in a multitude of different ecological relationships, how exactly are humans to be the guardians of all? This is further complicated by the facts that: 1) we have no idea of the identity or requirements of most of these species; 2) many species are antagonistic to one another; 3) organisms of other species are constantly in jeopardy from environmental conditions that are beyond our control; and 4) most of the organisms currently living will suffer and die in the process of natural selection. What, in such a system, is the role of the steward? Where is the harmony in nature, and as a major selection pressure on most other species, how can humans be the keepers of harmony? Such questions imply that stewardship-based understandings of the natural world are non-rational artifacts of romanticism and cultural tradition. To Gould and others, the reality is that we are but one of many species, no more favored by some omnipotent being but seeking, like all living things, an opportunity to survive and to provide for our own (Gould, 1990).

What can we say, then, about the sanctity of nature? In my estimation, the evidence for genetic and neurobiological foundations of spirituality should give pause to both extremes of the conceptual continuum. It becomes difficult, given this evidence, for the ardent spiritualist to insist that the directive to protect sacred places and species comes from a supernatural power. Neither should the material environmentalist dismiss the spiritual, for it is clear that spirituality plays an important role in both body and community. It is instead a better argument for both sides to emphasize the mental, physical, and social benefits that come from promoting and celebrating ecological and human communities alike.

Spirituality in balance

Undeniably, spirituality and religiosity provide psychological and social benefits for many. We are not so far removed from the late Pleistocene savanna—we still have the need for connection with nature and with other people, particularly as we deal with pain, with grief, and with the unknown and uncontrollable. In part, human spirituality has always been (and perhaps will always be) about contemplating the mysteries of our existence and the wonders of our world. For many people, immersion in the sacred elements of the nonhuman world can be a process of coping and healing. Likewise, religion provides social structure and mutual support. It offers a context for the sharing of personal stories and trials, achievements, and failings. It is a generator of great compassion. Religions can function as "mighty engines of collective action for the production of benefits that all people want" (D.S. Wilson, 2002: 187). That these better elements of our character are regulated by neurotransmitters which are coded for by genes should not lessen their appeal. That we are beginning to understand how spiritual mindsets and religious practices stimulate such character should not cheapen them. To the contrary, understanding spirituality and religion should facilitate their role in providing comfort, healing, and compassion (Box 8.1).

Still, for all their beneficial qualities, spirituality and religion are also implicated as major barriers to societal change. Religious spirituality, along with racism and ethnocentrism, can feed our deep-seated instinct for parochial xenophobia. It is telling that the Golden Rule to "Do unto others . . ." does not define who the others are. In a perfect world, "others" would encompass our entire species. But that is not how we have evolved. The tribal morality of our ancestors was authenticated by group-specific spiritual beliefs and religious practices. Hence, "others" are—at least in an evolutionary sense—those of your group, those who share the same belief system and the same customs. They are

---

Box 8.1 Religion and environmentalism

"For environmentalism to succeed," in the words of philosopher Roger Gottlieb, "it must offer a universal vision of community" (Gottlieb, 2007: 83). Gottlieb argues that religion can provide just such a vision. Religious groups offer social engagement that is not centered on consumption. They offer moral expectation, compassion, and mutual support. Most importantly, perhaps, the best examples of religion provide a model of political engagement that is inclusive, nonviolent, respectful, and principled. Accordingly, Gottlieb suggests that religion is good for environmentalism.

Of course, there are examples of religious failings, "tendencies towards self-righteousness, careerist leaders, male posturing, and irrational claims which ignore evidence to make a point" (Gottlieb, 2007: 84). Religious groups can be xenophobic, exclusive, discriminatory, and condescending. Gottlieb acknowledges these shortcomings but points out that secular groups are equally susceptible to antisocial behavior. In the best cases, religious communities at least provide mechanisms of introspective humility that can overcome counterproductive attitudes and actions.

David Sloan Wilson postulates that the worst attributes of group behavior—inequity, discrimination, exploitation, and so on—are "individual-level adaptations with consequences that are often dysfunctional at the social level" (D.S. Wilson, 2002: 36). Social control mechanisms, such as moral systems, cultural mores, and religious codes, can constrain individual transgressions. In this way, religion is an important adaptive response of human evolution. It minimizes exploitation, maximizes equity, and coordinates behavior within the group. These same characteristics are applicable to socioecological systems; they are, in fact, excellent descriptors of environmentalism.

In small foraging groups, human social bonds are simultaneously—and inseparably—social, spiritual, religious, economic, cultural, and ecological. Group interactions in large-scale, modern, hierarchical society are rarely so entangled. But there are advantages to sociocultural entanglement. Just as the interpersonal accountability of religious groups can coordinate support and action, cross-linkages among groups might encourage the common purpose and mutual accountability that environmentalism needs.

---

the ones you should treat well, for they are the ones who will be treating you. Outsiders, strangers, interlopers—these are not of one's group, and are therefore not subject to the same courtesy. Unfamiliarity breeds distrust. This is, effectively, another kind of dualism, in that we separate our own social circle from others. Equally disconcerting is recent research that shows a correlation between strong religiosity and respondents' belief that the prevailing social state of the world is just and that disparity is acceptable. Trust in a god or gods may thus promote a contented complacence and reduce the perceived need to break down sociocultural barriers. Religious spirituality, in Lerro's words, can be "a sedative which justifies group inequalities" (Lerro, 2000: 308; Gross and Ziebertz, 2009; Jost *et al.*, 2014).

Of course, we are no longer on the late Pleistocene savanna. Many big-hearted, empathetic people can and do treat all sorts of "others" with compassion and respect, and the major world religions all encourage such behavior. But the tribal mindset is one of the innate characteristics of our evolutionary inheritance, and xenophobia is psychologically difficult to overcome. A quick browse of the news will confirm the fanatical, religiously dogmatic xenophobia in the modern world. Xenophobia—like religiosity—is also in part a learned behavior, and we humans tend to follow the lead of authority figures and go along with the majority.

In sum, modern environmentalism exists in a state of conceptual conflict. Animists, polytheists, Gaians, romantics, and true believers intuitively see the human spirit as being one with nature, or at least perceive humans as the stewards of natural sanctity. Many of the spiritual mindset reject material explanations of the world, and indeed see these explanations as the source of our problems. Meanwhile, objective, rational materialists seek to manipulate the natural world in myriad ways (ranging from beneficent to dubious), in many cases regarding the spiritual perspective as folly. Spirituality and religiosity can be affirming, constructive, and uplifting paths to mental, physical, social, and even ecological well-being, but they can also be divisive mechanisms of exclusion. Material reductionism can indeed explain, but for all its explanatory powers it so often misses the needs of the person, the community, and the culture. Clearly, material and spiritual worldviews are far from mutual understanding. Yet in the midst of these perspectives there is, or should be, common ground. Michelangelo may have provided us a map—the common ground is in the gray matter of the human brain.

Bibliography

Alper, M. (2006). *The "God" part of the brain: a scientific interpretation of human spirituality and God*. Naperville, IL: Sourcebooks.

Bohm, L.C., Curtis, R. and Willock, B., eds. (2009). *Taboo or not taboo? Forbidden thoughts, forbidden acts in psychoanalysis and psychotherapy*. London: Karnac Books.

Chemhura, M. and Masaka, D. (2010). Taboos as a source of Shona people's environmental ethics. *Journal of Sustainable Development in Africa*, 21(7), pp. 123–131.

Diamond, J. (2005). *Collapse: how societies choose to fail or succeed*. London: Penguin.

Diamond, J. (2012). *The world until yesterday: what can we learn from traditional societies?* New York: Viking Press.

Dissanayake, E. (1992). *Homo aestheticus: where art comes from and why*. New York: Free Press.

Gottlieb, Roger. (2007). Religious environmentalism: what it is, where it's heading and why we should be going in the same direction. *Journal for the Study of Religion, Nature & Culture*, 1(1), pp. 81–91.

Gould, S.J. (1990). The golden rule: a proper scale for our environmental crisis. *Natural History*, 9(90), pp. 24–30.

Gross, Z. and Ziebertz, H. (2009). Religion and xenophobia. In: H. Ziebertz, W. Kay and U. Riegel, eds., *Youth in Europe: an international empirical study about the impact of religion on life orientation*, Vol. 3. Berlin: LIT Verlag. pp. 181–198.

Hamer, D.H. (2004). *The God gene: how faith is hardwired into our genes.* Norwell, MA: Anchor Press.

Jost, J.T., Hawkins, C.B., Nosek, B.A., Hennes, E.P., Stern, C., Gosling, S.D. and Graham, J. (2014). Belief in a just God and a just society: a system justification perspective on religious ideology. *Journal of Theoretical and Philosophical Psychology*, 34(1), pp. 56–81.

Lerro, B. (2000). *From Earth spirits to sky gods: the socioecological origins of monotheism, individualism, and hyperabstract reasoning from the Stone Age to the axial Iron Age.* Lanham, MD: Lexington Books.

Meshberger, F.L. (1990). An interpretation of Michelangelo's creation of Adam based on neuroanatomy. *Journal of the American Medical Association*, 264(14), pp. 1837–1841.

Milgram, S. (1974). *Obedience to authority: an experimental view.* New York: Harper & Row.

Nash, R.F. (1989). *The rights of nature: a history of environmental ethics.* Madison, WI: University of Wisconsin Press.

Northcott, M.S. (2015). *Place, ecology and the sacred: the moral geography of sustainable communities.* New York: Bloomsbury Press.

Orlove, B. (2005). Human adaptation to climate change: a review of three historical cases and some general perspectives. *Environmental Science & Policy*, 8(6), pp. 589–600.

Seybold, K.S. (2010). Biology of spirituality. *Perspectives on Science and Christian Faith*, 62(2), pp. 89–98.

Stamos, D.N. (2008). *Evolution and the big questions: sex, race, religion and other matters.* Malden, MA: Blackwell.

Tertullian, (1722 [c. 220]). *De praescriptione haereticorum.* Translation by J. Betty. Oxford: Oxford University Press.

Thacker, C. (1983). *The wildness pleases: the origins of romanticism.* London: Routledge.

Tippett, K. (2016). *Becoming wise: an inquiry into the mystery and art of living.* New York: Penguin Press.

White, L. (1967). The historical roots of our ecological crisis. *Science*, 155(3767), pp. 1203–1207.

Wilson, D.S. (2002). *Darwin's cathedral: evolution, religion, and the nature of society.* Chicago: University of Chicago Press.

Wilson, E.O. (1975). *Sociobiology, the new synthesis.* Cambridge, MA: Belknap.

9   Socioaesthetic evolution

Key points

- Aesthetic preference is a function of evolutionary inheritance and cultural influence.
- Romanticized aesthetics can create an expectation of ideal natural beauty, but many aspects of ecological systems do not fit this ideal.
- An informed aesthetic experience can offer a means of relating to the natural world and to other people.

Like spirituality, human aesthetics is caught up in a sort of intellectual skirmish between those who see it as a neurological product of human evolution and those who find evolutionary explanations to be somewhat unrefined. Some insist that reducing beauty to scientific explanation, to bits of material, or to mechanisms of selection is tantamount to the extermination of beauty altogether. Others find extraordinary beauty in material origins themselves. I will not settle the dispute here. But if natural beauty is one of our core environmental values—if it is one of the reasons we seek to lighten the human footprint upon the Earth—then we must wrestle with some basic questions of aesthetics. Why do we perceive some things as beautiful and others as repulsive? What is it that we find to be beautiful in nature? Are there universal concepts of beauty, or is it truly, and only, in the eye of the beholder? And finally, if there is such a thing as a common concept of natural beauty, is it something that we can protect and preserve for our children and grandchildren?

Evolutionary origins of beauty

To use a sub-heading like *evolutionary origins of beauty* is to step right into the fray, and to pick a side at that. The opposite perspective is that beauty is an inherent and eternal property of the universe, making it nonsensical to speak of its origins. But does beauty exist without one to behold it? I will hazard to answer that it does not. Beauty is a mental model, and it therefore requires a mind of sufficient capacity to conceive it. Now, whether the human mind is the only one capable of such consideration is anyone's guess. Did Neanderthals have an aesthetic sense? How about other species of our now-extinct cousins? How many branches of the evolutionary tree support a creative preference that is not solely for survival or reproduction, but instead based upon like or dislike?

A rather intriguing case can be made that some nonhuman animals do have an aesthetic taste. In most bird species, for example, it is the male with the bright plumage and hopeful song—hopeful, of course, that he can attract a mate. But philosopher David Rothenberg and biologist Richard Prum have posed some interesting questions about bird mate selection. We think we understand why the male sports the colors and sings the song that he does—these are advertisements for his fitness, driven by competition with other males of his species. This is sexual selection, and it certainly plays a role in natural beauty. More on this below. But what is it that makes the female bird settle on a mate? Is it completely because a particular shade of red or the ability to hit a high note equates with fitness? Why one shade, why one trill, and not another? Some birds, like the sedge wren, have been shown to *improvise* their songs on an individual basis (Kroodsma *et al.*, 1999). Could it be that the female wren chooses from many fit suitors because she happens to prefer the song of one over the others? This could be an instance of *aesthetic* selection, and if Rothenberg and Prum are correct it means that many species, not only ours, have the ability to perceive beauty (Rothenberg, 2011: 61–17; Suddendorf, 2013: 262–263).

An obvious thought, but one that is often overlooked, is that different organisms will perceive the world in different ways according to their needs. What is beautiful to one organism—perhaps a perfect spider web in the morning dew—is death to another. Value and meaning, in this sense, have everything to do with one's situation, with one's place in the ecosystem. Fittingly, James Gibson calls this ecological perception. To Gibson, every perception includes information of the perceiver and of the perceived. "The awareness of the world and one's comp- lementary relations to the world are not separable" (Gibson, 2014 [1979]: 141). What this means, beyond the banal observation that moths see the world differ- ently than humans, is that our (human) concept of natural beauty is *distinctly* human. It couldn't be the same experience for any other species (if indeed there are others that have aesthetic preference). This makes the whole notion of natural beauty a rather species-centric thought. Additionally, it hints at another potential engine of xenophobia, for while we humans have some common aesthetic pre- ferences, taste can vary with culture (Dissanayake, 1992).

Ecological perception also implies that aesthetic appreciation encompasses more than an observer and a disconnected object to be observed. Rather, as psychologist Heft (2010: 18–19) puts it, "entities exist and manifest the qualities that they do by virtue of their relationships within a dynamic system of mutual influences." To Heft, this means that beauty is a property neither of the object (or scene, or sound) being perceived, nor of the mind of the perceiver, but is instead a property of the associ- ation between the two. This has been called a relational aesthetic, and it suggests that preference is in part defined by the beneficial attributes of relationship.

Adaptive aesthetics

While we don't know the exact point (or points) on the branching tree of evolution at which aesthetic appreciation emerged, it is entirely plausible that prehuman ancestors had some sort of capacity for preference. To the extent this is true, it means that at least some aspect of the human sense of beauty is genetically inherited. This is the *adaptive* view of aesthetics, championed by Denis Dutton, among others. The idea is that our aesthetic preferences—not only in nature but also in art, music, literature, and performance—have at their foundation instincts that were critical for the survival of our species as it evolved. For example, our notions of beautiful literature (according to Dutton) are descended from the best of storytelling among our ancient ancestors. These are stories that ostensibly drew the attention of the listener and observer (and now reader and viewer) to dilemmas of the individual as he or she negotiates the social and environmental landscape; they are tales of survival, of overcoming strife to live and to thrive. Likewise, the beauty we see in performance recalls tribal rituals of social bonding, rites of passage, and even indoctrination to the rules and taboos of the group. The adaptive perspective postulates that our proclivity for creating objects of beauty may have originated as an element of ritualistic group bonding, especially in relation to the nonhuman world (Dissanayake, 1992; Aiken, 1998; Dutton, 2009).

We have no record of the song, dance, or tales of our ancient ancestors, and we have precious little of the objects, personal adornments, etchings, and paintings through which they expressed themselves. Some of the oldest remaining carvings and drawings depict scenes of the hunt, outlines of the human hand, and patterned images. Interestingly, the patterns of some prehistoric etching and painting have been linked with phosphenes, those images that we see when our eyes are closed. Humans universally see the same sorts of phosphenes—spirals, waves, radials, lattices, and others—because of our eye anatomy, optic nerve function, and brain physiology. The images are more common in times of fasting, sleep or oxygen deprivation, or under the influence of hallucinogenic drugs. But they occur even in the absence of such stimulation and there are striking similarities in phosphenes between different cultures. (As an avid doodler I find this fascinating, for many of the scribbles that appear in the margins of my notes I now recognize as phosphenes. I will admit to the occasional sleep deprivation, but not to the use of hallucinogenic drugs, unless caffeine counts.) Sundstrom (2004), author of *Storied stone*, argues that phosphenes were an important part of early spiritual activity and provides evidence that they are commonly depicted in rock-carved art. The human mind, in her view, attempts to make sense of these images by translating them into recognizable objects—like plants, animals, or humans. The psychologist Carl Jung (1875–1961) called these "images of instincts" (Jung *et al.*, 1978: 410). Thus, some of the oldest surviving examples of human art depicts people, animals, and phosphenes. We cannot know the significance of such drawings, but it seems plausible that these early artists were attempting to make sense of what they perceived, both when their eyes were open and when they were closed (Aiken, 1998; Rothenberg, 2011).

Beauty in nature

While the adaptive perspective can only partially explain the notion of beauty, genetic inheritance is undeniably part of the human aesthetic. In a similar vein, some have attempted to explain aesthetic appeal in terms of basic physical principles. The Scottish mathematician and biologist D'Arcy Thompson (1860–1948) proposed in his book *On growth and form* that fundamental features of symmetry and order are "embodied in the concept of mathematical beauty" (Thompson, 1992 [1917]: 2–3; Rothenberg, 2011: 53). The notion of mathematical beauty is that the elements of symmetry, balance, ratio, counterpoint, synchrony, rhythm, harmony, and perspective have sweet spots that most people would acknowledge as beautiful and sour spots that many find repulsive. Such principles suggest an ingrained aesthetic appreciation for order, uniformity, and consistency. Actually, it is more than a suggestion. Neurophysiologist Zeki (2002: 56) has confirmed that the human cerebral cortex responds to "precision, regularity and predictability," and that such neurological responses are correlated with expressed preferences for beauty. Perception of preferred images is associated with reward stimuli in the brain while perception of repulsive images is not.

At one level, it makes perfect sense that our idea of beauty is based upon (and constrained by) the anatomy and physiology of our sensory and nervous systems. It follows, then, that most of us have similar basic preferences for what is attractive or desirable and what is not. Dutton strengthens this argument by observing many innate, universal functions of the human mind, including:

> an intuitive physics that we use to keep track of how objects fall, bounce or bend; an intuitive sense of space, including imaginative mapping of the general environment; a feeling for probability, along with a capacity to track frequency of events; an ability to read facial expressions that includes an inventory of universally recognizable patterns; and a fascination with organized pitched sounds, rhythmically produced by the human voice or by instruments.
>
> (Dutton, 2009: 43–44)

Our brains have evolved to interpret the world in particular ways, and so it logically follows that we have common perceptions of like and dislike—a mutual aesthetic taste, you might say.

The psychologist Steven Pinker has argued that human perceptions of beauty and aesthetic preference are by-products of these evolved cognitive characteristics. To borrow from Dutton's examples listed above, it is our intuitive physics, our sense of space, our capacity to track frequency of events, and our ability to discern patterns that are adaptive in the sense of providing biological fitness. Aesthetic appreciation, like bike riding, is a spandrel that has emerged from this collection of mental skills. In Pinker's words:

> The mind is a neural computer, fitted by natural selection with combinatorial algorithms for causal and probabilistic reasoning about plants, animals,

objects and people. It is driven by goal states that served biological fitness in ancestral environments, such as food, sex, safety, parenthood, friendship, status and knowledge. The toolbox, however, can be used to assemble Sunday afternoon projects of dubious adaptive significance.

(Pinker, 1997: 524)

By this point some of the art connoisseurs among my readers will be howling. Beauty can't be reduced to the incidental and idle sensations caused by a few neurons firing at the sight of straight lines and tidy ratios! What of abstraction, innovation, surprise, juxtaposition, mystery, emotion? What of the enrichment and enhancement of the human condition? If I were truly itching for a fight I would point out that these too have a neurological basis. But I seek no such confrontation. Certainly, there are many aspects of aesthetic appeal that reach far beyond the basics of "mathematical beauty," but it is hard to deny that our brains, at some basic level, are searching for—and finding beauty in—order. The French artist Amédée Ozenfant (1886–1966) pondered this very thought:

Is the world geometric? Is geometry the thread that man has seized which links all things? Or is it that the laws which guide the brain are geometric, and so it is able to perceive only what fits into its warp and woof?

(Ozenfant, 1952 [1931]: 284; Rothenberg, 2011: 114)

The human penchant for order in nature is apparent in our aesthetic preferences. People from cultures around the world show similar attraction to certain natural settings at particular scales (Box 9.1). We are drawn to sheltered waterfronts, to landscape vistas and to tall trees, but are less enamored with inaccessible bramble and litter-strewn landscapes. We tend toward an "aesthetic of care," meaning that we generally find favor with well-kept, ordered land. This mental construct is "laden with good intentions and social meaning: a work ethic, personal pride, contributing to community" (Nassauer, 1997: 68). Modern landscape architects often design visitor experiences accordingly, with tall trees, vantage points, gentle curves, and clean lines. Trimmed, fenced grass and wooded lands with tidy, short groundcover are far more attractive to most people than unkempt overgrowth. As Nassauer (1997: 82) observes, "people make and manage landscapes not only for what they produce but for how they look and how they are *supposed* to look."

By the same token, people tend to view disturbed areas as less attractive. Flooded land, burnt vegetation, uprooted or standing dead trees are thus generally perceived negatively, while apparently unblemished landscapes are more desirable. The last several decades of scientific research have of course affirmed the ecological necessity of floods, fires, and other disturbances, but humans appear to have an aesthetic preference for stable landscapes and ordered resources nonetheless. The prehistoric impetus for this seems plausible, particularly given our species' coming of age during the climatic upheavals of the late Pleistocene. Stable landscapes and ordered resources, the thinking goes, meant survival in the moment, so they came to be regarded as beautiful. Even though we now know that

Box 9.1 Aesthetic perception and ecological function

Ecological processes occur across a wide range of spatial and temporal scales, but people typically perceive the nonhuman world on the scales of landscape and lifetime. Gobster *et al.* (2007: 959) have called this the *perceptible realm*, and they postulate that aesthetic experience at this scale influences our environmental preferences and actions. While such experience provides meaning and emotion to the human condition, it can be environmentally problematic, for ecological systems do not conform to human scales.

Our species, like others, seeks suitable habitat. Human habitat requirements extend beyond biological necessities to cultural desires; thus, we have a sense of what our ecological surroundings should be like. Gobster *et al.* (2007: 962) make the case that "perceived aesthetic value" can come to be equated with ecological quality, when in fact these may be very different attributes of ecological systems. Effective ecological structures, functions, and processes may include such things as disturbance, decomposition, migration, and competition, which are not readily perceived as aesthetic positives. Moreover, many important ecological processes occur at scales that render them unimportant to aesthetic perception. Human preference and ecological function may coincide, but are not identical (2007: 965).

Rectifying this disconnect requires: a) reformation of aesthetic values, e.g. through education; b) design of ecologically beneficial landscapes that conform to aesthetic expectations; or c) some combination of the two (2007: 962). This is complicated by the fact that perception differs by culture, and ecological function differs by both social context and geographic setting. Nevertheless, Gobster *et al.* (2007: 970) promote an ecological approach to aesthetics that attempts to align perception with function. Ecological aesthetics may be achieved through intentional landscape design and effective communication, such that a functional landscape incorporates attractive features and conveys purpose. Ecological function and aesthetic appeal must be integrated, in the opinion of these authors, for just as we need products and processes of the natural world, we also need to experience its beauty.

disturbance is important for long-term ecological viability, our perception tends to be a short-term assessment (Steg *et al.*, 2012: 42–43).

I do not mean to imply that natural beauty is only to be found in that which aids survival. Certainly, there are other factors at play. Carlson (2004), for example, has theorized that people find beauty in that which they understand. Intimate knowledge of an object, system, or process of nature may in itself be aesthetically pleasing. Mark Sagoff offers an alternative to cognitive aesthetics: we appreciate most that with which we have an emotional connection. We find beauty—in nature, just as with people, Sagoff argues—in that which we love (Sagoff, 1991).

Godlovitch (2004) proposes that we find natural beauty in mystery, in that which eludes our understanding. These perspectives may well have an element of truth, though of course they are all apt to be culturally variable. It is interesting, though, that they are all dependent on the person doing the perceiving, and they make little sense in the absence of that person. Godlovitch (2004: 120) points this out for the first two theories: "Cognitivism fences in nature as an object (or collection of objects) of human knowledge; affectivism reduces nature to that which falls within the bounds of our reverence." Equating beauty with the mysterious, I will add, relegates aesthetic appeal to that which challenges our understanding and piques our curiosity.

In sum, we have a number of ideas about natural aesthetic appeal. Order and uniformity, stability, cognitive understanding, emotional connection, mystery—all might play a role in the human perception of natural beauty. All suggest that natural beauty revolves in a conceptual orbit around people.

Nature's harmony and charisma

At some point in western sociocultural evolution the romantic notion of a natural world that is *normally* in a beautiful state gained popularity (León, 2010). According to Nassauer (1997: 68), this aesthetic "is drawn from the eighteenth century picturesque, in which the power of nature began to be seen as beautiful, as long as it was controlled." This is still commonly seen in environmental and nature writing; it is the "balance of nature" or "nature's harmony" sentiment which we have encountered repeatedly in this book. Even scientific ecologists long assumed (and some still assume) the Clementsian model—that natural systems seek mature, stable equilibria and will remain at equilibrium as long as they are protected from disturbance. The aesthetic corollary is that "the natural environment, insofar as it is untouched by man, has mainly positive aesthetic qualities; it is, for example, graceful, delicate, intense, unified and orderly, rather than bland, dull, insipid, incoherent, and chaotic" (Carlson, 1984: 5). But Henry Gleason and others have questioned these assumptions. Much ecological function, it seems, takes place in a state of disequilibrium, as the system in which it exists responds to random environmental fluctuations. This is a hard sell to many people, who are conditioned to perceive the world as a stable place. It has real implications in conservation ecology, for donors, visitors, and patrons often envision a certain ecological community and a particular successional state in iconic ecosystems. Late-successional plants, large and slow-dispersing animals, and orderly landscapes are the expectation. In reality, disturbance and changing stress regimes disrupt ecosystems. All ecological systems are constantly changing in response to environmental fluctuations. Ecological structures and functions are periodically "insipid, incoherent and chaotic." In short, the nonhuman world does not trend toward the order, balance, and harmony that humans prefer. This fact, however, has not prevented order, balance, and harmony from becoming central to our concept of natural beauty.

The romantic perception of natural harmony is premised on the idea that the various constituents of the natural world work together to obtain and maintain a certain ideal state. Humans, in this view, once were and can still be in harmony with all beings. When we remove ourselves from this connection, we upset the natural harmony. This belief system appears to incorporate an alternate under-standing of ecological systems, particularly what is meant by the word "fit" (Thomas, 1982). To the Darwinian evolutionist, fitness means the ability to survive and produce fertile offspring. In the romantic sense of the term, "fit" individuals are those that "fit in" the best with other organisms. Living things achieve this fit by communing with their environment, understood as "the ability to be open to and to contribute, from one's unique sense of self, to the well-being of the whole system" (Conn, 1995: 165). Hence, when humans "fit" with nature, there is balance and harmony. In a sense these two definitions are compatible. After all, an organism cannot survive to produce fertile offspring if it does not find some sort of working relationship with other organisms. Indeed, the biological concept of fitness may be achieved by cooperation through symbiotic relation-ships. On the other hand, biological fitness is ultimately a life-or-death compe-tition with every other organism that seeks survival. Competition and conflict do not lend themselves to peaceful coexistence with all other organisms. Here, then, is the familiar conceptual discrepancy. In one light, we may see the natural world as a cooperative effort to achieve and maintain an optimal state of harmony. In another, we may see individual struggles for existence in a universe of randomly fluctuating contingencies (Wilson, 2002: 37–40).

As we have seen, there is an evolutionary basis to this conceptual conflict—one, I suggest, that is even played out in the aesthetics of nature. For example, consider the human preference for landscape. The "ideal" landscape, the one to which modern humans the world over are drawn, is often called the "prospect-refuge" landscape (Appleton, 1975). It offers a view from an elevated position, with nearby water and some complexities, such as distant hidden areas for exploration. It holds the prospect of adventure! But there is also trepidation in the scene. There are unknown threats that might be hiding in plain sight. Thus, the vista is even better if there is shelter nearby; this is a refuge for the viewer in case the situation turns ugly. I don't want to make too much of this scene, for there is variability in this generalized story and humans are drawn to many other aspects of nature as well. Still, it is evident that some of our aesthetic preferences are ancient, and the prospect-refuge landscape nicely demonstrates the dueling character of the human aesthetic perception of the natural world. Nature is at once a source of sustenance and life and a threat of injury and death; we simultaneously experience biophilia and biophobia (Fenton, 1985; van den Berg *et al.*, 1998; Dutton, 2009: 21).

Aiken (1998) has argued for just this perspective in her book *The biological origins of art*. To Aiken, the aesthetic response is one kind of emotional response, and as such we react subconsciously to line, shape, color, sound, and motion in emotional ways. Basic patterns can elicit certain responses, such as gentle curves, regular rhythms, graceful motions associated with comfort, soothing and calm, whereas eyespots, sharp angles, aggressive motion, and the color red are associated with threat, fear, and defense. Of course, such responses are subject to cultural nuance. For example, personal association, say to a rocky crag, can engender feelings of familiarity and comfort, even though it is sharp and angular. Still, Aiken argues that our basic aesthetic perception has at its foundation the primal emotions of fear and contentment, and that simple cues in what we sense can trigger neurological and physiological responses. One can imagine other emotions that could be associated with perception—awe, anger, sadness, surprise. Aiken proposes that these are also neurophysiological responses to basic stimuli (Aiken, 1998).

We can see the propensity for emotional response in human attitudes toward wildlife. Many people express positive emotions for animals—we love to see birds at the feeder, dolphins leaping in the wake, and fish in the stream. Our strong attachment to particular species is the reason that zoos attract millions of visitors every year and that so many humans keep pets. But our emotional connection is selective. Strong negative reactions to some species—like snakes, spiders, cock-roaches, pigs, sharks, rats, mosquitos—make it clear that our love for animals is conditional. There is a reason that the logo for the World Wildlife Fund is the panda and not the dung beetle. We are attracted to charismatic species. In *Wildlife in the Anthropocene* (2015), Jamie Lorimer defines charismatic species as those that are readily identifiable, easy to individuate, have visual appeal, are subject by face and body movement to anthropomorphism, and are accessible for close, multi-sensory encounters. These qualities in some ways make certain nonhuman species ready extensions of human actions and emotions (Lorimer, 2015: 35–36). Placing ourselves mentally in the position of charismatic species—and thereby human-izing the species—is a powerful urge, and one that strongly influences ecological conservation efforts.

Moreover, aesthetic appeal is subject to the psychological effect called peak shift. This is the tendency to accentuate a favored or preferred stimulation in reference to the disfavored. Peak shift is postulated as a factor in sexual selection—a reason why we see runaway evolution of antlers, tails, horns, flowers, and similar charac-teristics to nearly preposterous proportions. Organisms are caught up in a game of evolutionary competition that trends toward bigger, more ornate, showier, or more sensational versions of whatever traits are successful in securing reproduction. Humans too are subject to peak shift, not only in sexual selection but also in other aspects of our perception of beauty. Applied to our aesthetics of nature, peak shift means that we are drawn to extreme forms of what we find to be aesthetically pleasing. The nature we seek can be, in this sense, a sort of Platonic ideal that does not exist in the real world (Endler and Basolo, 1998; Ramachandran and Hirstein, 1999; Davies, 2006).

At least in part, then, nature is beautiful to humans when it is harmonious with our existence: when it sustains us, flatters us, and comforts us. Simply stated, we love nature when we see ourselves or our prospects in it. There is nothing wrong with this as such, but the expectation that nature *should* be harmonious, sustaining, flattering, and comforting is problematic. The elements of the nonhuman world do not conform to our desires. In fact, the elements that engender biophilia are inextricable from those that engender biophobia.

I know of no better example of our aesthetic bias than the Old Man in the Mountain of Franconia Notch State Park in New Hampshire. High atop a peak, granite outcroppings formed the silhouette of a man's head that became an iconic symbol for the state and a destination for thousands of tourists every year. Then, in 2003, the Old Man crumbled. The massive slabs that formed the profile were gone, victims of weathering and gravity. There is still a peak to be seen. The air is still as pure, the landscape still as rugged. But the number of visitors to the park has plummeted since the Old Man fell (Goodnough, 2011). Why? I suspect it is because we find our own image, both literally and figuratively, to be the fascinating aspect of the natural world.

Sociocultural aesthetics

Admittedly, it is too simple to explain the concept of natural beauty as merely a matter of emotion-evoking lines, order, balance, and charisma that makes us feel safe and important. Rothenberg and Prum are correct that aesthetic perception is only partially adaptive. Much of what we consider to be beautiful (in nature and in art) is culturally conditioned. We are influenced by group value systems, by expert opinion, by marketing and media, and by popular opinion. As we have seen, cultural evolution has resulted in some dramatic shifts in the idea of "natural beauty" over the course of human history, from wilderness as loathsome wasteland to wilderness as nature's cathedral. So, while personal reaction might be visceral to, say, an alligator-infested swamp, cultural biases can overcome instinct to regard the swamp as a place that should be drained, a place that should be protected, or home sweet home.

This brings us back to the relational aesthetic, meaning that the perceiver is inextricable from the perceived. We are apt to think differently about the non-human world when we experience it directly, learn about it, co-exist with it, and interact with it. Stated in these terms, aesthetics sounds less like a neurological knee-jerk or the exclusive domain of the highly cultured and more like an exercise in the broadest sort of community relations. Rothenberg, in fact, uses the language of ecology to describe it:

> the more connections we identify, the better we know who we are and where we stand. The more the world means and works for us, the less it is random, terrible, dangerous or frightening. And if we know our place, we will be better able to maintain our place.
>
> (2011: 218)

Dissanayake (1992), in her book *Homo aestheticus*, theorizes that human aesthetics evolved as a relational experience, specifically through spiritual ritual. Ancestral humans, in her view, interacted with the nonhuman world and with one another through rites and ceremonies. Such ritual was intended to set apart certain times, places, events, and objects as *special*—as something different than the normal. Thus, ritual included adornment, dance, song, chant, and other displays to make it extraordinary. The social bonding, the connection with nature, the adornment, and the ritual itself were all one transformative experience. In fact, the special human connection with nature may have been indistinguishable from the action of the ritual. Dissanayake argues that adorned ritual made moments (like rites of passage), places (like burial grounds), events, and objects more real than everyday life. This instinct to:

> recognize an extra-ordinary as opposed to an ordinary dimension of experience ... to make important things special by transforming them from ordinary to extra-ordinary, often in ritual ceremonies, and to have the capacity to experience a transformative or self-transcendent emotional state ... all have a potential to provoke naturally aesthetic behavior.
>
> (1992: 71)

If Dissanayake is right, it is a short trip to see that ancestral humans also imagined certain ecological places and organisms as special, as more real than life—as iconically beautiful. In this sense, it is not a black bear or a waterfront but the *ideal* black bear, the *ideal* waterfront that are beautiful to the cultural imagination. As much as we like to consider our modern aesthetic tastes to be a matter of individual preference, we are not so far removed from the collective intelligence of our ancestors. That which makes certain aspects of our environment seem to us to be special, beautiful, and worthy of protection may be an ancient mechanism of connecting with other human beings (Dutton, 2009: 243).

In this sense, aesthetic preference is a sociocultural construct. If we add this together with the more genetically hard-wired aspects of perception, we begin to get a picture of what natural beauty means for our species. We are drawn to aspects of the natural world that we perceive to be orderly, regular, and predictable. We are attracted to landscapes of prospect (for our own utility) and protection (of our own status). We tend to prefer nonhuman species: a) that serve our needs; or b) in which we can see ourselves. We prefer that they, and the abiotic environment in which they reside, remain in situations that we consider to be correct, and by and large we are willing to manipulate our environment to these ends. Finally, our aesthetic tastes are a product of our culture. Through the sociocultural medium we may express both our adherence to group norms and the idiosyncrasies that make us unique.

All told, it seems that the human perception of natural beauty is rather narcissistic. This is not entirely a criticism, for it makes some practical sense. Many of the ecological services on which we depend are drawn from orderly, regular, predictable landscapes, and they are much harder to come by in chaotic, invaded, disturbed systems. But the reality is that ecosystems undergo succession, species migrate and out-compete one another, and much of the world is responding to disturbance much of the time. Iconic, charismatic species exist with and depend upon unsightly species and mundane processes. Our environment is not only a form, it is also a function. However we work to conserve or protect it, process and change are realities that must be acknowledged. The failure to reconcile process and change with mental models of beauty is part of the conceptual conflict of modern environmentalism.

A relational approach to natural aesthetics could promote such an understanding, just as it has for much of human history. Unfortunately, the current state of western affluent, synthetic society is not exactly promoting a relational lifestyle. Part of the task of environmentalism, then, might be to reconnect aesthetic pleasure to socioecological function. Nassauer (1997: 82) has phrased this elegantly: "If we align the aesthetic experiences that people already value with the ecological health that they do not yet know how to recognize, we can build landscape ecological structure while we are building new cultural expectations for ecological health." Aesthetic experience, in this sense, can promote social cohesion around ecological services. This is the sort of natural beauty that we may be able to protect, promote, and share. Admittedly, this is a rather instrumental and anthropocentric approach to natural aesthetics—but perhaps human perception of natural beauty has always been instrumental and anthropocentric. In any case, whatever our aesthetic preferences say about human nature, our sense of the beautiful appears to be one of the things that draws us together.

Bibliography

Aiken, N. (1998). *The biological origins of art*. Westport, CT: Praeger.

Appleton, J. (1975). *The experience of landscape*. London: John Wiley and Sons.

Carlson, A. (1984). Nature and positive aesthetics. *Environmental Ethics*, 6(1), pp. 5–34.

Carlson, A. (2004). Appreciation and the natural environment. In: A. Carlson and A. Berleant, eds., *The aesthetics of natural environments*. Calgary: Broadview Press. pp. 63–75.

Conn, S.A. (1995). When the earth hurts, who responds? In: T. Roszak, M. Gomes and A. Kanner, eds., *Ecopsychology: restoring the Earth, healing the mind*. San Francisco: Sierra Club Books. pp. 156–171.

Davies, S. (2006). Aesthetic judgements, artworks and functional beauty. *Philosophical Quarterly*, 56(223), pp. 224–241.

Dissanayake, E. (1992). *Homo aestheticus: where art comes from and why*. New York: Free Press.

Dutton, D. (2009). *The art instinct: beauty, pleasure and human evolution*. New York: Bloomsbury Press.

Endler, J.A. and Basolo, A.L. (1998). Sensory ecology, receiver biases and sexual selection. *Trends in Ecology & Evolution*, 13(10), pp. 415–420.

Fenton, D.M. (1985). Dimensions of meaning in the perception of natural settings and their relationship to aesthetic response. *Australian Journal of Psychology*, 37(3), pp. 325–339.

Gibson, J.J. (2014 [1979]). *The ecological approach to visual perception*. 2nd edition. Hove, UK: Psychology Press.

Gobster, P.H., Nassauer, J.I., Daniel, T.C. and Fry, G. (2007). The shared landscape: what does aesthetics have to do with ecology? *Landscape Ecology*, 22(7), pp. 959–972.

Godlovitch, S. (2004). Icebreakers: environmentalism and natural aesthetics. In: A. Carlson and A. Berleant, eds., *The aesthetics of natural environments*. Calgary: Broadview Press. pp. 108–126.

Goodnough, A. (2011). On a somber mission to restore the missing face of a mountain. *New York Times*, June 12, 2011, A22.

Heft, H. (2010). Affordances and the perception of landscape: an inquiry into environmental perception and aesthetics. In: C. Thompson, P. Aspinall and S. Bell, eds., *Innovative approaches to researching landscape and health*. New York: Routledge. pp. 9–32.

Jung, C.G., McGuire, W. and Hull, R.F.C. (1978). *C.G. Jung speaking: interviews and encounters*. London: Thames & Hudson.

Kroodsma, D.E., Liu, W.C., Goodwin, E. and Bedell, P.A. (1999). The ecology of song improvisation as illustrated by North American sedge wrens. *The Auk*, 116(2), pp. 373–386.

León, M.J.A. (2010). Positive aesthetics: claims and problems. *Enrahonar: Quaderns de Filosofia*, 45, pp. 15–25.

Lorimer, J. (2015). *Wildlife in the Anthropocene*. Minneapolis, MN: University of Minnesota Press.

Nassauer, J.I. (1997). Cultural sustainability: aligning aesthetics and ecology. In: J. Nassauer, ed., *Placing nature: culture and landscape ecology*. Washington, DC: Island Press. pp. 67–83.

Ozenfant, A. (1952 [1931]). *Foundations of modern art*. Translation by J. Rodker. New York: Dover.

Pinker, S. (1997). *How the mind works*. New York: Norton.

Ramachandran, V.S. and Hirstein, W. (1999). The science of art: a neurological theory of aesthetic experience. *Journal of Consciousness Studies*, 6(6–7), pp. 15–51.

Rothenberg, D. (2011). *Survival of the beautiful: art, science and evolution*. New York: Bloomsbury Press.

Sagoff, M. (1991). Zuckerman's dilemma. *Hastings Center Report*, 21(5), pp. 32–40.

Steg, L., Van den Berg, A.E. and De Groot, J.I.M., eds. (2012). *Environmental psychology: an introduction*. New York: Wiley.

Suddendorf, T. (2013). *The gap: the science of what separates us from the other animals*. New York: Basic Books.

Sundstrom, L. (2004). *Storied stone: Indian rock art in the Black Hills country*. Norman, OK: University of Oklahoma Press.

Thomas, L. (1982). Are we fit to fit in? *Sierra*, 67(2), pp. 49–52.

Thompson, D. (1992 [1917]). *On growth and form*. Cambridge, UK: Cambridge University Press.

Van den Berg, A.E., Vlek, C.A. and Coeterier, J.F. (1998). Group differences in the aesthetic evaluation of nature development plans: a multilevel approach. *Journal of Environmental Psychology*, 18(2), pp. 141–157.

Wilson, D.S. (2002). *Darwin's cathedral: evolution, religion, and the nature of society*. Chicago: University of Chicago Press.

Zeki, S. (2002). Neural concept formation & art: Dante, Michelangelo, Wagner. *Journal of Consciousness Studies*, 9(3), pp. 53–76.

Part 3
Environmentalism evolving

10 Psychological discord

Key points

- Psychological comfort is associated with controlled, personified nature; this can create conceptual environmental problems.
- The physical and social benefits of connection with nature can be overwhelmed by antagonistic social cues.
- The task of environmentalism is to create more ecologically and socially meaningful communities.

It should be clear by now why modern environmentalism is so multidimensional and so conflicted. Capitalism, socialism, and sustainable development; individualism and holism; materialism and spiritualism; the aesthetics of order and the realities of disorder—all are artifacts of biological and sociocultural evolution, and all are competing for sociocultural dominance. These rival mindsets present dilemmas in the lives of individual people, for they complicate the ways in which we relate to our environment and to others of our species.

In this book I have made the case that environmental problems are social problems. They are questions of resource utility and allocation, of intercultural and intergenerational fairness, of self-interest and cooperative reciprocity. They are the product of social transactions that take place within the context of many social norms and pressures. In a general sense, these are the same dilemmas of self-interest-versus-common-good that have long been governed by sociocultural rules of interaction. Social contexts have changed, however, and while some people still have a close connection with the land and with one another, those in affluent extractive and synthetic societies often do not. The loss of social cohesion can generate ecological stress and it can hinder a concerted response to that stress.

I have also suggested that environmental problems are conceptual problems. They are the product of conflicted mental models. Romanticized notions of nature, for example, create unrealistic expectations of ecological systems. Human spirituality is in some respects a romanticized model of the universe. Similarly, human aesthetic preferences have a tendency to idealize the nonhuman world. This does not mean that romanticized and idealized notions of nature are without value, only that they are not easily reconciled with ecological realities of process, selection, and change.

Simply stated, the social and conceptual aspects of environmental problems can generate psychological tension. People are subjected to many conflicting social cues, and a desire to act for the common good can clash with the lure of hedonic selfishness. Moreover, our environmental ideals are not always compatible with the world we encounter, and existence within the biosphere is not always amenable to the protection of the biosphere. Exploration of the personal interaction with the environment, then, may help us understand some broader human behaviors—both those that are environmentally positive and those that are detrimental to the self, the society, and the species.

The purpose of this chapter is to consider some of the factors that influence our environmental behavior (Saegert and Winkel, 1990). Many such factors exist, including "childhood experience; knowledge and education; personality; perceived behavioral control; values, attitudes and worldviews of various kinds; felt responsibility and moral commitment; place attachment; norms and habits; goals; affect; and many demographic factors" (Gifford, 2014a: 544). I do not seek to review all or even most. Rather, I will consider three theoretical models in partial explanation for why we interact with our environment as we do. The first model is based upon the notion of physical well-being. In this paradigm, we interact with our environment according our own physiological need for comfort, control, and stress relief. A second model proposes that we interact with our environment to achieve emotional well-being. The third model holds that our behavior is an integrated response to both environmental and sociocultural cues, and that collective behavior influences both ecological and social well-being. These models are not mutually exclusive; indeed they are likely all occurring at once. Nor do they explain every aspect of our complex environmental behavior. Still, they offer a psychological framework for understanding our social and conceptual discord.

I will consider each of these models in turn, and along the way I will propose three points of psychological conflict that are central to our modern environmental dilemma.

Physical well-being

Our social interactions can be overwhelming. Consciously or not, we are always reading (or misreading) facial expressions and actions, wondering how we are perceived by others, pursuing self-interest without appearing selfish, empathizing and cooperating while minding the social contract. It is exhausting. The poet David Whyte (2016) has observed that time in nature is time away from all of this. Trees do not judge us, and the brook winds its way down the slope without treachery or deceit. We do not have to read expressions to discern the intentions of the forest or the stream. There is honesty here; there is truth. Thus physiological stress relief has been proposed as a basic impetus for our behavior toward the nonhuman world (Gifford, 2014b: 7–12).

The idea that interaction with nature can enhance physical well-being is supported by some physiological evidence. Time in a natural setting has been associated with lower heart rate, reduced level of stress-related hormones, and lower blood pressure (Park *et al.*, 2010). Dozens of clinical studies of both children and adults in settings all over the world confirm that time spent in nature has stress-reduction effects, including the relief of anxiety and depression (Kahn, 1999). Of course, it is hard to say if David Whyte is correct that the stress reduction is due to respite from human social entanglements (though this is a reasonable hypothesis which even has a name: directed attentional fatigue). Possibly time in nature is a stress reliever not so much because it is a break from social interaction, but rather because it facilitates social cohesion with fellow adventurers (Van den Berg *et al.*, 2012: 52). It could also be attributed to fresh air, exercise, or the thrill of the excursion itself. But other studies have documented health benefits of even visual exposure to a natural setting. Hospital patients with a view of greenspace or with nearby potted plants, for example, were shown in one study to have a shorter recovery time and less of a need for pain medication than those without (Ulrich, 1984). Children with natural settings near their home have been shown to have fewer instances of behavioral disorder and a higher sense of self-worth (Wells and Evans, 2003; Louv, 2008: 49). On the basis of such evidence, some scholars have advanced the idea that interaction with the nonhuman world can enhance people's physical condition.

The individual benefits of nature connection have been extended to studies of public health (Radkau, 2014: 36). Studies in the Netherlands, England, Denmark, Australia, and Japan, controlled for economic factors, correlate residential greenspace with better mental health and fewer physical health complaints as compared to peer groups without greenspace. Epidemiological studies have shown that the effect is more pronounced in poor communities than in affluent. The presence of greenspace has even been associated with the degree of difference in mortality rates between wealthy and disadvantaged people. Such research implies that nature is important for more than food sources, water purification, and carbon storage. It fills a psychological need, and human behavior is at least in part a response to stress and a desire for relief. The idea is not new—Emerson wrote about it in 1836—but in the research of environmental psychology it has been re-discovered.

Natural environments have been the subject of many studies on stress recovery, meaning that they seem to have restorative effects on human physiology (Campbell, 1983; Misra and Stokols, 2012). Stress, in this sense, refers to physiological responses to threats, demands, and fatigues of an individual's life. It is the body's reaction to a challenge, and while challenge can be a psychological positive (and our response to it is a critical evolved survival mechanism), *chronic* stress has been implicated in disease and decreased quality of life.

The field of neuroscience has come to understand much about stress and stress alleviation. Psychophysiologists have established that stress involves a stimulus, a mental process, and a hormone-mediated physical reaction; it is a complex interaction of the peripheral, central, and autonomic nervous systems with the endocrine and immune systems. The purpose of such a system—the reason it evolved at all—is apparently as a response to threats. This makes perfect sense for the physical threats of the ancient savanna, or even in the fight-or-flight situations we might find ourselves in today. More common for most modern humans are chronic mental and emotional stressors, such as guilt, anxiety, desire for acceptance, and fear of rejection. These too stimulate a physical response in the human body. Chronic stress can lead to fatigue in and declining performance of the endocrine system, which can result in a host of mental and physical health problems. Relief from stress, whether it be through exercise, meditation, a healthy diet, social support or some other activity, alleviates the endocrine load, reduces the blood concentration of stress hormones, and allows the body to return to homeostasis. Thus it is well established that both stress and the relief of stress are biochemical responses to stimuli (McEwen and Lasley, 2002).

There is great interest, then, in strategies to reduce chronic stress and to provide the individual with an opportunity for recovery. Roger Ulrich's stress recovery theory (Ulrich, 1983; Ulrich *et al.*, 1991) proposes that humans have a rapid and unconscious reaction to basic sensory exposure in certain natural environments. The sight or smell of vegetation, for example, or the symmetry and spatial depth of a landscape—these, according to the theory, are autonomic stress reducers. A companion theory called attention restoration theory has been proposed by Rachel and Stephen Kaplan (Kaplan and Kaplan, 1989). This model recognizes that humans have a limited capacity for attention and concentration, and that our mental centers of attention can become overwhelmed and fatigued with prolonged and monotonous demand. According to the Kaplans, situations that remove us mentally from obligations and that provide a sense of fascination, connectedness, and compatibility (i.e. that we are part of something interesting and that we belong there) can reduce our attention fatigue and restore our mental focus. Some scholars, in testing this theory, have found that natural surroundings provide a better restorative environment than built surroundings (Joye and Van den Berg, 2012: 60).

It does not necessarily follow that time in nature is *required* for physical and mental well-being. An equally convincing case can be made that regular exercise has a positive psychological outcome in cases of depression or anxiety (Byrne and Byrne, 1993). Yoga and dance have been shown to relieve stress and improve mood (West *et al.*, 2004). A recent study has shown that dancing with others in unison makes people better able to bear pain (Tarr *et al.*, 2015). Meditation is associated with improved emotion regulation and enhanced personal relationships (Sedlmeier *et al.*, 2012). Social identity and group belonging enhance feelings of self-esteem and positive affect (Crabtree *et al.*, 2010). While any of these can provide psychological positives, it may be that immersion in nature provides an experience that includes all or most at once (Mayer *et al.*, 2008). Indeed, the psychological benefits of nature exposure have been attributed to "recovery from stress and attention fatigue, encouragement to exercise, facilitating social contact ... [and] providing opportunities for personal development and a sense of purpose" (Gezondheidsraad, 2004: 16).

Other scholars have pointed out some problems with the stress/relief model. One issue is that environmental interactions of stress or relief are socioculturally specific. The same type of experience may be stressful in some cultures while offering relief from stress in others. Even within a given culture, different people may encounter nature differently due to their political and socioeconomic context. Similarly, stress occurs within individualized contexts that make it difficult to generalize behavioral responses. Despite the common architecture of our nervous systems, people will experience and react to the world in unique ways (Saegert and Winkel, 1990: 452).

Another issue with nature-derived stress alleviation is that it depends what we mean by "nature." Proximity to an avalanche, an unexpected rendezvous with a grizzly bear, or the knowledge that one has a nest of snakes in the crawlspace of one's home are all encounters with nature, but not particularly relaxing ones. Interestingly, psychophysiologists have established that *control* can be both a source and an alleviator of stress in humans, depending on whether we believe we have it or not. Time in nature is in this sense a stress-reliever if it is perceived to be under the control of authorities, such as parkland managers, or if we believe we are able to control the situation ourselves. The walk in the woods on a beautiful fall day is stable, non-threatening, and stress relieving. The approaching hurricane is beyond our control and likely to do damage, and is therefore a source of stress. True, many nature lovers find stress relief in the thrill of uncontrolled nature— whitewater rafting, mountain climbing, storm chasing, sailing on the open sea, and the like. As acute, intense experiences these are different than the unremitting stress of long-term lack of control; they may provide relief in the opportunity to forget, temporarily, the chronic stressors of life. It is not clear, moreover, that the intense experience must be a "natural" one to achieve the effect. One might find the same thrill on a roller-coaster. In any case, the relationship between control (or perceived control) and stress is interesting, and it may explain some aspects of the human relationship with the nonhuman world (McEwen and Lasley, 2002: 149).

A peculiar aspect of our desire for control is that we are not terribly good judges of environmental risk (Slovic *et al.*, 1979). Things that are unfamiliar, unavoidable, and beyond our understanding are typically perceived as a greater risk than things that are common and within our grasp. In the case of human health, for example, nuclear power plants, oil spills, and genetically modified organisms are often believed to be greater risks than smoking, automobile driving, and obesity, when in fact the opposite is true. In part this is attributable to the well-established notion of temporal discounting—humans are generally much more concerned about the present than the future. But discrepancies in risk perception are also attributable to *agency*. Generally speaking, when we feel that we know how something works or what it does, when we choose to do it, and when we perceive that we are in control, it seems to be more of an opportunity than a threat (Schmidt and Wei, 2006). Lawrence Axelrod and his colleagues extend this view to the human perception of natural hazards, like droughts and floods. According to this research, people usually see such events as being harmful to their well-being and are inclined to overlook the ecological benefits. We are predisposed to see disturbance as "a human rather than an ecologically-based event" (Axelrod *et al.*, 1999: 46). Further, the study shows that people tend to see manipulative practices like dams and irrigation as being low-risk and high-reward propositions. In general, it seems, we do not perceive the long-term consequences of evolutionary change as well as we perceive the short-term rewards of ecological management. Manipulation of nature is generally seen as being worth the long-term environmental risk (Axelrod *et al.*, 1999).

Some social theorists have observed that the ways in which we identify and mitigate risks are themselves a product of our culture, and that cultural bias has much to do with wealth and power structures (Wildavsky and Dake, 1990). Those that benefit from a hierarchical power structure (i.e. those with wealth), for example, place great trust in societal and technological solutions to environmental problems. Wealthy people also have a propensity to see social deviance as a potential threat to their position. Individuals with the means to work the market tend not to perceive the risk of environmental scarcity; rather, they trust in technology and innovation to present future solutions to the problem. Members of less affluent social groups, by contrast, tend to fear authority-imposed technology in response to environmental risk, instead preferring the response of collective social action. In this difference of cultural response we can see how environmental policy controversies are inextricably linked with socioeconomic context.

How can all of this help us understand our environmental behavior? The physical well-being model suggests that we act at least in part to advance our own prospects. According to this theory we have an affinity for natural settings and transactions that reduce our stress, that allow us actual or perceived control of our environment, and that minimize our perceived risk. These are in keeping with a human characteristic that we have already encountered: our predilection for self-interested utility and stability.

To the extent that this model describes our actions, I suggest that it raises our first point of psychological discord. Modern humans, particularly in western affluent society, might find comfort and stress relief in nature, but only in *benign* nature. Nature that is docile, predictable, benevolent, and under control—this is the nature of physical well-being, not the forest fire, the drought, or the infectious disease. In synthetic society, where so much is controlled, there is the expectation of stability even in wilderness, just as there is the expectation that consumable natural resources will remain in constant supply. There is more than a little romanticism at play here. As we have seen, the human perspective of the non-human world has not always been one of comfort. To the contrary, wilderness was long regarded with fear and dread. Instead, it is *managed* nature—the garden, the domesticated plants and animals, the reliable and predictable source of food—that has been the source of comfort for much of human history. Romanticism changed social perception of the western world by creating the expectation that all of nature is a source of repose and inspiration. We have already encountered a number of corollaries of this notion: the perception that there is a *correct* version of nature, that particular species belong in particular areas, that ecosystems mature into climax communities, and that ecological functions are regular and predictable. Likewise, we have seen the human preference for charismatic species and iconic landscapes.

These attitudes are not entirely unjustified—to be sure, there is nurture in nature. But these expectations belie the system of incessant change that we find in the natural world. Harmonious stability is not a characteristic of nature. The nonhuman world has no interest in human comfort, and the perception of natural benevolence is imaginary. If benign, charismatic nature is what we aim to protect, we will surely fail. It is much more difficult, and much less psychologically pleasing, to protect the capacity for function in the midst of change. How well will mental models of permanence and control fare in an impermanent ecological world?

In summary, modern environmentalists are faced with a basic question: *What do we ask of the nonhuman world, and what exactly can it provide?* Given our physiological preference for nature's stress-relieving comfort, it is only logical that we wish to protect the calm, the beautiful, and the awe-inspiring. Given our desire for control, we tend to prefer stable and predictable nature. We can indeed manipulate the nonhuman world to temporarily achieve these goals. But this is nature with a fence around it. It is our own mental version of Eden; it is nature that caters to human interests. Protection of a natural world that includes the unpredictable, the destructive, the repulsive, the mundane—this is difficult to reconcile with the romantic ideal.

Emotional well-being

Our interactions with the natural world—be they acts of protection, manipulation, or communion—can stir emotions in ways that rival interpersonal intimacy. People can and do experience love of a place and grieve for its loss; we can care for an animal or plant as though it were our own offspring; we can feel guilt and despair when confronted with environmental destruction. The reasons we feel such emotions and their relation to our actions might be described as an affective model of environmental behavior.

In *Life is a miracle*, Wendell Berry states that "people exploit what they have merely concluded to be of value, but they defend what they love" (Berry, 2000: 41). Berry associates the love of nature to the pleasure we take in the individual uniqueness of living things and in the mystery of that which is greater than ourselves. E.O. Wilson, in *Biophilia*, also sees the human love for nature: "the innate tendency to focus on life and lifelike processes" (Wilson, 1986: 1). Wilson's reasoning is evolutionary: that humans seek out connections with organisms and landscapes that have long provided utility and fascination. While these two scholars share a recognition of human love for the natural world, they differ on the origins and meaning of the emotion. Wilson's perspective is that of a materialist. In this view our emotional connection to nature is genetically influenced. It stems from our evolutionary reliance upon the Earth and its living things for sustenance. Harold Fromm summarizes this succinctly: "that nurture, in other words, *is* nature" (Fromm, 2009: 164). Our emotions themselves, our hopes, our spirits—all have at their core our genetic predilection for life, as expressed in the chemistry of our central nervous system. Berry's love, on the other hand, is a belief that nature is a manifestation of grace with which we can commune in ways that are beyond our ability to explain. It is an acceptance that there are vital forces greater than us, and that there are true and proper ways to co-exist within creation, just as there are false and improper ways. Berry and Wilson share a sense of natural wonder, but for Wilson it is a wonder to be understood, while for Berry it is a wonder of mystery beyond our comprehension.

Through Berry's vision we see the elements of sanctity. The sense of being a part of something larger, of drawing energy from and giving energy to an ancient life force too big to understand, of sharing a spirit with other beings—these are thoughts of sacred nature. Further, sacred views of nature often imply the ability to *connect*: to commune with other spirits, human or nonhuman, and to share per-ception and emotion. Above all there is a sense of oneness, perhaps with a single organism or place, but more broadly with all the universe of matter and energy. There are varieties of spiritualism, to be sure, including many that reject all others. But at its most basic the sense of sacredness in nature is "a more palpable sense of being part of a meaningful reality beyond the merely human world severed from its context and source" (Berry, 2000: 223).

For some people, nature is a metaphor for or actual embodiment of the super-natural. Thus we see variations of animism, pantheism, vision quests, creation myths, and holiness attributed to lands, organisms, and objects. To the spiritualist these are the pathways of communion with the essence of ancestors, nonhuman species, and the Earth itself. To the materialist they are evolutionary survival mechanisms—they are part of the sociobiological norms of a group; they are the beliefs and behaviors that define a people and thereby facilitate acceptance, protection, and provision (Wilson, 2012: 8). A materialist might argue that a literal interpretation of these beliefs is at odds with the realities of life, death, and existence. To a spiritualist these *are* the realities of life, death, and existence.

Whether you are persuaded by the materialist or the spiritualist—or by neither, or by something else altogether—the human affinity for the nonhuman world is hard to deny. As we have seen, of course, there are qualifiers: we have affinity for those certain aspects of the nonhuman world which we find to be attractive or useful, with less love (or outright contempt) for the ugly, annoying, and lethal. Biased though it is, emotion can be strong. Confronted with the loss of a beloved organism, species, ecosystem, or landscape, humans can experience feelings of grief. Just as we mourn the death of kin and close friends, some mourn the loss of nonhuman entities. This emotional and spiritual worldview is the driving force behind a movement called ecopsychology (Roszak et al., 1995; Gifford, 2014b: 11–12).

The basic premise of ecopsychology is that the personal emotion of grief can be extended to lost aspects of our environment. The loss of a species or a sacred place is irreversible; the despair this brings for some can be accompanied by sadness and depression. Some see the Earth quite literally as a being, a superorganism that can be healthy or ill. In this sense the experience of environmental degradation is like watching a loved one struggle with a disease—it evokes emotions of fear, anger, compassion, and rage. Various ecopsychologists speak this language: "The Earth speaks to us through our bodies and our psyches; she often cries, and many of us feel her tears;" . . . "The Earth hurts, it is in pain;" . . . "the planet is dying" (Windle, 1995: 138; O'Connor, 1995: 154; Conn, 1995: 161; Sewall, 1995: 214). The rational realization that things change or that species sometimes go extinct is of no more consolation than the understanding that everyone dies. The grief process is non-rational and neither brief nor pleasant, but for some people it is a necessary step in the process of coping with environmental change (Roszak *et al.*, 1995).

Ecopsychologist Paul Shepard maintains that connection with nature is a critical factor for wellness, and that it is not just nature-deprived individuals who are unwell; it is human society. He observes that in foraging societies, what he calls "tribal peoples," the maturation process of children is much different than that of more technologically advanced societies. Tribal culture teaches cooperation, leadership, and that "everyday life [is] inextricable from spiritual significance and encounter" (Shepard, 1995: 26, 32, 35). In the tribal childhood there is constant and consistent connection with both people and nature, often ceremonialized, and there is freedom to play and explore and wonder. He calls this our "normal" path of development and notes that it historically (and prehistorically) happened within a natural setting, not set apart from nature. By contrast, Shepard sees modern affluent childhood development as more about learning to change the world than to change the self. Nature and the synthetic environment are presented and learned as separate spheres of existence. In order to compete, one must learn to consume, control, dominate, and change. Needs are expected to be met immediately, use is careless, waste is common, ceremony is trivialized, and natural history is ignored.

Clinical psychologist Chellis Glendinning sees in this behavior many similarities with chemical addiction, including denial, dishonesty, mental disorder, and disconnection from feelings. The disease from which these symptoms spring "is the systemic and systematic removal of our lives from the natural world." The children of synthetic society cannot help but be influenced: "from this erosion of human nurturing comes the failure of the passages of the life cycle and the exhaustion of our ecological accords" (1995: 51). This manifests in adults as psychopathic and neurotic tendencies, stemming (in Shepard's view) from a loss of connection with—and indeed hostility toward—the nonhuman world. In this perspective, the human wellness afforded by connection with nature makes perfect sense, as it is a return to our evolutionary legacy and an expression of our inner child. It is our link to sanity amid madness. And yet we are, some of us, addicted to the lifestyle of madness (Glendinning, 1995).

Some see a loss of spiritual well-being in modern affluent society. Ecopsychologists Ralph Metzner and Theodore Roszak, for example, lament the human "blind-[ness] to the psychic presence of the living planet" (Metzner, 1995: 59) and recall the sensibility of animism, "listening for the voices of the Earth as if the nonhuman world felt, heard, [and] spoke" (Roszak, 1995: 7). There is more than a hint of mystical Gaianism here—Metzner cites Thomas Berry's lament that humans can no longer enter into a "communion relationship" (Berry, 1991) with the natural world, and Roszak notes that the Earth "seems to be crying out for a radical readjustment" (1995: 2). Even taken as metaphor, these sentiments signal a spiritual disconnect with our distant ancestral relationship with nature. Analogizing our species as an individual, Metzner sees similarities to the symptoms of amnesia, autism, addiction, and dissociation that stem, in his view, from the "trauma" of domestication and the adoption of agriculture. With agriculture, he argues, came the beginning of the division of the human spirit from the natural world, a split that has been exacerbated by western religion and consumerism. Thus our collective psyche is unwell, for it is considered to be superior to the world in which we live. It is, to Metzner, a "life-destroying dissociation between spirit and nature" (1995: 67).

And yet not everyone grieves for the lost species, the cleared forest, or the polluted oceans. In fact, the very idea is absurd to many in the industrialized world. These individuals, according to ecopsychologists, have separated themselves from the Earth and are exhibiting classic human conditions of avoidance, denial, and repression. They are victims of numbed senses and weak imaginations. Affluent, synthetic society encourages this detachment and provides a shallow substitute in the temporary pleasures of consumption.

This, to a rational materialist, might seem to be an unfair characterization. That humans have many adverse effects on nonhuman species is undeniable. The Earth, however, is not an organism, and the planet is not dying. In fact, many organisms and processes are thriving. They just increasingly happen to be organisms and processes that humans find undesirable. What we are losing, in the material view, are ecological functions that support human life. This should be alarming, to be sure, but it differs from the loss of a loved one. This loss does not call for grief or despair; it calls for rational planning. To ecopsychologists, though, rational materialism is not the answer to the problem; it is the problem. It is the mindset that artificially separates us from the other inhabitants of our planet (Sewall, 1995: 204, 214).

Here, then, is a second point of psychological discord. We tend to personify nature, or to think of it in terms of supernatural beings with human-like behaviors, sensations, and emotions. We seek agency in our surroundings, we create mental models that project human actions and emotions onto the nonhuman world, and we find solace in real or perceived connection with the spirits of nature. Of course, these feelings are a biochemically explainable part of our social nature. There is nothing wrong with them as psychological coping mechanisms. As the logic behind conservation efforts or environmental policy, however, spiritual personification of nature can be counterproductive. Ecological systems do not behave as people would, and they do not exist for human fulfillment. While this is widely understood in modern society, environmental appeals to personified nature are still surprisingly common.

In academic literature these viewpoints are often presented, when they are even discussed together, as irreconcilable (Reser, 1995). Much of the disagreement concerns the incompatibility of the objective and intuitive ways of understanding the world. However, the common element—that our actions are at times based on emotion—is not really in question. We are sensual organisms. We feel emotions intensely, we are expert mental modelers, and we project human thoughts, actions, and feelings onto the nonhuman world. We are at least subconsciously obsessed with social relationships among ourselves and our peers, and so it makes perfect sense that we are enthralled with personified nature. For some, the relationships we perceive with nature help us relate to other humans and to cope with life. On the other hand, we are also rational creatures. We seek to understand, and with understanding we seek to manipulate. We act as self-interested competitors, who at least subconsciously place ourselves and our own above all else. At the same time we are community members with a vested interest in the common good. These disagreements over material versus spiritual and individual versus collective are not describing enlightened humans and ignorant humans. They are just describing humans.

Nevertheless, these different worldviews pose another fundamental question of environmentalism. *How do we imagine the nonhuman world, and how does it actually function?* Do we seek to maintain connections with nature that engender feelings of love and togetherness, while easing the grief of loss? Do we seek to extend our social bonds to the nonhuman world? Or do we seek to maintain sustenance, stability, and process in a world that is not capable of feeling love for us and will not mourn our passing?

Social well-being

If connection with nature can bring us physical and emotional comfort, why are so many people averse to it? Why do we behave in such ecologically and personally damaging ways?

It is clear that our thoughts and actions are partly guided by the innate response of our genetic inheritance. Our ingrained attitudes toward the natural world include elements of personal and social wellness described above. We are drawn to certain aspects of nature and repulsed by others. Simply stated, we are attracted to those aspects that are useful to us—they hold the prospect of utility or adventure, they offer services, they make us feel good, they remind us of ourselves. Not surprisingly, then, our default disposition is to favor the nature that favors us.

But genetics only takes us so far. Much psychological theory holds that our behavior is often a response to signals we receive from our community (Lindenberg, 2012: 121). We are influenced by cultural cues that can encourage a wide range of behavior—from hedonic to altruistic. The actions that result from such cues affect not only our social groups but also the environment in which we all live. Hence, an understanding of sociocultural cues may help explain why we act as we do.

The people and places with which we interact on a daily basis are the strongest drivers of our culturally derived behavior. However independent we fancy ourselves, we pay a great deal of attention to the attitudes and actions of other people. Psychological research has shown that people are much more likely to behave in a particular way when they see others doing the same, and much more likely to forgo the activity when others refrain. Thus we see "bystander behavior" among groups of people who will passively watch a situation that calls for assistance and, alternatively, people responding to "cues of care" when they see others stepping forward to lend a hand. The classic research case for this (Rutkowski *et al.*, 1983) dealt with an individual's response to an injured roadside pedestrian, but the behavior is transferable to environmental situations like wasteful and polluting activity. We have already encountered some of the social biases that tend to influence our behavior in such situations. The example of others, particularly in a majority, can nudge us to action. Even more powerful is the observation (or suggestion) that a respected leader or celebrity acts in a particular way. The tendency is equally responsive to cues of inaction and apathy. Our default behavior, for better or worse, is to follow the crowd (Lindenberg, 2012: 123).

If it were this simple, we could just hire celebrities and throngs of people to pick up litter, recycle, and plant trees and the whole population would join in. But this psychological model suggests that we are also responsive to cues of personal gain and selfishness. Our ever-present competitive nature can be difficult to overcome. In comparing ourselves to others we are not just copying their actions to blend in, we are subconsciously measuring ourselves against the other, looking for an edge. In some situations this can drive positive behavior, as in the case of seeking the enhanced reputation of the hero or the leader. In many cases, though, human competitive behavior can seek an edge by devaluing the other, either figuratively by circumstance and reputation or literally by acquiring resources and status symbols that indicate superiority. Marketing specialists are well aware of our competitive instincts, and much of the world is bombarded by advertisements for products and behaviors that will make us look younger or appear to be more successful. Further, our hedonic instincts are easily triggered by sensual cues and further exploited by marketing for impulse buys, enticed by the taste, sight, and smell of immediate comfort and sex appeal. The acquisition of things becomes part of our identity. As a reward, we get a temporary physiological rush for acting on the impulse (Durning, 1992: 78).

Of course, people can and do overcome these competitive and selfish instincts, but it takes some effort. It helps if we are surrounded by others who are fighting the same fight, and it becomes nearly insurmountable if we are surrounded by others who routinely seek to satiate their competitive and hedonic desires. A third case is even more daunting: that of the "socially empty" environment. Psychologist Siegwart Lindenberg (2012) describes these as social spaces in which we are not easily observed by others, like empty parking garages or lonely work spaces. In such cases there are few or no norming cues, and thus our environmentally and socially detrimental behaviors are more likely. *What will you do with your empty soda can when no one is looking?* We could easily extend this thought to some environments in modern affluent society which, while full of people, can be socially empty. The anonymity of complex urban environments, the isolated working and living situations, the declining membership in civic and religious organizations—all contribute to an environment that lacks cues of cooperative reciprocity and therefore permits selfish behavior. *What will you do with your time and money when no one cares?*

The sociocultural cues we encounter are inseparable from the physical spaces in which we encounter them. Thus we might think of behavioral cues more broadly as environmental cues, inclusive of other people. How we perceive, interpret, and respond to a multitude of signals has long been a topic of considerable interest to environmental psychologists (Gibson, 1966; Barker, 1968). In general, theories of environmental perception propose that physical and social spaces can signal to the individual how he or she might function in those surroundings. Here again, the signals can only be interpreted within the context of culture. A forest scene might indicate recreation, threat, financial opportunity, or a source of muhacha fruits depending on one's perspective. But more to the point is the consequence of physical spaces that offer few or no signals that are representative of the nonhuman world. We might think of such spaces as *ecologically* empty environments. Synthetic society is in many ways ecologically empty.

The cues of personal behavior can present a dilemma when they are scaled up to greater socio-environmental behavior. Our large-scale motivations are not so different than our evolved interpersonal values of self-interest and cooperative reciprocity. However, when many people contribute to environmental problems over wide expanses of space and time it can be difficult to establish and reinforce behavioral norms. The problem is that the benefits of our actions are small, short-term, and local, while the social and environmental ramifications of collective behavior are large, long-term, and global. More critically, in synthetic society the immediate benefits of selfish behavior are obvious while the long-term costs are invisible. In the same way, the costs of contributing to a public good (like an environmental charity, for instance) are real, immediate, and local for the individual who writes the check, while the benefits are faraway and nebulous. It is easy to ignore the common cause and focus on more personal and parochial matters (De Groot and Thogersen, 2012: 146).

The point is that the cues of interpersonal behavior do not readily translate into a biospheric ethic. Awareness helps, of course, for knowledge of an issue makes the consequences of one's actions more apparent. But even when we are aware, the proper course of action is not always clear. We generally don't act for just one reason, for instance. My choice to come into work today was egoistic, self-interested, cooperative, reciprocal, and biospheric all at once. Would it have been better for me to not burn the gasoline to get here and, in so doing, sacrifice face-to-face conversation time with my students? Should I trade my car for an electric vehicle built by a corporation that is extracting metals for the battery (from where and at what cost I do not know)? Such questions are never-ending, and the best path of global environmental action is never entirely clear. The overarching question is more sobering: *Do my actions matter at all?* These are largely the same dilemmas we face in the small sociocultural circles of our lives, but we face the global problems with much less information. Not surprisingly, scholars of social dilemmas have found that we tend to act more selfishly when the dilemma involves large or undefined groups, when the problem itself is unclear, when the situation is poorly communicated among the participants, when participants are not convinced that their contribution will be significant, and when participants are unaware of the actions of other stakeholders (Von Borgstede *et al.*, 2012: 181–182).

The intimate relationship between individual behavior, social cues, and environmental consequence is known in scholarly parlance as the socio-nature hypothesis. This is the view that "social relations are inherently ecological and ecological relationships are inherently social" (Alkon, 2013: 683). It implies that problems of ecological stress and social strife are both founded in human relationships. If this is the case, it means that weakened mechanisms of social responsibility can diminish collective environmental action (Box 10.1). Accordingly, I present a third point of psychological discord: the separation of people from one another (and from the nonhuman world) removes a social preventative measure against destructive environmental behavior. Socially and ecologically empty environments can diminish function in human and nonhuman communities alike. This presents a third question for modern environmentalism: *What does it mean to be a responsible member of a society or an ecosystem when the intentions and actions of other members are isolated, excluded, or invisible?*

Another way of saying this is that the socioecological cage of synthetic, affluent societies is in need of repair. Adam Smith's "impartial spectator" is missing from socially and ecologically empty communities, leaving individuals vulnerable to a corporate capitalism that preys upon instinctive hedonic selfishness. This is difficult to overcome, even among individuals with a strong environmental ethic. It also poses a barrier for social change. Even in the resistance of selfishness, the proper course of action can be difficult to ascertain, for global problems lack personal social cues. The remedy, at least in part, may require meaningful interaction with other members of our socioecological system.

A mental muddle

What influences our environmental behavior? In this brief review I have considered only a few of the many potential factors, but even these form a complicated answer to the question. We may act in aversion to stress and in search of comfort. We may seek to control our surroundings to enhance our own prospects. In some cases our actions are driven by emotion, and in most cases they are influenced by our sociocultural context in ways that we probably don't even realize. These and many other forces simultaneously prompt us to treat the world around us in particular ways.

I submit that we have difficulty defining and building consensus around environmentalism because it is founded on socio-psychological discord. Our conflicted nature, our contradictory conceptual scenarios, and the confusion of behavioral cues we experience make it unclear exactly what we are trying to achieve and how our desires align with reality. Misconceptions of nature can hinder ecological action. Furthermore, the isolation within synthetic society removes its members from the natural world and renders the ancient mechanisms of cooperative reciprocity ineffective. Social separation can hinder social action.

Box 10.1 A relational approach to socioecological well-being

Environmentalism occurs at the intersection of individual behavior, sociocultural milieu, and ecological context. As such, environmental action is most successful when it is informed by all of these realms. This requires two things: understanding the ecological and social systems involved, and engagement of individuals and organizations with socioecological systems.

Bodin and Prell (2011) have promoted such understanding and engagement from a social network perspective. In their view, social networks must be understood in terms of their context and characteristics. Geography, cultural setting, natural resource base, institutions, and key stakeholders, for example, make each social network unique and define the ways in which it will interact with other networks and with ecological systems. Scale can be a particularly relevant factor. Small-scale networks occur at the level of individual stakeholders and specific ecosystems. Small networks are situated within larger networks, and ultimately within global networks of international organizations and biospheric processes.

James Miller (2006) has explored socioecological systems at the small scale. Small ecosystems, even in the midst of development, can play an important role in habitat provision for local biota and in the physical and mental well-being of local people. Access to local natural areas can reduce "estrangement from the natural world" (2006: 360) and provide a focal point for social cohesion. Large-scale integration of social and ecological systems is entirely compatible with, and indeed complementary to, local socioecological systems. Folke *et al.* (2011) have called for economic development standards and governance processes that prioritize ecosystem services, recognize key stakeholders, and integrate global networks with regional and local networks. The large-scale challenge, in the authors' words, is to "make the work of the biosphere visible in society, in human actions and in financial and economic transactions" (2011: 726). Ultimately, success at the large scale will depend upon the same thing that small-scale success requires: individual people connecting with one another to advocate for ecological systems.

Are we then adrift in a sea of environmental problems without social or psychological tools of navigation? In some sense it seems that we are. But environmentalism is a mental model. If we humans are good at anything, we are good at mental modeling. And mental models can change. The human relationship with the nonhuman world never has been just one idea. It has evolved along with our biology, our social structures, and our cultural perceptions of the planet we inhabit. It is evolving still. This evolutionary process takes place in our collective minds, as we compare the world we imagine to the realities we perceive and work to reconcile the two.

Bibliography

Alkon, A.H. (2013). The socio-nature of local organic food. *Antipode*, 45(3), pp. 663–680.

Axelrod, L.J., McDaniels, T. and Slovic, P. (1999). Perceptions of ecological risk from natural hazards. *Journal of Risk Research*, 2(1), pp. 31–53.

Barker, R.G. (1968). *Ecological psychology: concepts and methods for studying the environment of human behavior*. Stanford, CA: Stanford University Press.

Berry, T. (1991). *The ecozoic era*. Presentation for the E.F. Schumacher Society, October, 1991.

Berry, W. (2000). *Life is a miracle: an essay against modern superstition*. Washington, DC: Counterpoint.

Bodin, Ö. and Prell, C. (2011). Social network analysis in natural resource governance: summary and outlook. In: Ö. Bodin and C. Prell, eds., *Social networks and natural resource management: uncovering the social fabric of environmental governance*. Cambridge, UK: Cambridge University Press. pp. 347–373.

Byrne, A. and Byrne, D. (1993). The effect of exercise on depression, anxiety and other mood states: a review. *Journal of Psychosomatic Research*, 37(6), pp. 565–574.

Campbell, J.M. (1983). Ambient stressors. *Environment and Behavior*, 15(3), pp. 355–380.

Conn, S.A. (1995). When the Earth hurts, who responds? In: T. Roszak, M. Gomes and A. Kanner, eds., *Ecopsychology: restoring the Earth, healing the mind*. San Francisco: Sierra Club Books. pp. 156–171.

Crabtree, J.W., Haslam, S.A., Postmes, T. and Haslam, C. (2010). Mental health support groups, stigma, and self-esteem: positive and negative implications of group identification. *Journal of Social Issues*, 66(3), pp. 553–569.

De Groot, J. and Thogersen, J. (2012). Values and pro-environmental behaviour. In: L. Steg, A. Van den Berg and J. De Groot, eds., *Environmental psychology: an introduction*. New York: Wiley. pp. 119–128.

Durning, A.T. (1992). *How much is enough? The consumer society and the future of the Earth*. New York: W.W. Norton.

Emerson, R.W. (1836). *Nature*. Boston: James Munroe.

Folke, C., Jansson, Å., Rockström, J., Olsson, P., Carpenter, S.R., Chapin III, F.S., Crépin, A.S., Daily, G., Danell, K., Ebbesson, J., Elmqvist, T., Galaz, V., Moberg, F., Nilsson, M., Osterblom, H., Ostrom, E., Persson, A., Peterson, G., Polasky, S., Steffen, W., Walker, B. and Westley, F. (2011). Reconnecting to the biosphere. *AMBIO: A Journal of the Human Environment*, 40(7), pp. 719–738.

Fromm, H. (2009). *The nature of being human: from environmentalism to consciousness*. Baltimore: Johns Hopkins University Press.

Gezondheidsraad: The Health Council of the Netherlands. (2004). *Nature and Health*. Report to the Minister of Agriculture, Nature and Food Quality, June 9, 2004.

Gibson, J.J. (1966). *The senses considered as perceptual systems*. Boston: Houghton Mifflin.

Gifford, R. (2014a). Environmental psychology matters. *Annual Review of Psychology*, 65, pp. 541–579.

Gifford, R. (2014b). *Environmental psychology: principles and practice*, 5th edition. Colville, WA: Optimal Books.

Glendinning, C. (1995). Technology, trauma and the wild. In: T. Roszak, M. Gomes and A. Kanner, eds., *Ecopsychology: restoring the Earth, healing the mind*. San Francisco: Sierra Club Books. pp. 41–54.

Joye, Y. and Van den Berg, A.E. (2012). Restorative environments. In: L. Steg, A. Van den Berg and J. De Groot, eds., *Environmental psychology: an introduction*. New York: Wiley. pp. 57–66.

Kahn, P.H. (1999). *The human relationship with nature: development and culture.* Cambridge, MA: MIT Press.

Kaplan, R. and Kaplan, S. (1989). *The experience of nature: A psychological perspective.* Cambridge, UK: Cambridge University Press.

Lindenberg, S.M. (2012). How cues in the environment affect normative behaviour. In: L. Steg, A. Van den Berg and J. De Groot, eds., *Environmental psychology: an introduction.* New York: Wiley. pp. 119–128.

Louv, R. (2008). *Last child in the woods: saving our children from nature-deficit disorder.* Chapel Hill, NC: Algonquin Books.

Mayer, F.S., Frantz, C.M., Bruehlman-Senecal, E. and Dolliver, K. (2008). Why is nature beneficial? The role of connectedness to nature. *Environment and Behavior*, 41(5), pp. 607–643.

McEwen, B.S. and Lasley, E.N. (2002). *The end of stress as we know it.* Washington, DC: Joseph Henry Press.

Metzner, R. (1995). The psychopathology of the human–nature relationship. In: T. Roszak, M. Gomes and A. Kanner, eds., *Ecopsychology: restoring the Earth, healing the mind.* San Francisco: Sierra Club Books. pp. 55–67.

Miller, J.R. (2006). Restoration, reconciliation, and reconnecting with nature nearby. *Biological Conservation*, 127(3), pp. 356–361.

Misra, S. and Stokols, D. (2012). Psychological and health outcomes of perceived information overload. *Environment and Behavior*, 44(6), pp. 737–759.

O'Connor, T. (1995). Therapy for a dying planet. In: T. Roszak, M. Gomes and A. Kanner, eds., *Ecopsychology: restoring the Earth, healing the mind.* San Francisco: Sierra Club Books. pp. 149–155.

Park, B.J., Tsunetsugu, Y., Kasetani, T., Kagawa, T. and Miyazaki, Y. (2010). The physiological effects of Shinrin-yoku (taking in the forest atmosphere or forest bathing): evidence from field experiments in 24 forests across Japan. *Environmental Health and Preventive Medicine*, 15(1), pp. 18–26.

Radkau, J. (2014). *The age of ecology.* New York: Wiley.

Reser, J.P. (1995). Whither environmental psychology? The transpersonal ecopsychology crossroads. *Journal of Environmental Psychology*, 15(3), pp. 235–257.

Roszak, T. (1995). Where psyche meets Gaia. In: T. Roszak, M. Gomes and A. Kanner, eds., *Ecopsychology: restoring the Earth, healing the mind.* San Francisco: Sierra Club Books. pp. 1–17.

Roszak, T., Gomes, M.E. and Kanner, A.D., eds. (1995). *Ecopsychology: restoring the Earth, healing the mind.* San Francisco: Sierra Club Books.

Rutkowski, G.K., Gruder, C.L. and Romer, D. (1983). Group cohesiveness, social norms, and bystander intervention. *Journal of Personality and Social Psychology*, 44(3), p. 545.

Saegert, S. and Winkel, G.H. (1990). Environmental psychology. *Annual Review of Psychology*, 41(1), pp. 441–477.

Schmidt, M.R. and Wei, W. (2006). Loss of agro-biodiversity, uncertainty, and perceived control: a comparative risk perception study in Austria and China. *Risk Analysis*, 26(2), pp. 455–470.

Sedlmeier, P., Eberth, J., Schwarz, M., Zimmermann, D., Haarig, F., Jaeger, S. and Kunze, S. (2012). The psychological effects of meditation: a meta-analysis. *Psychological Bulletin*, 138(6), pp. 1139–1171.

Sewall, L. (1995). The skill of ecological perception. In: T. Roszak, M. Gomes and A. Kanner, eds., *Ecopsychology: restoring the Earth, healing the mind.* San Francisco: Sierra Club Books. pp. 201–215.

Shepard, P. (1995). Nature and madness. In: T. Roszak, M. Gomes and A. Kanner, eds., *Ecopsychology: restoring the Earth, healing the mind.* San Francisco: Sierra Club Books. pp. 21–40.

Slovic, P., Fischhoff, B. and Lichtenstein, S. (1979). Rating the risks. *Environment: Science and Policy for Sustainable Development,* 21(3), pp. 14–39.

Tarr, B., Launay, J., Cohen, E. and Dunbar, R. (2015). Synchrony and exertion during dance independently raise pain threshold and encourage social bonding. *Biology Letters,* 11(10), p. 2015.0767.

Ulrich, R.S. (1983). Aesthetic and affective response to natural environment. In: I. Altman and J. Wohlwill, eds., *Behavior and the natural environment.* New York: Springer. pp. 85–125.

Ulrich, R.S. (1984). View through a window may influence recovery. *Science,* 224(4647), pp. 224–225.

Ulrich, R.S., Simons, R.F., Losito, B.D., Fiorito, E., Miles, M.A. and Zelson, M. (1991). Stress recovery during exposure to natural and urban environments. *Journal of Environmental Psychology,* 11(3), pp. 201–230.

Van den Berg, A.E., Joye, Y. and De Vries, S. (2012). Health benefits of nature. In: L. Steg, A. Van den Berg and J. De Groot, eds., *Environmental psychology: an introduction.* New York: Wiley. pp. 47–56.

Von Borgstede, C., Johansson, L.O. and Nilsson, A. (2012). Social dilemmas: motivational, individual and structural aspects influencing cooperation. In: L. Steg, A. Van den Berg and J. De Groot, eds., *Environmental psychology: an introduction.* New York: Wiley. pp. 175–184.

Wells, N.M. and Evans, G.W. (2003). Nearby nature a buffer of life stress among rural children. *Environment and Behavior,* 35(3), pp. 311–330.

West, J., Otte, C., Geher, K., Johnson, J. and Mohr, D.C. (2004). Effects of Hatha yoga and African dance on perceived stress, affect, and salivary cortisol. *Annals of Behavioral Medicine,* 28(2), pp. 114–118.

Whyte, D. (2016). Interview. On being. National Public Radio, April 6, 2016.

Wildavsky, A. and Dake, K. (1990). Theories of risk perception: Who fears what and why? *Daedalus,* 119(4), pp. 41–60.

Wilson, E.O. (1986). *Biophilia.* Cambridge, MA: Harvard University Press.

Wilson, E.O. (2012). *The social conquest of Earth.* New York: Liveright.

Windle, P. (1995). The ecology of grief. In: T. Roszak, M. Gomes and A. Kanner, eds., *Ecopsychology: restoring the Earth, healing the mind.* San Francisco: Sierra Club Books. pp. 136–148.

11 Dimensions revisited

Key points

- The conceptual dimensions of environmentalism can be resolved, thereby reframing social and ecological relationships.
- Environmental actions should be judged by the degree to which they promote access to ecological services for all people.

In the preceding chapters, we have seen how various aspects of environmentalism have arisen through sociobiological evolution and developed through socio-cultural evolution. Our sociobiological character provides motivation for cooperative reciprocity that checks our selfish instinct. Our social skills include the ability to share mental models that afford a capacity for empathy. Sociocultural evolution has resulted in normative cultural codes of acceptable and unacceptable behavior with regard to our social group and its environment. These, I have proposed, are the tools that prime our species for an environmental ethic.

But we have also encountered the ways in which these tools have been compromised, particularly in synthetic society. Cooperative reciprocity requires meaningful interaction that has in some instances been replaced with socially and ecologically empty exchange. Mental models of the natural world are in some instances idealized and romanticized, such that the notion of preserved nature is contrary to the reality of functional process. Normative cultural codes in synthetic society—and increasingly the world—are providing behavioral cues for consumption to excess in pursuit of short-term gratification and an economy of continuous growth.

The resulting exploitation of natural resources has stressed the ecological processes on which we rely. Disparity, disconnection, and division have strained social structures, such that collective responses to environmental problems are hampered. We are seeing the ramifications in our mental, physical, and social health.

While the factors that gave rise to environmentalism remain, the social and ecological context in which they occur has changed. I suggest that environmentalism must change accordingly. Specifically, I believe that a reconsideration of the different conceptual dimensions of environmentalism is in order. In the second chapter I proposed five such dimensions. Now, armed with evolutionary context, I revisit each with a critique.

Anthropocentrism and biocentrism

From humble beginnings as one species of many on the branching tree of life, *Homo sapiens* has improvised its way to an exploitative society that is dominating the other species on the planet. Seeking a more biologically just world, some have advocated for extending human rights to all living things. Others have argued that humans must use other species for the greatest good—that being our own welfare. At the heart of this debate lies Darwin's paradox: that organisms must struggle to compete for individual survival even as our kinship with all living things implies cooperation. A well-meaning environmentalist may be pulled in both directions. Most people have a genuine appreciation, even love, for certain manifestations of nature, and we now recognize that connection with nature has profound and positive human health effects. At the same time, we typically do not hesitate to use, kill, or manipulate other species to service needs of our own, our kin, or fellow humans, usually in that order.

Having reviewed the biological and social evolution of our species, I believe that we can see a way out of this apparent conceptual impasse. It is a recognition that we are anthropocentric organisms, and that anthropocentrism is not only the approach we have always taken (whether we care to admit it or not), but also that it is the most viable approach to our environmental problems.

Let's re-consider biocentrism. In some versions it means that all organisms are of equal value, while to others it means that each organism has intrinsic worth. Equality among organisms (or even species) is a difficult position to defend. In Darwinian ecology, it just doesn't make much sense. Biological evolution is a process of *inequality*, with some taking advantage of others to live and reproduce. We are products of natural selection, and it shows in our behavior toward other living things. We interact with trillions of other organisms every minute of every day (that is if we count microorganisms, and why would we not?). Some are beneficial, some are harmful, most are neutral. Our every action places stress or visits death upon some organisms while benefitting others, though to most of this we are oblivious. Our species has done this throughout its history, from our earliest days as hunters and horticulturists through our modern use of genetically modified organisms. In fact, you could make a convincing case that much of the ecological world exists as it does because of some past or present selection pressure exerted by humans—pressure that valued some organisms over others. In what sense, then, have organisms or species ever been treated as though they have equal value? If this were truly our goal, how would we even go about pursuing it?

I contend that it is not our goal, never has been, and, due to the mechanisms of evolutionary selection, is unachievable if we ever were to adopt it as a goal. We are incapable of treating other species as equals. Rather, we find value in the non-human world as it relates to ourselves (Thompson, 1990).

Granted, when we are aware of the suffering we cause, many of us feel compassion toward nonhuman species and some feel a sense of loss at their demise. As far as we know, we are unique in this respect. Aldo Leopold recognized this long ago: "For one species to mourn the death of another is a new thing under the sun" (Leopold, 1949 [1947]: 110). But what do we mourn, exactly? Perhaps it is a perceived loss of some essential quality of living things; perhaps it is the feeling that living things have intrinsic worth. It seems, though, that our grief is usually more selective and conditional. We mourn the loss of things that we value the most. These tend to be the aspects of the nonhuman world that contribute to—or remind us of—our own existence.

I don't intend any disrespect for the admiration of living things. In fact I share it. Like many people, I've kept a long series of pets in my life. Dogs, cats, fish, gerbils. A few lizards for a while. And, like most people, I developed a sense of attachment to each, and I felt sadness at their passing. Okay, less for the lizards. Similarly, people can and do become emotionally attached to domesticated farm animals, and even wild animals with which they have recurring contact. We even become enamored with plants, like the grand old oak in the back yard. But just as there are species we love there are those that we despise. For every *Canis familiaris*, there is a *Canis lupus*. We tend to dislike species that cause us discomfort or harm, like hornets, rats, lice, spiders, mosquitos, tapeworms, the influenza virus, and poison ivy. These, we are eager to kill.

As we have seen, such attitudes toward our fellow species are an ancient part of our evolutionary psychology. The moral question of how we should treat nonhuman organisms is a transference of human social morality: how should we treat other humans? This mental extension makes much more sense when it is applied to organisms in which we perceive desirable qualities of people: companionship, loyalty, grace, strength, beauty—*charisma*. In other words, we favor organisms that are easily personified. We also favor species that serve us directly, and many of these are domesticated and changed so much through artificial selection that they bear little resemblance to their wild ancestors. We favor organisms that favor us. The value we so often find in other species is an instrumental value, even if the service they are providing is psychological comfort, a perceived spiritual connection, or an aesthetic catharsis. To argue that we ought to behave differently—that we ought to see that each species has intrinsic value—is problematic, for we are the only beings capable of assigning worth. As Harold Fromm has observed, the philosophical pronouncement that each species has intrinsic worth is nothing more than a denial that we humans are the sole judge of the concept of value (Fromm, 2009: 71). How meaningful is it to take the position that every species has value when we arrange them in descending order based on their importance to us? How does such a position differ from anthropocentrism? I argue that it does not differ at all, and this leads to a startling conclusion: *our biocentrism is anthropocentric.*

This is disconcerting, to be sure. But it does not mean that we should treat other species with disrespect. If we retreat a bit from true biocentrism we might still advocate biocentric-like behaviors. For example, I might recognize my human bias for certain species but support a general notion of equity among nonhuman species: that everything has a right to exist out there in the world, on the condition that it is not bothering me. There is nothing wrong with this attitude, as long as we also recognize that we live in a world of Darwinian evolution. As a major selection force on the biota of the world, our choices have ecological ramifications. Every species we select *for* means that we have selected *against* others. So we drive the evolution of other species; there is no shame here. If we truly wish to encourage co-existence among species, though, we might heed the lessons of a century and a half of ecological research. Ecological stress limits mutualistic relationships. Alleviation of stress encourages them. Reducing the stress that we exert on the natural world will benefit us and some of the species we hold dear. Unfortunately, many human activities are ecologically stressful and select for the very organisms we despise, at our own peril and at the expense of the species we cherish.

Another biocentric-like behavior is animal welfare. This is an acknowledgement that we do indeed harvest other species for our own survival, but that we can and should do so with compassion. This is also a fine attitude, and regrettably one that is suppressed by the anonymous and opaque system of livestock treatment in industrial agriculture. But again, let's recognize it for what it is: comfort for our own psychological state of mind. Knowledge of the gory details that put the beef in our stew may cause some to feel guilt. Acts of compassion alleviate guilt. Access to the free range may or may not be better for the chicken, but it makes some people feel better about themselves. Advocates of animal welfare call for certain nonhuman organisms to be treated as humans—to be treated *humanely*. Choosing to do so in the ways we personally treat animals, by what we purchase, and by what we eat does not seem to have a downside, and indeed it may have real psycho-social benefits. We could use more compassion, not only in how we treat animals but also in how we treat people.

My point is not that we shouldn't care for other species, only that the biocentric/ anthropocentric debate is long since over. The notions that each organism has equal value and that each species has intrinsic worth simply do not work in the Darwinian world. We are anthropocentric creatures. Our primary responsibilities are toward one another. Embracing our anthropocentrism need not signal the death of environmentalism, however. To the contrary, it can liberate us to see that "nature" is a world of our construction. For better or worse, the biosphere responds to the pressures we place upon it. If we are anthropocentric then let's be anthropocentric and interact with the nonhuman world for the long-term and inclusive benefit of the human species. This will necessarily include many of the things that biocentrists hold dear: biological diversity, functional ecosystems, and connection among living things.

Materialism and spiritualism

Many people—perhaps most—believe that some essence of being exists separately from the material universe. Cartesian dualism has been remarkably persistent. Actually, the notion is far older than Descartes and far wider spread than the western world. Animism, pantheism, Gaianism, cyclic reincarnation, the vital spirit, angels and demons, the eternal soul, the omnipotent One God: all are manifestations of human spirituality. The ubiquity of spiritualism is evidence that it is part of our ancient evolutionary inheritance. And, since we have no evidence of spirituality in any other species, it seems to be uniquely human.

Without a doubt, the spiritual–material debate has profound implications for environmentalism. A sincere belief that there is spiritual energy in the nonhuman world and that one's own spirit is linked to the greater spiritual realm is a powerful worldview. Anthropological evidence points to many cultures, both existing and extinct, that confer great respect to the natural world as a matter of spirituality. Of course, spirituality can also enable the hierarchical dominance of nature (and people) if the belief implies that one's spirit is on a higher plane than others. Spiritual belief, and the accompanying religious practice, can thus be a justification for a wide variety of behaviors.

The nature of human spirituality is a matter of some contention. Some believe it to be gift from the Creator, in whose image we are made. Other spiritualists might argue that the prehistoric evolving human mind reached a point of cognitive ability that allowed us to sense the spiritual presence in ourselves and in the universe. Materialists propose alternative physical explanations. Some have postulated that spiritualism is a spandrel—a by-product of our propensity to create mental scenarios, to search for causation, and to seek agency in everyday events. But spandrels do not contribute to biological fitness. Spirituality does seem to confer an adaptive advantage, both in the relief of anxiety and in the community-building aspects of ritual. If the capacity for spirituality is heritable, this implies some set of genetically coded traits that are subject to natural selection. Hence, whether you believe that spirituality is a divinely inspired characteristic of the human mind or that spiritual beliefs have arisen because they confer adaptive advantage, the mechanism of spirituality appears to have a biochemical basis.

The notion of spirituality as a biochemical phenomenon has been disparaged by some as the removal of sanctity from the natural world in favor of an insensitive appraisal of instrumental value. A central criticism is that the recognition (or belief) that the river, the mountain, the salmon, and the willow are only packages of energized atoms has made them easier to exploit—just as the same perspective makes people easier to exploit. There are, therefore, modern environmentalists who insist that materialism is incompatible with an environmental ethic—that it is the *antithesis* of environmentalism. This attitude, in my estimation, is incorrect.

Too often, an other-worldly and extra-biotic spirit is presented as the sole domain of cooperation and compassion, while materialism is cast as the absence of these qualities. In fact, cooperation and compassion are products of evolution—they are materially derived traits. Compassion exists not in spite of the material world, but because of it. Similarly, spirituality and religion are too often exempt from critiques of the socioeconomic systems that are driving many of our greatest environmental problems. To the contrary, the worst characteristics of religious spiritualism are implicated in social problems of inequality and xenophobia (Jost et al., 2014). My point is not that spiritualism is imperfect and materialism is ideal. My point is that we should not differentiate between the two at all. Evidence that spiritual thoughts and actions are tied to the architecture of the human brain, that such feelings are physically and chemically inducible, and that spirituality is variable across human populations all point toward a neurological basis for spirituality. What this means is that *the spiritual is material*.

I propose an environmentalism that acknowledges our instrumental need for ecological services—*and that recognizes the best of spirituality as one of those services*. Just as we need food, fuel, fiber, and function, we need mentally restorative and physically healing connections with the nonhuman world. Likewise, we need the social structure that ritual, tradition, recognition, common purpose, and acceptance can provide. Such cultural bonding, religious or secular, has long taken place in the context of the natural environment. It is only recently—with the emergence of synthetic society—that some people have become isolated from both group and place. Connections with the people around us and knowledge of the places in which we live are now understood to confer real psychological benefits. That we have come to recognize these benefits as fundamentally biochemical does not lessen our need for them. And it matters little that our spiritual imaginations are sometimes unscientific. We have an entirely rational need for the non-rational.

This sort of environmentalism is a rejection of Cartesian dualism. It accepts that the mind is of the body and that humans are of the natural world. Such a worldview—a material environmentalism—seeks to promote spiritual well-being as a function of physical and social well-being. It may provide the added benefit of shedding the us-versus-them mentality that overtly zealous religiosity has engendered. In truth, there are not people with the right or wrong ways of seeing the beauty of nature or wondering at its mystery. There are only people with material needs, be they neurological, psychological, physiological, social, or ecological. This should be our common spirituality.

Ecocentrism and egocentrism

Another dimension of environmentalism is the question of human interference with nature. It is not really a question of *if* humans interfere with the nonhuman world, for that ship has long since sailed. The history of our species is a legacy of management, from the use of fire to clear land, to the selection pressures of hunting, to domestication, fragmentation, extraction, emission, and effluent. Global environmental change is a reality—we have created and entered the Anthropocene epoch (Crutzen, 2002). As such there is no area of the biosphere that is untouched by humans. In fact, we cannot help but change the nonhuman world as a reality of our existence. We are ecological engineers, and always have been. But we should not wring our hands over the fact that our species alters its environment. Every other species does it too.

A more common environmental question is *should* we manipulate the nonhuman world to our own egocentric ends; or should we instead restrict our activity and leave some ecological systems as nature intends? As we have seen, one argument for ecological preservation is the idea that ecological systems have a natural state—that biological communities have a proper arrangement. This is the

Clementsian climax community, expressed as Leopold's notion of that which is right: the integrity, beauty, and stability of the biotic community (Leopold, 1949). The idea that living things assemble themselves according to a preordained order is attractive; it implies the harmony and balance that people so often seek in nature. But we have seen the counterargument that natural associations are temporary and transitional. In a state of constant transition, it is unclear exactly what is meant by natural balance and harmony—and if we call these concepts into question we must also question concepts of ecological integrity and health. It seems that these too are human conceptions of nature as a superorganism. Furthermore, the desire to protect ecological systems is decidedly uneven. We often advocate for charismatic species and iconic landscapes at the expense of less desirable aspects of the natural world. That so much of our environmentalism is aimed at serving our own needs, preferences, and pleasures simply means that *our ecocentrism is egocentric.*

The reality is that there is no "correct" version of nature, and never has been. There is no more a goal to the evolution of the biosphere than there is a goal to the evolution of species; nature doesn't intend anything. Rather, the natural world is one of change and response. To be sure, some of our actions impose stress on the nonhuman world and jeopardize ecological services on which we depend. Such services include items that we harvest and processes that we cannot easily replicate, but they also include cultural and psychological benefits of connection with nature. It is precisely because of anthropogenic stress that we must manage our world. Ecological systems are not superorganisms, and they do not naturally revert to an ideal state on their own. Without human intervention (both in terms of stress reduction and ecological manipulation) our ecological support structure will fail. In some respects, it is failing now. It is no longer a question of whether we *should* manipulate the world. We must act to protect the ecological functions that support our own species.

There is a difference, of course, between this sort of manipulation and the sort that involves exploitation, desecration, and cruelty. Certainly, some manipulation of the nonhuman world is done for short-term gain without regard for socio-ecological consequences. As self-interested organisms, we tend to think and act for immediate personal benefit. But the remedy for this is not the sequestration of human activity from natural activity. Rather, we need to interact more fully with ecological systems to understand the factors that promote and impede critical processes. We need to develop better criteria for considering the long-term ramifications of our actions, and we need to act on these criteria to nurture ecological function.

But ecological systems can have many different functions. If there is no proper state of the nonhuman world, on what basis shall we judge the appropriateness of our ecological engineering?

The answer is this: we can judge our ecological interventions by the benefits they offer and the costs they impose upon humans. We all need ecological services. We need oceans that support fish, forests that sequester carbon, grasslands that fix nitrogen, and wetlands that transform wastewater. We need beautiful landscapes, iconic species, and awe-inspiring vistas that inspire creativity and imagination.

Increasingly, it takes effort and management to maintain such services. So yes, we must be managers of nature, and yes we are egocentric. The task before us, I believe, is to become better ecological engineers who more effectively minimize anthropogenic stress on the ecological systems that are critical to our collective survival.

Individualism and collectivism

Since the industrial revolution, the utilitarian perspective has come to dominate the world. In theory, this approach ensures the greatest use of resources for the greatest number of people. Admittedly, problems can emerge if everyone is a utilitarian (Kaufman, 2003: 9–11). One problem is that some uses, while good for a great number, are directly or indirectly detrimental to many others. Another problem is that certain uses degrade common resources, jeopardizing future use by anyone. Third, some actions may simply be immoral, and not justifiable by any benefit for any number. But a larger problem occurs in the absence of the responsibility to meet certain ethical standards toward one another and with regard to the resources at hand. This is the direction in which synthetic society trends.

Some modern environmentalists find capitalism to be the selfish extension of utilitarianism and curse it as the driver of environmental degradation and injustice. These arguments often call for a return to an earlier model of human interaction, one perceived to be more egalitarian and less competitive. Indeed, for thousands of generations the predominant system of social conduct among our kind was a face-to-face social contract. Such a system encourages cooperation and reciprocation. The skills and resources of one are enhanced by exchange with the skills and resources of others, to the general benefit of all participants. Cheaters—those who seek to take but not give—are subject to social sanction. And, in the best-case scenario, group production is available for mutually profitable trade with other groups.

Fundamentally, though, this sort of tribal economy is not devoid of possession, competition, or self-interest. Nor is it a system of equality. It is a system of commerce. It is a system in which capital (not only tangible items but also knowledge, creativity, skill, status, loyalty, and wisdom) is bartered for like capital as a means of achieving an end. In this sense, our evolved system of cooperative reciprocity is itself a market-based economy. I suggest, therefore, that it is not market-based exchange that is the problem, but rather the removal of social responsibility from the transaction (Hawken *et al.*, 1999).

Champions of capitalism argue that it spurs innovation and problem-solving. It is seen (by some) as a system of freedom; it is the socioeconomic system that has done the most to raise the standard of living, to address problems of resource scarcity, to alleviate threats to human health, and to promote democracy. Indeed, it is hard to argue that human wealth and comfort have not been elevated in the era of capitalism. The availability of food, the access to health care, the opportunities to advance one's life through education and self-improvement have never been higher. Still, the benefits and costs of capitalism are unevenly distributed. Income disparity has risen dramatically in recent decades, such that much of the world's wealth is concentrated in the hands of a few while billions struggle with basic survival. Too often the burden of extraction, exploitation, and pollution are borne by the poor. Similarly, the benefits of capitalism often come at the expense of ecological services that are not easily translated into market value. This is not a system of mutual benefit for all participants. How is it that our system of cooperative reciprocation has been compromised?

The brand of capitalism featuring transnational corporations in a loosely regulated global arena is a far cry from the face-to-face responsibility of interpersonal reciprocity. The trend toward impersonal capitalism has removed the social checks and balances of selfishness from the system, allowing for exploitation of unknown people and degradation of unseen ecological systems. Further, a core of the workforce in developed nations has achieved a level of comfort in terms of salary, benefits, and possession. This status is tied to the success of the corporate model—indeed many residents of synthetic society are financially invested in the corporate system. Such affluence has created a situation in which many people of means have little reason to question the source of their wealth or the destination of their waste. Even for the curious, information on source, destination, and effect is difficult to acquire and seemingly not worth the effort. Economic comfort and environmental ignorance can limit the desire to challenge the prevailing system.

Hence, a deficiency of global corporate capitalism is that it separates the consumers (and investors) from resources, labor, and modes of production, making it difficult to judge whether economic actions harm others, degrade the commons, or are immoral. Accordingly, any manipulation of nonhuman species, natural resources, or human individuals may be economically validated by default. The end user, too often, has little basis to judge whether the means to the end are right or wrong. In short, the socio-economic systems of synthetic society have become non-relational.

It may be argued that our ancient system of cooperative reciprocity incorporates a moral basis into the ways in which we interacted with the natural world and with other humans. In groups regulated by collective governance, responsibility to other group members keeps self-interest from becoming selfishness. This evolutionary moral code is as close to a universal system of right and wrong as we are going to get. Today, most of us are far from tribal culture, with no plans to return to a foraging lifestyle any time soon. We are often removed from cooperative relationships with other producers or consumers. This does not mean that all of our actions under the auspices of corporate capitalism are immoral. It means that they are amoral. The question of right or wrong has simply been removed from the equation.

The task that falls to us, in this vision of environmentalism, is to mend the social cage that has been broken through the course of sociocultural evolution. What this means is that our transactions and interactions need to take place in a socially meaningful way. We need to feel the eyes of the impartial spectator upon us. We need to understand that the entities with whom we are dealing are people, and that our behavior toward others will influence their behavior toward us. The benefits here are not only socially meaningful, they are ecologically meaningful. In a socially meaningful world I must recognize that others have a home, that they drink water and breathe air and have children just as I do. It means that what I purchase, what I consume, what I choose to do with my money, and how I spend my time can all affect another person's home, and the way their home is treated can affect mine. It means that my actions matter, and so do yours. It is a recognition that *action for the collective good is an act of self-interest*.

Parochialism and globalism

Undeniably, there are problems with the extension of small-group morality to global socioeconomics. It can be hard to identify all the stakeholders, for one, and once identified they are sure to have conflicting interests. For some activities, like those that alter the climate, the manipulation is biospheric and the stakeholders number in the billions. Considering and including all affected parties in business transactions would internalize social and environmental externalities; it would therefore raise costs and lower profits in some cases, and halt economic activity in others. For this reason alone it has been and will continue to be resisted.

Here's an interesting observation about the global economy, though. It relies on the stability of social and ecological systems all over the world. The collapse of a major fishery, a region disrupted by war, a major demonstration of labor unrest, the death of a coral reef—increasingly, these are all directly related to the global market. Affluent people in synthetic societies may be ignorant of other social and ecological systems, but they have come to depend on them nonetheless. It is difficult to see a future in which this co-dependence does not grow stronger. People in developed nations need people in developing nations, not only for their natural resources but also for their creativity, energy, and ingenuity. *Parochial viability depends upon global viability*.

Social responsibility makes sense among our families, peers, and acquaintances. Indeed, we often follow it subconsciously, for at the small scale the social contract is enforceable by reputation. The greatest task facing humanity is to embrace the widening circle by extending social responsibility to those who are not of our group—to those of other cultures, ethnicities, religions, and skin colors. This is a question of environmental justice, of fair access and fair burden. It means overcoming xenophobia, a powerful evolutionary legacy of our species. It means calling *others* to the decision-making table. This will force restraint and encourage moderation. It will extend protection and conservation to other species and ecosystem services as a matter of course. It means that we must consider new models of compensation, representation, and projection—new models of cooperation and reciprocation.

And what of our responsibilities toward future generations? Choosing to favor our own current interests by saying we don't fully understand what our descendants will value is a cop out. We know what they'll value, at least in the near future. They'll be of the same evolutionary line as we are. They'll value clean air, uncontaminated water, and a reliable source of food. They'll value natural resources, ecological processes, and ecosystem services. They'll value stability, beauty, and spirituality in an anthropocentric way, just as we do. As to equity, we can only hope that we leave them a better model to follow than the one we are currently demonstrating.

Environmental morality

In my reconsideration of each of these dimensions of environmentalism I have collapsed them. While they are often portrayed as opposites in environmental literature and rhetoric, I believe they are false dichotomies that have too long occupied the environmental movement with unproductive arguments. I believe that this reduction of environmental dimensions can help us reframe both social and ecological relationships.

I have suggested that an environmental morality based on intrinsic worth and equal rights for all living things is untenable. Further, I have argued that spiritual approaches to morality are fundamentally material, and that their personal psychological benefits must be promoted over their social divisiveness. I have rejected an environmentalism that calls for an end to ecological manipulation, for we are a species of manipulators that has already transformed the planet. Rather, I suggest that the right and wrong of our ecological actions must be judged by how they promote or restrict access to ecological services for other humans.

I am convinced that there is no such thing as an intrinsic morality of nature. Environmental morality is therefore a social construct. Once, and still for some people, morality was defined by intimate social connections. But many people in affluent, synthetic society are insulated from the traditional mechanisms of cooperative reciprocity. Instead, we develop an individualized system of ethics over a lifetime of evaluating and responding to the norms of our social circles. Personal ethics may include biospheric feelings of moral obligation toward the environment; they likely also include feelings of obligation to self, family, and social circles large and small, all heavily influenced by our cultural milieu. Ultimately our actions flow from these personal values (Steg and Norlund, 2012).

Extension of personal ethics to other people in other places could encourage large-scale social cohesion. Unfortunately, social cohesion is at present hampered by social structures and cultural cues that promote hedonic, selfish, parochial, short-sighted behavior. Some see the inability to reduce the social distance between one another as a moral failing, and perhaps it is. If so, the remedy may be found through socio-psychological appeals to our sense of empathy, equity, and responsibility. These are the mental models that shape our behavior toward one another, and the way we behave toward one another will shape our future environment. The ecological consequences, should we fail, will be matters of cold probability. Natural selection always is.

Bibliography

Crutzen, P.J. (2002). Geology of mankind. *Nature*, 415(6867), p. 23.

Fromm, H. (2009). *The nature of being human: from environmentalism to consciousness*, Baltimore: Johns Hopkins University Press.

Hawken, P., Lovins, A. and Lovins, L.H. (1999). *Natural capitalism*, Boston: Little, Brown and Company.

Jost, J.T., Hawkins, C.B., Nosek, B.A., Hennes, E.P., Stern, C., Gosling, S.D. and Graham, J. (2014). Belief in a just God and a just society: a system justification perspective on religious ideology. *Journal of Theoretical and Philosophical Psychology*, 34(1), pp. 56–81.

Kaufman, F. (2003). *Foundations of environmental philosophy*, New York: McGraw-Hill.

Leopold, A. (1949 [1947]). On a monument to the pigeon. In: A. Leopold, *A Sand County almanac, and sketches here and there*, New York: Oxford University Press. pp. 109–110.

Leopold, A. (1949). The land ethic. In: A. Leopold, *A Sand County almanac, and sketches here and there*, New York: Oxford University Press. pp. 224–225.

Steg, L. and Norlund, A. (2012). Models to explain environmental behavior. In: L. Steg, A. Van den Berg and J. De Groot, eds., *Environmental psychology: an introduction*, New York: Wiley. pp. 185–195.

Thompson, J. (1990). A refutation of environmental ethics. *Environmental Ethics*, 12(2), pp. 147–160.

12 Evolving still

Key points

- Ancestral and progressive environmentalism are problematic for the conceptual and social discrepancies they present.
- An environmentalism based on material, anthropocentric, and relational principles can guide a return to responsibility thinking.

I find it interesting that some of the major transformations of human social development have been associated with climate change. It was during the wildly fluctuating climate of the last ice age that the human population nearly went extinct, only to emerge from the bottleneck and colonize the world. These foraging ancestors of ours were unlikely conquerors, but their mobility, ingenuity, and ability to cooperate made them resilient. Then, as the ice age waned and climate warmed, our ancestors learned to cultivate and domesticate other organisms. Through agriculture, human agency swept the world once again. Later it was climate change that initiated the Black Death, and—indirectly—the Black Death that triggered the mechanization of industry and kindled the flame of enlightenment. Thus were the climate-driven trials of famine and disease a threshold to a new way of life. In all of these cases our species responded to environmental upheaval with sociocultural evolution that, more than anything, was a change in mindset.

None of these sociocultural leaps were planned, of course. They were the collective transmission of millions of individual ideas, lessons, and choices that solved some problems even as they created new ones. Despite their imperfections I believe that we should look on these past adaptations with pride, for in these difficult times our ancestors found ways not just to survive, but to flourish.

And now we are in the midst of another changing climate, this one of our own making. It is a global ecological stress—one to which humans will have to adapt. That's an important point, I think. It's not that there is anything wrong with the environment, or the atmosphere, or the ecosystems of the planet. These systems are merely responding to the stress that humans have generated. We will have to adapt in return. How adaptable are modern human societies? How amenable are we to changing mindset, lifestyle, and patterns of cooperation? We may be about to find out.

A number of qualities likely made our ancient ancestors adaptable—versatility, tenacity, creativity, resourcefulness—but their tight-knit social structure may have had as much to do with their success as anything. They were necessarily accountable to each other, and that may just have been the characteristic that enabled them to survive. We still see glimpses of this, even in the most individualistic social situations. Our species has a way of bonding in the midst of a catastrophe—a response known as disaster convergence. In all sorts of sociocultural situations people draw closer together when there is a calamity, voluntarily risking their security and even their lives to assist strangers. The worst circumstances, somehow, bring out the best of our social behavior. Of course, much of our lives are *not* spent in response to disaster, but rather in the navigation of more mundane opportunities and trials. Social support systems are more variable in the chronic stress of everyday life; indeed, in some modern situations the desire for individualism has compromised social support in general. As we face a future of environmental change, do we have the social capacity to meet the challenge?

It is not my intention to speculate on future human reactions to imagined environmental dilemmas. A more productive exercise is to reflect on the evolutionary journey of our species and to consider some of the potential paths that lie before us. The good news is that we have some degree of choice in the matter. Though we are products of biological evolution, it is not our genes alone that will determine how we as a species react to future scenarios. It is our flair for sociocultural change—ironically a primary source of our environmental problems—that affords us the opportunity to choose our path. Sociocultural evolution is, and has always been, a great improvisation.

I have made the case in this book that environmentalism is an ideology full of contradictions. Far from a well-defined school of thought, it is a collection of worldviews that lacks a concerted focus. Our trip through the biological and sociocultural evolution of our species explains our state of contradiction. We are conflicted beings. We are at once self-interested and cooperative, xenophobic and empathetic, utilitarian and preservationist, spiritual and material, in need of the natural world and eager to be separated from it. It is no wonder that our relationship with the nonhuman world is inconsistent and our direction is vague.

And yet, it is from this collective discord that our next sociocultural improvisation must emerge. The stakes are high, for our evolutionary legacy has left us with a world of haves and have-nots, a world of ecological stress, and a world in which natural balance and harmony are looking more and more like illusions. In theory, environmentalism should be the collaborative effort that provides us with a road map. In practice, it has had difficulty moving past its own internal disagreements.

I contend that an examination of our evolutionary legacy can provide us with a clearer picture of who we are, why we do the things we do, which disputes can be laid to rest, and where our collective efforts must now be applied. Before concluding with my own perspective, then, I will consider two common environmental views that, in my opinion, miss the point.

Ancestral environmentalism

The first case (which I prefer to call ancestral, rather than the pejorative terms degenerative or primitive environmentalism) is a conceptual amalgam based on the premise that foraging human cultures had it right, and that the relationship our ancient ancestors had with the Earth was ruined by the emergence of agriculture, technology, hierarchical relationships, materialism, and rational science. Various ideas to this effect are that ancient foraging cultures were egalitarian and unselfish, that they lived in harmony with the land and with other species, that they were in touch with—in fact, one with—the collective spirit of the human and nonhuman world. The arguments are that people were happier, the Earth was healthier, and there was less oppression and exploitation of both humans and other organisms. Correspondingly, then, actions that decrease our reliance on material wealth and technology, that simplify our lives, that replace competition with cooperation, and that reject reductionist science in favor of non-rational intuition will bring us into balance with one another and with the Earth (Lerro, 2000: 298–301).

To be sure, there are attractive aspects to ancestral environmentalism. Foraging societies, based on what we know from modern ethnography, are indeed more egalitarian than industrial and synthetic societies. People in such tightly bound social circles are accountable to one another. The consumption patterns of the affluent are clearly driving much ecological stress; thus a simpler, less consumerist lifestyle would lighten our collective footprint. Incessant competition does seem to be driving us apart, and so a cooperative social model has obvious appeal. These features can and should be part of a new vision of environmentalism.

Why, then, do I claim that the ancestral approach misses the mark? I offer several reasons.

1   Foraging cultures were (and are) successful social models at very low population densities. It is not at all clear that such a system could work on a large scale with current population densities, or that sociocultural evolution could revert to an earlier stage.
2   The romanticized view of the forager's life ignores the short life span, high infant mortality, infanticide, banishment of nonconformists, and susceptibility to starvation that accompany such an existence.
3   Similarly, the romantic perspective of within-group harmony tends to ignore the prevalence of xenophobia and warfare among foraging groups.
4   It promotes a vision of a correct, benign, and personified nature that exists only in the human mind, and thus it is counterproductive to real-world conservation efforts.
5   The rejection of reductionism would presumably be a rejection of the many innovations that science has provided for modern society. It would be difficult, for example, to exist in blissful happiness without modern medicine, domesticated plants and animals, synthetic materials and new technologies, all of which were made possible by reductionist thinking. It is not at all clear that foraging cultures reject reductionism; indeed, many

ingenious examples of tool construction and aesthetic expression employ reductionist science.

6   Insisting on a rejection of objective rationalism in favor of intuition, emotion, and imagination is asking that we ignore a major aspect of our cognitive function. Given what is now known about cognitive psychology and neuro-biology, it is not even clear that we are capable of ceasing rational behavior and it is certainly not established that this would be a good thing.

7   Modern evolutionary ecology has cast doubt upon the notion of natural harmony; it is not clear that there is or ever was such a harmony or what it would look like if there were.

8   Modern neurophysiology has shown spiritual sensation and aesthetic appreci-ation to be biochemical in nature. While this does not discount the human need for them, it does imply that they are not extrabiotic characteristics of a supernatural realm, but rather material characteristics of the natural world.

9   To date, no intra-organismal connective energy has been identified. It is therefore unclear what being one with other entities might mean.

Ancestral environmentalism seems to be most effective when its adherents believe in it. Certainly, there are such people today, and I do not resent their position. For most of the world's population, however, the purported benefits of the ancestral lifestyle will not outweigh the drawbacks. Ancestral environmentalism simply does not present a convincing case for change. I do not, however, reject this sort of environmentalism altogether, and I will return to the relational aspects later. First, though, a consideration of the other end of the environmental spectrum.

Progressive environmentalism

Sometimes known as technocentrist environmentalism, this view holds that progress in societal infrastructure and superstructure is inevitable and, ultimately, where we must turn for solutions to our problems (Lerro, 2000). For example, the progressivist observes that specialization, technological innovation, individu-alism, centralization, and globalization have promoted freedom of choice, longer life, greater access, and more efficient use of resources than ever before. Complex societies that facilitate material wealth acquisition will raise the tide for all ships, so to speak, and eventually make everyone less reliant on unpredictable natural fluctuations. It is the reductionist, rationalist, and technology-based harnessing of nature that allows us to alleviate poverty, and free market enterprise has been the best system for generating the wealth to do so. Alleviating poverty, in turn, is our best approach to environmental protection.

It is clear that the progressive approach—via free market capitalism—has come to dominate our global political economy. Before considering the draw-backs to an environmentalism based on such a system, let's review some positives. It is undeniable that technological innovation (and even reductionism) have lengthened life spans, eased suffering, and enabled the self-actualization of billions of people. It is even a fair argument that technological progress has been, and continues to be, a primary means of reducing anthropogenic stress on the world's ecosystems. And alleviation of poverty is certainly a boon to both social and ecological systems; global progressive capitalism has accomplished this for some.

Therein lies the first of several criticisms:

1   Progress has been uneven, to say the least. While global material wealth has indeed grown with extraction and industrialization, so has disparity. The tide is raising the boats of some, while others are underwater. In short, progress has alleviated poverty on a select, localized scale; globally, it has exacerbated inequality.
2   Uneven regulation leads to exploitation of the poor and their resources to the benefit of the wealthy minority.
3   Complex, hierarchical societies can be isolating, socially empty environments that remove individuals from human connection. This can have negative psychological consequences.
4   Corporate capitalism removes consumers from producers. It often means that the consumer (or investor) has little knowledge of the materials or means of production, and thus cannot make value judgements on them. This can have negative ecological consequences.
5   An emphasis on individualism reduces the pressures of social obligation, and hence diminishes reciprocal cooperation. This can have negative social consequences.
6   The progressive system is intended to spur consumption far beyond need. This stresses ecological systems at the front end of extraction and at the back end of emission, effluent, and waste disposal.
7   Technological innovation tends to insulate the affluent from their socioecological environment altogether, resulting in a population ignorant of ecological, social, and personal stress.
8   The expectation of a continuously stable natural environment in synthetic society is contrary to ecological disturbance theory and therefore ecologically untenable.
9   The progressive system is designed for short-term thinking, while ecological and social resilience require long-term planning.

Progressive environmentalism is thus as much or more a part of our environmental problems as it is a part of viable solutions. Innovation is certainly a strength of our species, and we will need every bit of it to face our current and future challenges. But innovation that isolates, divides, polarizes, and dehumanizes will not solve our societal ills, and societal ills are driving our environmental ills.

A hybrid environmentalism

I propose, therefore, a hybrid model; one that draws on the best of both ancestral and progressive environmentalism. It is a material, anthropocentric, relational environmentalism. Drawing from arguments I have presented through-out this book, let me now make the summary case for these three characteristics.

Material

We have seen that our fundamental environmental needs are based on ecological services; that is, we need food, fuel, fiber, and function from the nonhuman world. These are material needs, and our greatest ecological challenge is to understand and protect the ecological processes that provide such services to our species. We have also seen that many of our needs are less tangible. They are the spiritual contentment, the aesthetic expression, and the psychological, physiological, and social wellness that we experience when we have regular connection with nature. *These too are material needs.* They are neurobiological necessities just like the natural resources we rely upon for ecological provision and process.

In advocating for a material environmentalism I am not excusing wasteful, ostentatious, or frivolous consumption. Materialism and consumerism are not the same thing. Rather, I am describing an environmentalism that embraces the ways in which human physiology, psychology, and ecology actually work. A material approach, broadly conceived, illuminates the need to protect and nurture the ecological and social conditions on which our species depends. Reckless con-sumerism, narrowly conceived, jeopardizes those conditions.

The change in mindset I propose can be seen from two directions. First, spir-itualists will need to recognize that the positive emotions and inspirations we draw from nature are biochemical processes that occur within our own bodies, and that people have widely varied abilities to experience such feelings. Further, knowing as we do that romantic conceptions of nature are not accurate depictions of reality, emphasis should be placed on the protection of functional ecosystems, not necessarily idealized ecosystems. Materialists, for their part, will need to accept that spiritual, aesthetic, and psycho-social needs are real aspects of human inter-action with nature, and that meeting such needs is incompatible with wholesale removal of humans from the nonhuman world. The concept of instrumental utility must be expanded to encompass aspects of nature that do not have a market value. This is an *inclusive* materialism (Thompson, 1990).

Anthropocentric

I have argued that the concept of intrinsic value is difficult to defend, particularly when the species and systems we value the most are personally or collectively beneficial, while other species and systems are despised. What this means is that our biased sense of intrinsic value is itself a form of instrumental value. Accord-ingly, an environmentalism based upon the protection of pristine nature for nature's sake is untenable. There is no pristine nature. Ecosystems do not auto-matically revert back to desirable structure or function in the midst of—or even upon relief from—ecological stress. An anthropocentric environmentalism (or, more correctly, a *sapiens*-centric environmentalism) is a recognition that the nonhuman world has been sculpted by our species for ages, and that it is instrumental value (broadly imagined) that does and will continue to drive our manipulation of nature. Nonhuman life, in this perspective, is best protected through alleviation of ecological stress. And ecological stress is best alleviated through the promotion of social equity.

But let me be clear. By arguing for an anthropocentric environmentalism, I am not suggesting that humans are the pinnacle of evolution or the center of the universe. To the contrary, our species is but one of millions of branches on the tree of life, occupying a charming, but small speck of dust in a vast universe. I am simply observing that our species prioritizes its own interests and always has—even in the ways it has valued other species. By acknowledging our species-centric, egocentric nature, perhaps we can better understand exactly what it is that our species truly needs for its own long-term survival.

Nor should this be seen as a green light for ecological destruction or permission for cruel treatment of animals. Far from it, in fact. If we can indeed come to understand environmental values as inclusive of spiritual, aesthetic, and psychological needs, then anthropocentric manipulation of nature becomes constrained by a broader group of socioecological factors. It means, for example, that we need to recognize and defend ecological processes, systems, and services on which our species depends. It means that extraction or pollution that destroys the ecological basis of a culture is unacceptable. It means that individuals, communities, states, corporations, and third-sector organizations must collaborate to alleviate stress on ecological and sociocultural systems alike. It means that our actions are bound by intergenerational responsibilities. This is a *collective* anthropocentrism.

Relational

I have made the case that much of our modern environmental dilemma flows from extractive, synthetic society generally, and from the disconnection engendered by corporate capitalism specifically. Affluent society has trended toward the removal of social obligation and the blind consumption of and investment in modes of extraction and production that exacerbate inequality. We have also seen that both socially and ecologically empty environments can leave us psychologically adrift and perhaps less apt to care about self, others, and the nonhuman world. By a relational environmentalism I mean that we need to re-connect these loose ends— to restore social cohesion and to re-establish meaningful relationships with our ecological foundation. A relational mindset recognizes that the individual person, the human population, and the natural environment are not disconnected but rather of the same system.

In practice, a relational environmentalism means that consumers must have the capacity to know the processes that bring a product to market and the opportunity to understand the effects of their purchases. It means that more human interactions should be cooperative and reciprocal, that all communities should have access to, ownership of, and responsibility toward regional ecological systems, and that economic development should allow broad stakeholder input. These are characteristics of a relational society.

In my estimation, many approaches to environmentalism miss these relational imperatives. We have marvelous educational materials, detailed ecosystem management plans, and effective lobbyists for new regulation. All of these are fine, but if we fail to curb social dysfunction we will not begin to approach workable solutions. I am convinced that we cannot achieve environmental sustainability without social sustainability. And social sustainability, I believe, begins with individual connection. To recall the Minnesota farmer with whom I introduced the book, the important point might not be which of us was behaving as an environmentalist, but instead that he got to know me, and I him.

An environmentalism that is inclusively material, collectively anthropocentric, and broadly relational provides clarity—if not simplicity—of purpose. The tasks of the environmentalist are aspects of responsibility thinking. We must identify and protect ecological structures and functions that are critical for human life, and we must be mutually accountable to all other members of our species.

The next improvisation

I am not so naïve as to expect that it will be a simple matter to bring materialists and spiritualists together at the neurological table, or that corporations will suddenly invite dozens of concerned stakeholders to development strategy meetings, or that marketing firms will happily disclose the dirty secrets behind every product, or that cities and communities the world over will devote money, time, and personnel toward greenspace creation and management. Selfishness, parochialism, short-term thinking, and xenophobia are powerful instincts, and not easily overcome. Throughout most of our existence as a species, social pressures have kept such individualistic instincts at bay. Only very recently in our evolutionary history have social constraints been weakened, but the effects have quickly come to dominate the world. Once freed from the social cage, we are not so eager to return.

Others, notably Alexandra Maryanski and Jonathan Turner, have celebrated the fact that people in affluent, post-industrial society are becoming more removed from social pressures—that humans are "breaking out of the social cage" (Maryanski and Turner, 1992: 139). Their argument is that humans are by nature individualistic and resistant to restrictive social structures, and that the decline of such structures promotes "individualism, autonomy, and freedom" (Maryanski and Turner, 1992: 166). They are correct, to a point. Much progress may be credited to self-determination. But we ignore the benefits of collective action at our peril. The social cage, whether we imagine it constructed biologically, culturally, or (as I have portrayed it in this book) by a combination of the two, has repeatedly enabled our species to overcome challenges that it could not have faced as individuals. Moreover, hedonic selfishness, short-term thinking, and xenophobia are drivers of our current environmental crisis. A future that promotes these aspects of our character at the expense of cooperative reciprocity is bound for deeper inequality, unchecked degradation of ecosystem services, increased social strife, and ultimately a declining functional capacity of our species. An alternate path—one which maintains individual autonomy within a social structure of mutual responsibility—is by no means a guarantee of success. But it stands a chance of reaching beyond blind consumption to encourage equitable access to ecological services in the broadest sense.

Ironically, it is those with the most individual freedom—those of affluent, synthetic, democratic societies—who are best placed to initiate global interactions that favor cooperation, reciprocity, and the maintenance of ecosystem services. Actions for collective benefit might be encouraged by incentives that make them viable choices for individuals and organizations. I see some encouraging signs that such incentives are becoming more common. Cities and towns are recognizing that parkland raises property values and draws people who wish to live, work, and raise a family in such a place. The same can be said for certain historic and prehistoric landmarks, for which a newly appreciated economic value is protecting ancient cultural values. Some corporations have chosen to disclose their suppliers and processes as green and socially conscious marketing strategies. Some are even listening to community stakeholders. More people are accepting that a variety of socio-spiritual approaches—including none at all—can be compatible with healthy communities. A growing number of consumers are asking questions about the things they buy and insisting on socially and ecologically sensitive production. Groups of concerned individuals are pooling resources to conserve land, to protect rivers, and to enhance ecosystem services.

We certainly have a long way to go, but this is a start. What I find to be particularly promising is that at least some of this is achievable through market-based approaches. Capitalism, as we have seen, is directly or indirectly responsible for many of our problems, but it can just as easily provide products and services that alleviate environmental and social stress. The market does not care, it only responds to supply and demand. And profit margins are thin. So we don't need 100% of consumers to carefully consider the ecological and social impacts of their purchases and demand better. What if 5% more consumers refuse to buy products with unsustainably harvested palm oil (or timber, or seafood, or unsustainable natural resources of any kind)? How about 10% more? What if 10% more consumers demand full disclosure of extraction and manufacturing processes? What if 10% more investors choose investment options that build social and ecological relationships over those that do not? At what point do you force corporate action? Election margins are also thin. What if 10% more voters support candidates who prioritize ecosystem services? How many voters will it take to successfully demand comprehensive product labeling? How many more votes are needed to advance the transition to renewable energy? At what point do you force political action? Communities too are primed for change. How many citizen volunteers will it take to start a community engagement program? What if 10% more people buy their produce in-season from a local vendor? What if 10% more consumers seek to purchase goods from facilities that pay their workers a living wage and ensure safe working conditions? How many people does it take to identify and secure protection for critical ecological processes in their region? How many environmentally proactive communities will it take to encourage other communities to do the same? At what point do you force social change?

I believe that the barrier to achieving these ends is not a lack of concerned and dedicated people. Rather, the barrier is one of mindset, and this is not effectively countered by a divided and conflicted environmental movement. It is time to move beyond old dichotomies to join forces for our next sociocultural leap. Sociocultural evolution, after all, can be guided. It could be our greatest improvisation yet—one that yields functional ecosystems, mutually supportive communities, and mentally healthy individuals. There is no promise of harmony or balance here, and no guarantee of a happy ending. We probably won't be around to see the outcome in any case. But our descendants will. And who knows? Maybe they will look back upon us and say that we were environmentalists—and maybe they will know exactly what that word means.

Bibliography

Lerro, B. (2000). *From Earth spirits to sky gods: the socioecological origins of monotheism, individualism, and hyperabstract reasoning from the Stone Age to the axial Iron Age.* Lanham, MD: Lexington Books.

Maryanski, A. and Turner, J.H. (1992). *The social cage: human nature and the evolution of society.* Stanford, CA: Stanford University Press.

Thompson, J. (1990). A refutation of environmental ethics. *Environmental Ethics,* 12(2), pp. 147–160.

Index